My Psychic Search

Thank you for all of
your friendship and
support!

Gail

My Psychic Search

**Discovering what psychics do,
what psychics know, and
how they can help us
improve our lives**

Gail Kushner

Kushner's Kreations Press Tucson, Arizona

Contact the author or order
additional copies of this book at
www.MyPsychicSearch.com

This edition was prepared for printing by
Ghost River Images
5350 East Fourth Street
Tucson, Arizona 85711
www.ghostriverimages.com

cover design by Troy O'Brien

ISBN: 978-0-9848396-0-5

Library of Congress Control Number: 2011961800

Printed in the United States of America
May, 2012
10 9 8 7 6 5 4 3 2

Acknowledgments

I want to thank each of the psychics and energy workers for sharing their stories with me. I want to thank them for being honest and for being willing to go public with who they are, what they do and what they know. It's a big step forward for many of us.

I want to thank my family for supporting me in this research and writing adventure. Yes, I know dinner was sometimes a little late . . .

I want to thank my invisible, energetic support system for keeping my calendar free enough to allow me to work on this Project for three years. Somehow, my family has had the good health and the financial resources which have allowed me to complete this phase of my Project.

Dedication

This book is dedicated to my dog Pepper who lay in the room with me for years as I was writing and editing. The day I printed a "good draft," he became ill and passed on. Pepper was always there to remind me that snack time begins promptly at 1 p.m. Thank you Pepper!

Contents

Section III - Readings, Healings and Energy Work

Section IV - The Wheel of Incarnation or **Life Continues (for us and our Pets) and it Circles Back Around**

Section VII - References

Preface - How Psychics have Influenced my Life... for the Better

Even before I knew I was psychic, I glimpsed what I needed to do. I understood that I had to interview psychics, talk to "regular" people, and strengthen the connections between these groups. I knew that psychics had profound messages to share and I knew that people had eager minds ready to embrace these messages. How did I know this? A psychic told me.

I had seen psychics off and on for many years. When I was single, I wanted to know if I was going to find a husband. The psychics knew I would marry, but it wasn't until shortly after a psychic told me, "He's coming soon," that he showed up in my life. Years later, when we thought we needed a larger home for our family, I asked another psychic, "Will I buy a new home?" She told me that we were moving and that the home would be pink. Just a few weeks later we found a home for sale . . . with pink rocks in the front yard and pink carpeting in the rooms. We have lived in this house for 15 years now. It's been the perfect home for our family.

How can this be possible? How can someone I don't know, see my future more clearly than I can see it? How can someone be psychic?

This is ***My Psychic Search*** to answer questions about what it is like to be psychic, how psychics glean information, and what they know about the Universe. I have interviewed more than 20 psychics and asked them how they know what they know. How does information come to them? Where does information come from? What do they know about humanity, the Universe, life and death (and all that goes on in between the points of that cycle)? What is it like to live a psychic life? Their answers, in their own words, are enlightening and their experiences are extraordinary. During the interview process, I discovered my role in this Project: I am a point of connection standing on the wide bridge which connects the physical world to the spiritual world, then extends out to the Universe. I am a signpost gently suggesting that there is an interface between these worlds and that this interface is a psychic face.

Just as we are guided by lights along the paths to our front doors, or lights along the airplane floor ready to help in an emergency, let this book be a small guiding light along your path to understanding your unique place in the Universe. While this book is only a small point of light (like a laser!), it has a big job: helping people move towards fulfilling, inspired, expanded lives. The message is simple: "It is okay to amble further down your spiritual path. It is okay to ask questions and take spirituality seriously. It is okay to talk to a psychic and discover the answers to your questions."

If you have picked up this book, you are probably as curious about psychic abilities as I am. If you already connect to intuitive information, this book will help you understand your gift. If you think you might want to employ a psychic to enhance your connection, this book will show you how to find a reader and how to get the most from a reading. If you want to learn about your soul's evolution or about humanity's progress, this book presents the psychics' views on these topics.

Come with me on this journey of discovery. ***My Psychic Search*** can be ***Your Psychic Search***.

Section I

An Introduction to the Project, the Words, the Psychics

Chapter 1 - Introduction

What would happen if you asked 20 psychics the same question? Would they all have the same answer? What if you asked how they accessed information or if psychic ability ran in their families? What about life, death, and our work here on Earth? What about personal questions: Is it easier or harder to date when you know what the other person is thinking? What if the other person knows that you know what they are thinking? Is it easier to raise children when you are psychic? What if the children are psychic too?

I have always been fascinated by psychic ability. Why can some people tap into unseen information sources while other people struggle to make a connection? How can someone who I have just met know things about me and my family?

Whenever I don't know something, I ask someone who knows; someone who has direct experience or knowledge. To figure out how being psychic works, I interviewed more than 20 psychics. I talked to Tarot card readers, an astrologer, Mediums, a numerologist, palm readers, and psychics who don't use tools to make connections. I asked plenty of "yes" or "no" questions, for example, "Do psychic readings work over the phone?" and I also asked open-ended questions such as, "What do you think will happen in 2012?" Some responses are factual and some are speculative. The psychics agree on many answers and disagree on other points – and that is what makes this project so fascinating. Is there agreement as to what happens after death? Mostly. Is there a consensus as to what the Afterlife looks like? Not yet. Wouldn't it be interesting if they were interviewed independently about unseen worlds and all agreed on *anything*? Join me as I ask and answer questions about what life is like when a person is psychic, how it is possible for people to tap into invisible information sources, and how psychic insights can benefit all of us.

This is my job: I am asking psychics how they do their work, what it is like to be a professional psychic, and what they know. I am listening intently to their answers and forming my own world view. I have learned so much! This is ***My Psychic Search***.

Who am I? Why am I working on this Project?

When I began this Project, I didn't consider myself to be "psychic" or "intuitive." I have always been a normal person who is very curious about psychics and how they know the things they know. In the past, I have had psychic readings, some of which have been helpful and some of which haven't panned out. It's an adventure. I don't take the readings too seriously, but I do use them as a jumping off point for personal introspection. If a psychic tells me something about myself, I take the time to think about whether or not it's true. Either way, their reading has helped me think about my personal development. I am one of those people who is always thinking, always evaluating, always wondering how best to use my life. The downside of all of this self-evaluation is that I sometimes get stuck; I just don't know which path to select. And that takes me to more introspection and, sometimes, to another psychic reading.

In 2008, I told one of my psychic friends that I was getting bored with the work I was doing and I needed a new "thinking" project. She suggested that I interview psychics and learn more about their work and their lives. Eureka! What a great idea! I began interviewing people for ***My Psychic Search*** the following month.

Later, one of the psychics told me that my curiosity about psychic phenomena is more than an intellectual pursuit, it is one of the reasons I am here. According to Leah Taylor:

> "You are sharing a passion and joy of life with others. The psychic curiosity comes in because we need beacons of light and beacons of hope because it is dark right now. If you can carry your one little candle out into the dark and people can see that light, then it will change everybody's life. Then they can take a light from your candle. That is the purpose of your project."

Wow! That's pretty encouraging!

This same psychic tells me that there is a mass change in consciousness happening right now. People are wondering why we are here on Earth. People are asking, "What is going to happen when I die?" Her impression was that this project reminded people that it is good to ask those kinds of questions. It is okay to explore the possibilities of human consciousness and what it means to be human. She also told me that very slowly there will be a change from looking at human beings as living machines to trying to find the sacredness in each person. A study on psychics, and the people who are interested in psychics, brings that change of thinking into a wider consciousness.

So, here I am on ***My Psychic Search***. I am hoping to discover whatever it is that psychics tap into. Perhaps I will figure out how to tap into it myself. In the meantime, I am listening to the psychics as they tell their stories. These are the true experiences of people who are working on the frontlines to assist others and who are willing to speak publicly about their gifts. If you are as curious about psychics as I am, maybe we can both learn something from ***My Psychic Search***, and this will be part of ***Your Psychic Search*** too. If you are skeptical, maybe this Project will help you to see that psychics are very similar to you and I. They are real people who are working through their own personal issues while exploring an invisible world of knowledge and energy.

What am I doing?

I am talking to professional psychics, intuitives, readers, healers and energy workers to discover and share their stories. I want to find out how psychics feel about their unique abilities. Are these abilities considered gifts or burdens? How did the psychics know they were psychic? Does this talent run in families? Where does the information come from? How does this knowledge affect their lives?

I am also talking to clients and potential clients. I want to find out what people expect when they come for a psychic reading. I am asking whether or not psychic readings have helped clients live better, richer lives. I am interested in helping people get the most from a psychic reading. Clients may be interested in finding the best reader for their needs and psychics may be able to use information from clients to make their readings more successful. This is an on-going Project to voice different viewpoints and bridge the gaps between the public, the clients, the readers and the Higher Realms.

During psychic readings, clients often ask about love, relationships, family members, work, finances, health, life lessons, spiritual path, loved ones who have died, and the future. This book turns things around and asks the psychics about these same topics. They talk about their life stories (Chapter 3), gifts and challenges (Chapters 4 through 7), personal lives, relationships and "day jobs" (Chapters 8 and 9), work (psychic readings) (Chapters 10 through 16), life and death (Chapters 17 through 22) and the future (Chapters 23 and 24).

Who should read this book?

This book is for:

1) **People who are interested in what it is like to be psychic.** These people are curious about how all of this works and if there is anything "out there." Reading about the actual experiences of people with psychic abilities may answer some of their questions.

2) **People who would like to have a reading,** but don't know how to find a reader or what it is like to meet with a reader. This book provides basic explanations of what psychics do, how they do it, and how people can benefit from a reading. Talking to a psychic often provides a new perspective on life issues, a second opinion for approaching a problem, or an explanation of an issue so that the issue suddenly makes sense. Readings lead to a greater understanding of a person's life and the direction that their life is flowing.

Chapters 10 through 13 provide tips for finding the right psychic for a reading, tips for getting the most from a session, and suggestions for using the information from the reading. The trick is to find someone with a natural gift and the maturity to use it wisely. A reading can provide great insights with relatively low risks. Who wouldn't pay a few dollars for answers to life's mysteries?!

3) **People who think they might be psychic, but aren't sure**. These people may have had odd experiences which they can't explain. They don't know if they had a psychic moment, a random premonition, a coincidence or a strange dream. Did they really hear a voice or see a spirit? Professional psychics have fascinating stories about how they were either born knowing that they had abilities or how they figured out what was going on. Many readers thought that they were crazy until they realized that they were psychic. Once they understood what was happening, they were able to integrate their psychic abilities with their everyday lives and live their truth. People with psychic abilities are not alone. Many other people are leading similar lives. Information from the psychics about how they knew they were psychic, or about what they experience daily, may help people in this group understand what is happening in their lives.

Chapter 2 includes a *Psychic Skills Checklist* which can help people figure out, and name, their psychic abilities.

4) **People with psychic ability who are curious about other psychics**. People with psychic abilities are often curious about what other psychics experience, how they live their lives and how they do their readings. They want to know how other psychics prepare for readings and why they use certain tools. They are also interested in how other psychics navigate a world full of skeptics while working "day jobs," dating, and raising families.

5) **People who want to know the answers to life's big questions**, for example: what happens after we die? is reincarnation real? will we see out pets again? Chapters 17 through 22 discuss the psychics' perspectives on many of these issues.

In addition to meeting the needs of these groups, I also think it is important to have a written record of the psychics' lives and work. Times are changing and this Project records some of the work being done to prepare for the upcoming shifts. Psychics are extremely unique and interesting people who are working to heal our world and to help us understand our own growth. They live between worlds and have extraordinary true stories. Eventually, I plan to publish a book which contains the psychics' actual interviews.

A model for this Project

While working on this Project, I kept seeing images of pyramids in my mind. I think that pyramids represent this work. The pyramid base represents the four equally-important, essential contributors to this project:

1) the unseen sources of original information (angels, Spirit Guides, and God);

2) the psychics who bring information into this physical dimension;

3) the audience which can use the information to enrich lives; and

4) the author (me) who compiles and presents the information.

When communication is moving between these four participants, energy swirls upward through the pyramid, converges at the apex and creates successful inter-realm communication. If it's just me and the audience, I have nothing to say. If it's me and the psychics, I can only listen. If it's me and God, I am unsure of the truth. When all four elements work together, we make magic. We move generations forward.

What will people think of me? Is this the psychics' dilemma?

When I am not at a psychic fair, or talking with psychics, I frequently tell people that I am working on this Project and I receive a very cold response. They roll their eyes. They don't ask questions or want to know anything about my work. I don't know if they think I am crazy, or if they are just suspicious of the entire topic.

More often, I tell people I am working on this Project and they are curious about what I am learning. I tell them about the people I have met and the interesting insights psychics have shared about what it is like to be intuitive. Sometimes when I tell people about this Project, they open up with their own stories and experiences. One woman told me how she receives regular updates regarding her life at 4:42 a.m., and another woman told me how she saw her deceased sister help their father as he was passing away. A third woman told me that she knows when people are going to die within three days (even people who are not ill). People have stories to share, but need to know that they have a safe place to share these experiences.

During the course of this Project, I was picking and choosing who to tell about ***My Psychic Search***. I was not ready to "go public" and tell all my friends and family. I worried that they would think I was crazy. I didn't think I was crazy; I was curious! Similarly, some of the psychics have told me that they worry about being judged. Many of them go through periods of hibernation where they try to put their gifts aside and live a "normal" life, but this is not possible. Being psychic is who they are. They find that when they deny their abilities, they are not living authentic lives. In some ways it's easier to be who they are and risk judgement. Part of working as a psychic is getting used to being thought of as crazy, and learning to tolerate this mis-judgement. With this book, we are all going public!

Both psychics and non-psychics have a world of information floating beneath the surface, just waiting to be shared with someone they trust. People need to know that it is safe to share their stories without fear of being judged. We are moving into a new era when psychic insights will be more and more socially-acceptable.

Why do I talk to psychic readers?

I talk to psychic readers because I cannot, yet, make my own clear connections. I enjoy psychic readings because I like to receive the information and begin working with it rather than waiting for my own murky answers to appear. I meditate and am strengthening my connection, but when I am seeking straight-forward counsel, I enjoy talking to a psychic reader. In addition, I think psychic readings are fun and I am fascinated by the process. I am still awestruck when someone accesses my information.

Psychic connections require people to remain open to insights and to trust the information which is received. People who make their own clear connections are very fortunate. People who are not able to hear, see, or feel the messages on their own can take classes and develop these skills, or they can talk to someone who is already connected. Just as clients consult other people to learn from their training, skill and expertise, they can consult psychics. When I need assistance with medical conditions, I talk to a doctor. When I need assistance with my taxes, I talk to an accountant. When I need a new perspective on a life issue, I talk to a psychic reader.

A few notes on how this book is written:

1) A wide variety of answers are paraphrased and presented.

When I asked multiple psychics the same question, I often received a wide variety of answers. The clearest way to present these answers is to use summarized, paraphrased, lists. It is often more important to look at the wide range of perspectives on each issue than to determine which psychic presented a particular idea. However, if the answer came from just one person, I have indicated the person's name in parentheses after the thought. These quotes and near-quotes provide the most direct insights into psychics' lives and minds.

2) Imaginations may be stretched.

When reading about the psychics' lives, people may need to suspend their disbelief until they see if the information makes sense, and is useful, to them. The psychics' stories are amazing, but people who haven't had these kinds of life experiences may have their imaginations stretched. Keep in mind that these are true stories and real answers which are presented in the psychics' own words, or paraphrased solely for clarity.

3) The notation "G-d" is used.

One of the psychics explained to me that everyone thinks of God differently and that I shouldn't just write "God." I should do something different. Psychics believe that their information comes from a Higher Source, a Divine Energy, a Universal Source, by whatever name people want to call it. The word is just a label and they don't want people to be put off by a label with which they are not comfortable. The psychics tell me that God doesn't want us to confine Him or name Him. The energy and information source can be thought of as a Higher Power.

In the Jewish tradition it is disrespectful to say or write the name of God, except when praying. When writing, the name is hyphenated as "G-d." In this book I have adopted the notation G-d, hoping that people understand that I am referring to a positive, universal energy source which is not interested in being labeled or limited.

4) Only 24 of the 26 people interviewed are quoted by name and profiled.

For this Project, I interviewed 26 people about their personal and professional lives. Twenty-four psychics have approved their interviews and are allowing me to quote them. The other two psychics have not yet approved the use of their interviews for publication. The interviews have been analyzed, but the psychic's full names have not been used. They are referred to as "Nancy, an energy worker" and "George, an artist." Chapter 3 includes psychic snapshots for the 24 people who gave final approval to use their names. These people are working professionally in this field. I interviewed professional psychics because I thought that they would have strong gifts and be willing to share their information with the public. They are living public lives as psychics.

5) I only interviewed 26 people for this book.

This book provides a quick study of psychics. Each person has a unique story and a unique style of working. This is not a complete picture of what it is like to be psychic, but it is a nice introduction. I plan to interview additional psychics so that the ideas in this book can be further refined.

What do the psychics know about why we are here on Earth?

We are each on a journey of self-discovery. We are here on Earth to learn, to teach and to have a physical experience. We are here to taste food, interact with each other, explore emotions, love and travel. We are learning about birth, death and family. We are exploring a magnificent environment.

Those on the other side wish they were here to experience Earth as much as those of us on this side seek to understand universal dynamics. Spirits on the other side have the advantage of seeing the big picture, but we have the sweetness of physical life. Fortunately, we can live with a foot in both worlds. We can experience the beauty of this world while seeking knowledge and truth.

According to the psychics, understanding the cycle of birth, learning, death, integrating, and birth again, makes us more able to enjoy life and passion. As long as we are living in kindness, we can live with gusto, taking risks, knowing that the reason we are here is to try new things and to learn from our experiences.

Just like you and I, psychics may be challenged to learn about self-esteem, trust, interpersonal relationships, or how to be non-judgmental. These challenges help their souls evolve. There is a broad acceptance of reincarnation and a deep knowing that there is more to life than a single lifetime here on Earth.

It is my hope that this book helps people understand and enjoy their personal voyage of self-discovery. I have learned so much on ***My Psychic Search***. Let me tell you all about it . . .

• • •

If you want to follow this on-going interview Project, you can check the website and blogs for current study information, presentation dates, and coupons. The website can be found at: www.MyPsychicSearch.com

Chapter 2 - The Language of Psychics

What do people mean when they talk about psychic ability? What does it mean when psychics say that they talk to Spirit Guides? This chapter explores the definitions of "psychic," "intuitive," "Spirit," and many other commonly used terms in this book. This chapter will help people understand what psychics do and the variety of ways that people with psychic abilities can assist the rest of us. The first part of this chapter discusses the types of readers. The second part discusses the invisible information sources and the third part talks about what psychics do and how they do it.

Are you psychic too? This chapter contains a ***Psychic Skills Checklist***. Scan the list and see which skills you have, then discover the name for each skill. The more you know, the more you understand . . .

People who bring in Information

What is a Psychic?

This simple question has many answers. The word "Psychic" is used to describe people who gather information using more than the five natural senses of sight, taste, hearing, smell, and touch. Psychics tap into an unseen information source and help people find answers to some of life's mysteries. Using more than the five natural senses is often called extra-sensory perception (ESP), but psychics rarely refer to this term.

I interviewed 26 "psychics" for this Project. This word is in quotes because they don't all think of themselves as psychics. Most of the people I interviewed don't like to be labeled at all. They want people to see them as complete human beings, not to hear a label and assume they know something about these extra-ordinarily skilled people. However, in order to communicate a bit about themselves, they call themselves "psychics," "intuitives," "gifted," "readers," "healers," "Mediums," and "energy workers." I think of them as "well connected" to other realms.

Do the words psychic, intuitive, gifted, reader, channeler, spiritual counselor, Medium, shaman, empath, animal communicator, energy worker, healer and Light Worker mean the same thing?

In this book, I use the word "Psychic" as an umbrella term which covers all of the people with extra-sensory abilities. However, some people use that title in a more-limited way. Let's look at some of the different terms, as clarified by the people I interviewed.

Psychic

Some people feel that the word "Psychic" means "to see" and only applies to people who can see the future or see energy, and the flow of energy, around a person. Psychics often see the auras (personal energy fields) around the person with whom they are speaking. Psychics can ***reliably*** tap into an unseen information stream. They can ask for information from their Spirit Guides and other entities and bring that information forward for the rest of us. They see where we are in our lives and the direction in which we are going. In most cases, psychics were born with these talents. They are natural gifts.

Some psychics are clairvoyant (able to see images), clairaudient (able to hear messages), clairscentient (able to feel impressions), and/or claircognizant (able to know). Some psychics are also intuitive.

Intuitive

Intuitive means "to know." Intuitives have the gift of ***spontaneously*** knowing or saying things, but don't feel like it is a talent that they can summon every time they seek information. People with intuitive talent often remark, "The information just pops into my head and I know it is true," or "I just say the words without knowing why I say them." They have valuable information, but it comes on its own, in its own time. Many intuitives don't think of themselves as psychic. They explain that intuition provides a specific piece of information or a focused view of a situation, as opposed to the broad view of issues which can be seen by people who are psychic.

One psychic remarked that psychic and intuitive abilities are completely different because they come from different layers of our personal energy systems. Another psychic felt that intuition came from his Higher Self (his own knowledge), while psychic information came from an outside source.

Many interviewees commented that everyone is intuitive. All people experience synchronicities and intuition. People have hunches and can receive discrete pieces of information. Those who choose to work with these skills can develop them into larger gifts of insight. However, most people are not aware of their abilities, or choose not to use them.

Gifted

People who consider themselves "gifted" work with intuition. This word is often used as an adjective. People think of themselves as "gifted" astrologers or "gifted" card readers. They work with astrology, Tarot cards or some other tool, but in addition to understanding the information presented through the tool, they also receive intuitive information. They combine the information obtained using the tool with their own additional insights. This information comes in at the right time and goes out at the right time. It's not always there.

Reader

Anyone who does psychic or intuitive readings or consultations is considered a reader. They talk to clients and provide information and insights.

Channeler

A person who communicates with non-physical entities is known as a Channeler. These people may talk to non-physical individuals or to spiritual groups. The entities and groups are clearly distinct from the individual who is channeling them. Some people use the term "channeling" whenever they talk to someone who is not another aspect of themselves, such as a Spirit Guide or a person who has died and crossed to the other side.

Sometimes, channeling information feels like receiving a block of thought all at once, then having to find the words to describe it. Other times, channeling information feels more like a conversation. This kind of communication is known as "Conscious Channeling."

The other kind of channeling is called "Trance Channeling." This is when spiritual entities are allowed to enter a person's body and the person in that body steps aside and just listens to the information. The non-physical individual or group talks through the person's voice. This kind of work often addresses broad issues relating to humanity, such as why people come to Earth and how reincarnation works.

Spiritual Counselor

Spiritual Counselors talk with clients and help them understand why things happen in their lives and how to cope with problems. These people provide a new way of thinking about issues. Problems often surface because there are lessons which people need to learn. Spiritual counselors see "the big picture" of clients' lives and, perhaps, their past lives or the reasons they are here, and can help people understand how to deal with current issues.

Medium

Mediums talk to people who have died and crossed to the other side. They communicate with the spirits of the deceased and bring messages from the other side to this side. All Mediums are psychics, but not all psychics are Mediums.

Shaman

Shamans are "way showers." They are aligned with nature and help people find their way on Earth.

Empath

Empaths feel the emotions of other people. They don't just think they know what someone else feels, they actually feel it.

Animal Communicator

These readers connect with pets (living and dead) and other animals.

Energy Worker

Each person lives in an energy field and has energy moving through his or her body. Energy workers direct energy into a client's body. They can also remove blockages which thwart the flow of energy. Energy workers may, or may not, receive intuitive information while working.

Healer

After medical issues have been identified, healers can uses psychic, intuitive, or energy connections to assist patients in healing. There are many kinds of healers. In general, these people guide energy into clients' bodies so that clients can heal themselves. They pointed out that they don't do the healing; they facilitate the healing by bringing in energy. The person has to rise to the occasion and accept the energy in order for healing to begin.

Light Worker
Light Workers draw light (as energy and information) into this physical universe. They help human consciousness evolve. These people volunteered, before birth, to help heal the planet and its population. Some Light Workers help individuals bring in enough energy to vibrate at a higher frequency. Increasing a person's vibration helps them connect to their own information sources.

Many more definitions can be found in Chapter 26, "The Glossary."

Should all of these workers fall under the term "Connectors" or the term "PRISMS"?

Personally, I would like a new word which encompasses all of these workers. Many people dislike the word "Psychic" because it has been associated with fakes. In contrast, the people I spoke with are all well-connected to unseen energy and information. Should we use the all-encompassing term "Connectors?"

How about the word **"PRISMS"?** It stands for **P**sychics, **R**eaders, **I**ntuitives, **S**piritual Counselors, **M**ediums and **S**hamans." It also encompasses Healers, Energy Workers, etc. I believe that PRISMS take the light (energy and information from the other side), bend it through their brains, and shine the colors so everyone can see them.

In this book, I use the words "**Psychics**" and "**PRISMS**" as terms which encompass all of the people who connect with the other side, bringing information, energy and healing to our side.

Sources of Information

What about the term "God" (G-d)?

All of the psychics believe that some form of God is involved in their work although they don't always use the term "God." They work with a high level of energy and each of the psychics has their own concept of God. They surmise that God is an energy which is around us and is a part of us. Some psychics are reluctant to use the word "God" because the term is too closely connected with organized religion and they feel that religion and spirituality are not always the same thing. They comment that the concept of God is huge and should not be referred to in a way which limits the God energy. They refer to this energy as the Supreme Creator of the Universe, the Holy Spirit, a Higher Power, a Universal Energy which connects all of us, a Universal Consciousness, a Universal Intelligence, a Divine Source, and "The Force."

Several psychics thought that it might be more-effective to call this energy "Source" – what all of creation comes from.

One of the psychics pointed out that the word "God" is a defining label and that there is more to God than what people usually think of as God. She feels that the name "God" limits our thinking. She pointed out that in the Jewish tradition, the word "God" is never spelled out; it is hyphenated as "G-d." In her opinion, "G-d" is less limiting; it enlarges the concept and allows G-d to be whatever a person thinks it is. I use the term "G-d" when writing so that everyone can honor their own understanding of the G-d concept.

What about the words "Spirits," "Spirit," and "Spirit Guides" ?

Psychics often refer to "spirits," "Spirit," and "Spirit Guides." They use the term "spirits" to refer to souls who have crossed to the other side. While alive, people have souls. After death, they are spirits.

The word "Spirit" refers to a universal source of energy and information. It can either be singular or plural, depending on the psychic. Some psychics believe Spirit is made up of multiple energies.

Laurie Hays explained:

> "Spirit is similar to a glass of water in that water is a bunch of drops, just like Spirit is a group of individuals. If I take one drop, it's still water. To me, Spirit is a collective group. They could individualize, but why? It takes away its intensity, clarity and power."

In this case, I refer to Spirit as "them." It can seem like a grammatical error, but now you understand why some psychics refer to Spirit as an individual entity and some refer to Spirit as a group of entities.

The term "Spirit Guides" refers to people who have lived on Earth, crossed to the other side, and volunteered to stay in the spirit world so that they can gently guide incarnated people. They are neither male nor female; they are energy. When asked about its role, one Guide said that it preferred to be called a "Cosmic Servant." Some psychics communicate with individual Spirit Guides while others communicate with a group of Spirit Guides.

Who are the Ascended Masters?

Ascended Masters are individuals who were formerly embodied on Earth and learned their life lessons during their incarnations. They are enlightened beings who have undergone a process of spiritual transformation referred to as "Ascension." From the realms of Spirit, the Ascended Masters serve as the teachers of mankind. Examples of Ascended Masters include Jesus, Buddha, Confucius, Mary the Mother of Jesus, Kwan Yin, Saint Germain, Djwal Khul, Elijah and Saint Patrick.

What are angels?

Angels are spiritual messengers who have not lived life in a physical body. Angels convey advice and wisdom, but don't interfere with free will unless people are in mortal danger. People have Guardian Angels who protect them, as well as angels who bring whispered messages.

What about the phrase "Higher Self"?

The Higher Self is an aspect of each person which resides in the non-physical realm. Each person's Higher Self knows why he or she is here and understands the lessons which must be learned.

Does it matter where information comes from?

The people who were interviewed for this Project stressed the importance of working with positive energy and positive entities. They did not work with dark energies. They set boundaries which repelled negative energies. Within their sphere of positive energy, they were often able to identify their information sources. They called upon angels, Archangels, Spirit Guides, Ascended Masters and G-d. Although some people made a distinction between talking to their Higher Self and talking to other sources, most psychics agreed that it didn't really matter where the information came from. The source didn't need a name because it was all the same connection to Spirit. The need to name this connection was a human need.

My intention in trying to define and name things is not to limit concepts, but to ensure that when we communicate with each other, we understand what each of us is trying to say; we have a common language. These definitions are evolving as I talk with more and more people with psychic connections.

Related Definitions

What does the word "Psi" mean?

"Psi" consists of extra-sensory perception (ESP) and psychokinesis. Extra-sensory perception is the power to know by some means other than the five senses. Psychokinesis is the ability to use thought to change physical things and is often referred to as "Mind over Matter." Examples include healing prayer, levitation, and using mental powers to bend spoons or to sail furniture across a room.

What is Ascension?

Ascension is the concept of awakening to a higher level of consciousness. At the ascended level, people understand who they really are and what they have been learning on Earth. Some people liken ascension to entering Heaven alive, with a body. Death is normally the end of life. Through ascension, people no longer need to go through the pain and fear of death in order to return to the spiritual world. It is believed that all people will eventually go through the ascension process and move forward in spiritual evolution.

Psychic Abilities and Tools

What do people with psychic abilities have to offer?

Psychics, Readers, Intuitives, Spiritual Counselors, Mediums, Shamans and energy workers (PRISMS) can offer a fresh take on events in a client's life. Just as a person would talk to a wise friend and see if the friend had insights which could help them, they can talk to a psychic or Intuitive and see if the reader can help them move forward in their life. Most psychic readings are not like a bolt of life-changing information. They are more like a gentle sprinkling of wisdom which helps re-frame the issues being examined. Talking to a psychic reader brings in a different perspective. If someone listens with an open mind, they can see issues in a new way and come up with strategies for dealing with problems. Psychics offer the opportunity for people to understand who they are, what is happening in their lives and their choices for moving forward.

Psychics can explore situations, describe options and help people choose their best course of action. Psychics don't choose for them, people make their own choices.

In addition, talking with PRISMS can open minds to a world of potential. There is comfort in hearing that people are not alone in this world; that there is a greater picture of humanity and that there are reasons why people are here on Earth. Magic, mystery and a world of wonder do exist.

The people who were interviewed for this Project provide the following types of services:

Psychic Readings

A client can sit down with a reader and the reader can access information about that client and help the client understand the larger picture of what is happening in their life. Psychics are often asked about love, health, jobs, finances, and life path. Information from a psychic can provide a new perspective on an issue and can help a person clearly see their choices. Each choice shapes the future and psychics can help people understand how to create the future they want by making the choices which keep them on the path to the future they seek. It's like talking to a friend who has insights, but you don't have to keep going out to lunch with them!

Energy Work

Each person has an energy field which encompasses their physical body. Energy workers clean blockages out of this field, bring in fresh energy, and keep energy flowing through the body.

Healings

A client can sit down with a healer who can help them draw positive energy into their body so that they can facilitate their own healing. This can be physical and/or emotional healing. Sometimes the healing doesn't cure the illness, but helps the client cope with the illness, or make peace with the problem.

Do psychics all do the same thing or do they have specialties?

In the world of psychic connection, there are many specialities. Some psychics do it all, but most psychics have an area of expertise. Some psychics predict the future, while others provide inspirational messages (but not facts), communicate with the dead, communicate with entities who are not in this physical world, communicate with animals and/or help with healing. Other psychics predict financial markets and international issues.

Why do PRISMS do this work?

No matter how we define abilities, the people working professionally in this field mentioned that their mission is to help people. Helping people is why they do what they do publicly. Personally, they do this work because it is who they are. However, life could be easier if they kept their gifts to themselves. Society doesn't always treat people who have intuitive talents very well. People who are working as psychics are going public with what they do because they find it very rewarding to help other people sort out their lives.

Do psychics use tools when they do their work?

Many readers use tools to access information. For example, they may read astrological charts, explore numerology, read Tarot cards, read palms or use crystal balls. Several of the readers felt that these approaches opened the energy so that they could access information from the non-physical world. Other readers used these devices just because their clients liked them. Clients preferred to think that the information came from the tool (such as Tarot cards) rather than thinking that the psychic could read their mind. Other psychics mentioned that they liked having something like a card layout between them and the client. It gave people something to look at and provided a little physical space between the reader and the client. For more information on why PRISMS use tools, check out Chapter 12, "Tools of the Psychic Trade."

Psychic Skills Checklist

Psychics are born with a variety of natural skills which often include the ability to see or hear information. In addition, psychics can learn new skills like Reiki (a way to channel energy) and can also learn to use tools, such as Tarot cards and crystal balls. Below, is a list of the skills mentioned by the psychics. To get a clear picture of someone's abilities, ask them which gifts they use. Remember, having more gifts isn't better or worse than having fewer gifts. If a reader has only one gift and receives all of the information he or she needs, that one gift is plenty.

If you think you might be psychic, check off the gifts which you have.

<u>Natural Skills</u>

Do you:

- ❏ Hear voices? (known as Clairaudience or clear-hearing)
- ❏ See images? (known as Clairvoyance or clear-seeing; the ability to see with the "third eye")
- ❏ Smell aromas? (known as Clairalience or clear smelling)
- ❏ Taste something which isn't actually there? (known as Clairgustance or clear-tasting)
- ❏ See auras?
- ❏ Feel auras?
- ❏ Have a physical feeling in your body when you talk to someone?
- ❏ Have an emotional feeling in your body when you talk to someone?
- ❏ Feel another person's emotions or physical pain? (known as Clairsentience or clear feeling, for example, getting a "gut feeling" about someone you just met)
- ❏ Experience another person's emotions? (known as Empathy)
- ❏ Experience total knowing? (known as Claircognizance or clear-knowing)
- ❏ Know other people's thoughts? (known as Telepathy)
- ❏ Have information just "pop into my head"? (an aspect of Intuition)
- ❏ Have information "just come out of my mouth"? (an aspect of Intuition)

- ❑ See the future? (known as Precognition; the ability to have thoughts or visions about events before they happen)
- ❑ Have feelings about the future? (known as Presentiment; like a hunch about what is going to happen)
- ❑ Know things about a person by holding one of their belongings, like a wallet? (known as Psychometry)
- ❑ Communicate with the deceased? (known as Mediumship)
- ❑ See ghosts?
- ❑ Communicate with alien entities?
- ❑ Astral travel?
- ❑ Speak in tongues?
- ❑ Have prophetic dreams?
- ❑ Have medical intuition?
- ❑ Have a sensitivity to energy?
- ❑ Perform automatic writing?
- ❑ Channel information?
- ❑ Move physical objects with your mind? (known as Psychokinesis)
- ❑ Connect with someone else's energy?
- ❑ Help others connect with their Higher Self?
- ❑ Take on others' illnesses?

- ❑ Receive information about past lives?
- ❑ Help with past-life regressions?
- ❑ Remember your own past lives?
- ❑ Communicate with plant Devas?
- ❑ Communicate with nature spirits?
- ❑ Communicate with animals?
- ❑ Create intuitive art?
- ❑ Use music to link to the Divine?
- ❑ Help people heal energetically?
- ❑ Lay on hands to assist healing?
- ❑ Track energy?
- ❑ Perform spiritual counseling?
- ❑ Lead Shamanic journeys?

<u>Learned Skills</u>

- ❑ Perform Reiki?
- ❑ Perform bodywork?
- ❑ Perform cranial/sacral work?
- ❑ Perform massage therapy?

- ❑ Perform chakra balancing?
- ❑ Perform psychic surgery?
- ❑ Use Emotional Freedom Techniques?
- ❑ Work with flower essences?
- ❑ Perform exorcisms?
- ❑ Perform cord cuttings?
- ❑ See what is happening in a far away location using your mind? (known as Remote Viewing)

<u>Tools and Modalities</u>

- ❑ Read Tarot cards?
- ❑ Read palms?
- ❑ Read Akashic Records?
- ❑ Read a crystal ball, mirror or other reflective surface? (known as Scrying)
- ❑ Work with astrology?
- ❑ Work with numerology?
- ❑ Other

<u>Identification</u>

Are you:

- ❑ A Psychic?

- ❑ An Intuitive?
- ❑ An Empath?
- ❑ A Medium?
- ❑ A Healer?
- ❑ A Shaman?
- ❑ An Energy Worker?
- ❑ A Light Worker? (someone who works with light as energy and information)

<u>Communication</u>

Do you communicate with:

- ❑ Spirit Guides?
- ❑ A group of non-physical entities?
- ❑ Angels?
- ❑ Archangels?
- ❑ Ascended Masters such as Mother Mary, Kwan Yin, Buddha, Christ and/or Djwal Khul?
- ❑ Another person's Higher Self?
- ❑ G-d? Source? The Divine? The Creator by any name?

Now, that we understand the basic concepts and definitions, let's find out more about the people who were interviewed for this Project.

Chapter 3 - Psychic Snapshots

While psychics can pull information from unseen sources, I have to glean information from professional psychics. I interviewed 26 people for this Project. They all work as professional psychics, intuitives, energy workers and/or healers. Their life stories are fascinating. This chapter presents a brief introduction to 24 people who were interviewed between June 2008 and January 2011. They are presented in the order in which they were interviewed. Two other people, Nancy (an energy worker) and George (an artist), were interviewed but have been unable to formally approve their information so they are not highlighted in this chapter. However, their information and insights are used throughout the book.

1) Patricia Kirkman - Numerologist, Intuitive

Patricia Kirkman has offered intuitive readings in the Tucson area since 1994. She always knew she had abilities, but she didn't realize that they were *psychic* abilities until she was in high school.

Years later, after her first husband passed away, Patricia went to an astrologer who provided an insightful reading for her and she started taking lessons. After learning about astrology, she learned about numerology and it fit like a glove. Patricia is a numerologist/astrologer/intuitive who appears on local radio and TV shows.

Occasionally, people come to Patricia before their baby is born and ask about the numerological influences of baby names. Patricia thinks people choose their own names and that is why several names are planted with the parents. Even if a parent picked a name so that there were no holes, no Karmic lessons for the child to learn, the child would have a little bit of each lesson. People get the name they need.

Patricia believes that anything she can do to help someone make their road in life easier is a blessing. When she sits down with a client, she asks for their birth name and date. Thoughts come to her and answers come out of her mouth. She believes that we all have intuitive abilities, we just use them differently.

When Patricia sees clients, she gives them "a road map of their life" that they can take when they leave so they can do their own work. She is a guide. She shows clients around their lives, but their actions are their own choices. She tells people about their options and their potential lessons. According to Patricia, people know that there are certain lessons that they need to learn, but they don't always recognize them until they are in the middle of the lessons. Sometimes people repeat patterns and it helps to have someone point out what is happening. Then, it is up to the client to make changes. If people repeat issues and have trouble understanding their life lessons, Patricia can help them learn to change the way they use their energies.

At one point, Patricia worked in the Human Resources department of a large corporation. Her intuitive abilities helped her understand which candidates would be good employees and showed her ways to cope with workplace issues.

Patricia organizes and runs the monthly *Mystic Messengers Psychic Fair* in Tucson, Arizona. She co-authored *The Complete Idiot's Guide: Numerology Workbook* (Alpha Books, 2009).

2) Cecilia Nemmers - Psychic

As a child, Cecilia Nemmers knew she had a gift, but she didn't know what it was called. When she was 18, she met a palm reader who explained her abilities to her. The palm reader looked at her hand and said, "You should be reading mine!" Then she looked into Cecilia's eyes and said, "I've been waiting a long time to meet you." She had been told that Cecilia was coming to her. At that point in her life, Cecilia discovered that she was psychic. The palm reader became Cecilia's mentor.

As a young adult, Cecilia moved in with a family who lived in a mortuary. Bodies were laid out in caskets in the living room. Here, Cecilia had her first experience of watching spirits walk up to their coffins, look at their bodies, and walk away. She thought that was odd . . .

Cecilia communicates with a group of Spirit Guides which is like a family to her. When she was younger, her abilities were "on" all the time and she didn't know how to shut them off. The group members all talked at the same time and kept her up at night. Finally, she told them to stop talking simultaneously and to select a single spokesperson. After that, it was easier for Cecilia to work with her Guides. Now, she talks to her group of Guides about planetary changes, the economy, and other issues relating to humanity.

To begin a psychic reading, Cecilia examines her client's palm so that the energy opens. When she touches someone's hand, she can travel through their energy field. Cecilia asks each client if he or she has questions. When people ask questions, it opens their energy and allows someone to give them answers. From that point on, the reading becomes personally tailored to each client's needs. Cecilia receives information through her Guides, the client's energy field, and the spirits for whom the client has questions. Her gifts are multi-faceted. She can see, hear and feel any beings who are in the room at the time of the reading. The information comes through clearly and in words which can be easily understood by the person being read. The readings are never rushed, and the sessions do not end until the clients have all the information which they seek.

Some clients expect Cecilia to give them answers. What she does is confirm, or not-confirm, their feelings. People often think that they need to do something, but Cecilia sees that they are acting out of fear. By the time clients leave, they may have decided to change their course. They may think that Cecilia told them what to do, but they decided for themselves, using their own free will.

Cecilia believes that all people are energetically connected to each other and to G-d. In her view, G-d is a creator, but he doesn't get overly-involved in daily life. When people make a mess, it is up to them to clean it up. As a group, people need to find the solutions to the problems which they create on Earth. However, there are angels, Guides, and people who have gone before, who can help solve problems.

Cecilia values her psychic abilities and would not want to live without them. She has memories from before she could talk and memories from before she was born. She remembers standing on a cloud bank, waiting to jump into this lifetime.

According to Cecilia, the world is going through a period of chaos right now because people need chaos to make changes. No change is ever made when things are going well. There needs to be a change in government, a change in thinking, and a change in the fact that people think they need government. This change will affect the whole world. Instead of thinking of themselves as citizens of a particular nation, people will begin to think of themselves as citizens of Earth. Cecilia believes that people are inter-dimensional beings who are evolving.

3) Cynthia Rae - Intuitive Empowerment

Cynthia Rae is intuitive. According to Cynthia, the word "intuitive" means "knowing," while the word "psychic" is closer to "seeing." When Cynthia talks to people, words fly out of her mouth and she doesn't always know where they came from. She believes that everyone is intuitive and already has their answers, but they don't always trust what they know. Her job is to empower people.

Psychic talent runs in Cynthia's family. Her grandfather was a spiritualist minister with healing gifts. In addition, Cynthia had a near-death experience (NDE) as she was being born and this experience may have opened her abilities. At 21, she had a second NDE.

Cynthia works as a medical assistant/receptionist/co-office manager for a doctor who practices preventative and alternative medicine. Originally, she worked for several years as a medical assistant with a different group of doctors. She knew she had intuitive gifts, but those doctors would not listen to her medical input. In order to work one-on-one with patients, Cynthia attended massage therapy school. There, she discovered that she could feel things through clients and that she could lay hands on clients and help them heal themselves.

When working on clients, Cynthia feels pulses between each section of the body. Each section has its own rhythm and the rhythms need to be in sync with each other. If there is pain in a muscle, Cynthia can put her fingers on the patient in a particular way and feel the inconsistencies. She holds her fingers in place until there is a consistent pulse. When she takes her fingers away, the pain is gone.

When talking with clients, Cynthia doesn't work with a specific set of Spirit Guides. She is open to whomever wants to provide the highest and best information for her clients. She believes:

> "When you give the entities who are providing information a name or a label of any sort, you are narrowing down the information and the opportunity to get information. If you only call on Archangel Michael, then that's all you are going to get. I take whomever is out there and wants to give information."

Cynthia always asks the Higher Realms to bring the information which her clients seek. Sometimes she sees a vision, has an emotional feeling or receives a physical feeling. There is an internal conversation and the information comes to her. Her job is to give the information with the purest of heart. Whatever clients do with that information is their responsibility.

Cynthia believes that we are here on Earth to experience and grow in ways that no other soul has the opportunity to do. We are honored to be here. We each have the opportunity to affect other people's lives. We are the lucky ones who can taste, see, hear, touch, smell and physically experience life on Earth.

4) Beth Hays - Flower Essence Practitioner

Beth Hays is clairvoyant (sees things), clairscentient (feels things), clairaudient (hears things) and claircognizant (knows things). She finds it very rewarding and purposeful to help people. Beth connects with the Spirit Guide and Angelic Realms. She works with her own Spirit Guides and angels, as well as her client's Spirit Guides and angels. She creates a sacred space before working with clients. In this energetic environment, the Guides speak to her. Beth hears and sees things. Ultimately, she has a feeling of total "knowing."

Beth is a certified Flower Essence Practitioner and she makes her own flower essences. These essences help clients achieve their goals. Flower essences come from flowers which are cut and placed in water. While they are in the water, there is a process which allows the qualities of the flowers to be transferred into the energy of the water. The water holds the energy. People can drink this essence mixed with water, or spray it on their skin, and benefit from the plant's essence. According to Beth, our bodies vibrate at a certain natural frequency and our emotions modify that vibration. When a person uses the correct essence, it shifts their vibration so that they can vibrate at the frequency of having achieved their goal. Essences should be used each day in order to maintain the new vibration.

Originally, Beth used flower essences developed by other practitioners. Through meditation, Beth was inspired to make her own essences. She understood that the essences she would make would not re-invent products which were already available. The new essences would be intuitively guided. When she accepted the role of making essences which were guided and inspired, the desert began speaking to her.

Beth's company is called "Integrated Essences." She distills essences from Santa Catalina Mountain wildflowers. Beth also creates crystal and stone essences which work in the same way as the flower essences.

Beth's work is very goal-oriented. When clients come to her, they need to know what is wrong and they also need to know what they want. It is often easier to say what is wrong than it is to pin down what people really want. They have to know what their answer *feels* like. Then, Beth can custom blend a flower essence which helps the client vibrate at the frequency of the solution to their problem.

5) Gina Stanfill - Intuitive, Reiki Master

As a child, Gina Stanfill knew she was different from other people. She spent most of her time in her bedroom because that was where she could deal with the realms and the spirits who came to visit. The spirits were her friends and she hung out with them. During the day, Gina went to school and functioned, then she immediately returned home and hid in her room. At night, she astral traveled. Although she was happy, she worried that she was crazy.

It wasn't until Gina was an adult that she found a mentor who explained that she wasn't crazy; she was intuitive. She can read a client's energy and tell them if their energy is going to help them get where they want to go. If it isn't, she can help the client understand how to change their energy in order to achieve their goals.

Gina reads Shustah Divination and Meditation cards which are similar to Tarot cards. The cards trigger something in her and she tells the client whatever comes to mind. Words pop out of her mouth. Along the way, Gina has learned to trust the information which comes to her. She likes it best when people are direct and ask specific questions. She pinpoints questions because the Universe answers general questions in a general way and detailed questions in a more-detailed way. Gina remarked, "If people don't take the time to figure out what they are asking, how can the Universe provide an answer?"

Gina doesn't hear voices or see images; words just come out of her mouth. People say things which trigger her response and, as they talk, people are helped. Gina finds that people don't trust their own feelings because their egos have led them down a stray path so many times that they are confused about what they feel or don't feel; what is good for them and what is not good for them. Ego confuses people. It wants to control people. Once people see that they have options which are not driven by their ego, they are free to make new choices.

According to Gina, there is no such thing as the future; there is only the "now." The past no longer exists and the future isn't here. People invent the future every time they take a breath and a step. The past provides wisdom which can be drawn upon, but it can't be allowed to dictate the future. People grow and change and just because something didn't work 20 years ago, doesn't mean it won't work today. When people make decisions based on who they used to be, they just repeat cycles and lessons at an older age. If they listen to who they are now, and make decisions based on who they are today, they make wise decisions. They move into the future. People are here to experience things and the sooner they experience them, the faster they move to the next thing they have the opportunity to experience. However, people spend a lot of time going in circles.

Gina is also a Reiki Master. She can guide energy into a client's body and help the energy move to wherever it needs to go. The energy flows through her. She calls it in and is a conduit for it, but the client has to be willing to accept the energy into the body for his or her highest good.

In addition to working as an intuitive reader and an energy worker, Gina also has a bookkeeping business. While working on business accounts, clients often talk to Gina and find that they benefit from her knowledge and insights. Teachers come in all guises – even as bookkeepers.

6) Leah Taylor - Psychic, Medium, Medical Intuitive

Leah Taylor has always known she was psychic. As a child, she knew what other people felt and thought, and what was happening with them. She remembered her past lives. She was born into this life knowing which gifts she had.

When Leah reads for a client, she sees their past and their future. Because everyone has free will, there may be several possibilities for the future. Leah can see which way a client's energy is going and that knowledge helps her predict what will happen. She sees the client's life, their childhood, their thoughts, their heart, their relationships, and their living and dead relatives.

Leah sees images and hears messages in her mind. She speaks with Spirit Guides and can converse with her client's Higher Self. She hears these voices in her mind, not with her ears.

Leah is also a medical intuitive and an energy worker. When working with a client, Leah sometimes has a whole body image come up in front of her. She can look up and feel with her hands what is going on with someone's body. Because of her abilities, Leah can often see and heal medical conditions. She diagnosed her mother's cancer and helped her to recover from a debilitating condition. To help her mother, she suggested a combination of traditional medicine and other healing techniques, such as Reiki and herbs.

Leah does trance channeling which allows her Guides to speak through her. She also communicates with animals and often sees them on the other side with their deceased owners. Because she is a Medium, Leah can communicate with clients' deceased friends and relatives.

According to Leah, people who die will leave their body and usually be escorted to the other side by their relatives. Their relatives still love them and want to help as they are going through this transition. On the other side, spirits can learn with teachers or explore, then eventually reincarnate if they so choose. When Leah sees the other side, she sees people with friends and family members. Sometimes she sees multiple generations of people together. She might see people smoking or cooking, but she thinks it is just a symbol of those things. She believes that we have an etheric (energy) body which gets less and less dense the longer we are not incarnated. Leah feels that our personalities are physically based and are influenced by our human experiences. After death, we can enjoy being with people who we might not have liked on Earth. However, she knows it is not totally different on the other side. People are still people.

In addition, while there is much to be learned on the other side, Leah believes that most of our building is done in this life. People can learn lessons in the soul world, but to build a true spiritual legacy, develop a talent, or refine a deep character trait, that work is best done in the flesh.

Leah thinks that there is more that we don't know about human consciousness than we do know. There are possibilities out there and, even if it isn't the norm to have miracles and healings, miracles happen. She encourages people to explore the limits of human potential and consciousness.

7) Richard Schickel - Psychic, Medical Intuitive, Healer

Richard Schickel has survived three near-death experiences (NDEs). After he turned 40 and had a healing, his gifts opened up. He found that he could speak in tongues and understand what he was saying. Richard is a medical intuitive and a healer. He assists with past-life hypnotherapy, talks to pets, sees auras and performs exorcisms and cord cuttings. Cords are energetic attachments between people.

When clients come to Richard, they put their hands on top of Richard's hands so that their hand chakras connect. Richard connects with each person's energy and understands what the person is thinking. He sees the client's energy and knows what is in this person's mind and heart. He sees the truth even if the client is lying to himself. He provides past-life connections, sees spirits around clients, sees auras and hears voices. However, just because he receives all this information doesn't mean that he can share it. It can be too much to share with a client all at once.

Richard is also a "hand trembler." He can put his hand over someone's body and do a scan. If his hand trembles, he is feeling trapped energy. Because he is a medical intuitive, he sees and feels medical issues. He has to be cautious about what he says and remember to refer people to doctors. However, Richard is also a healer. In order to facilitate healing, he sometimes has to guide clients back in time and help them finish off past lives. If people can release their anger and fear, healing can take place. According to Richard, anger and fear are the basis for disease.

Richard works with the Higher Spirits, the energy of G-d, the Ascended Masters and a group of Spirit Guides. They come in at different times for different people. They tell him what he needs to know, when he needs to know it, for each particular person.

According to Richard, Heaven is whatever people want it to be. It is spiritual enlightenment. It is a wonderful, peaceful place. However, after a while, souls feel drawn to more learning. It becomes boring to be in perfection all the time. At that time, souls can chose to reincarnate. On the other side, surrounded by perfection, it is harder to learn lessons. On Earth, the lessons are harder, but it is easier to learn them.

Richard doesn't see any conflict between the concepts of Karma and G-d. He believes that Karma is used to burn off negative issues so that people can get closer to the G-d energy. People can only deal with a few issues during each lifetime. People need many lifetimes to learn all of their lessons. It's like people are rough diamonds. They need to polish one facet of their diamond, then return to polish another facet.

Richard's mission on Earth is to wake people up. He has had "normal" lives on Earth before, but this life is different.

8) Shirli Millmond - Psychic, Life Coach

Shirli Millmond was only five or six years old when she began having terrifying dreams and hearing voices. She knew things about other people and these people began asking her for advice. As a teenager, she was often surprised when people wanted her guidance, but she found that she was capable of providing the advice they sought.

In her teens, Shirli trained in Judo and qualified for Olympic sports. However, while training, she became sick with mononucleosis which limited her ability to compete in her sport.

At 21, she began working in a mystical shop and giving Tarot card readings. She knew the answers without the cards, but people liked to see the cards. One day, she did a reading and the client started to cry. Shirli realized that she didn't want the responsibility of being a card reader so she turned in another direction and began teaching Judo to children. When she worked with children with special needs, she found that she knew exactly what these children needed. Her intuition provided guidance.

Shirli wanted to help people in a way which gave them power and moved them towards their goals so she earned a Business Degree and started a life coaching business. She developed the skills to help people and to give them a push. Now, as part of her life coaching business, Shirli uses her intuition to understand what people need to hear. She sees the future and helps people make the most of it. She helps them reach their potential. Her work is very goal-oriented. Shirli feels that life coaches can help people exercise their brains until they learn to think differently. When people talk to psychics, coaches or teachers, they can hear a different perspective. If they listen with an open mind, they can gradually change their lives.

In addition to life coaching, Shirli also provides Tarot card readings. These readings address life issues and personal lessons. According to Shirli, people get the same lessons over and over until they learn the lessons and make changes. If they don't change, they repeat the lesson. If they can't understand the lesson on their own, they should seek help. A psychic reader can provide a fresh perspective on the situation.

During Shirli's readings, she discusses work, relationships, family and health. She helps people be the best that they can be and attain their full potential. Clients receive tools and abilities to deal with their problems. They clearly see their life and the things which they want to achieve.

According to Shirli, "You always get what your heart wishes for; not what your mind wishes for, but what your heart wishes for."

9) To-Ree'-Nee' Wolf - Energy Tracker

Since she was a small child, To-Ree'-Nee' Wolf has known that she was different from other people. She remembers Jesus teaching her lessons in her dreams. She identifies with wolves and often feels as if she is part of their pack. To-Ree'-Nee' can remember portions of her past lives here on Earth. In fact, she remembers negotiating a contract before agreeing to come to Earth for this incarnation.

When working with a client, To-Ree'-Nee' begins to prepare as soon as she hears from the individual. She usually receives a telephone call and the energy opens up when she hears the person's voice. She makes herself attentive to the images, thoughts and feelings which come to her. She prays and asks to be of the highest and best use, and to be able to give people the information which they seek. Before a client comes to her home, she sits on her porch and interacts with the nature realm. She works with ravens, hawks, and nature folk. She looks for unusual synchronicities and makes herself available for whatever information shows up.

During readings, To-Ree'-Nee' hears and sees information. Sometimes she sees images around a client. Sometimes she sees energy lines which go back to different times. Sometimes she feels things in her body. The client's issues drive the way she receives information. To-Ree'-Nee' identifies herself as an "Energy Tracker." She tracks time lines to see where problems originally arose and to determine if things can shift for her client. She tries to find the most positive, highest, best energy for each person.

To-Ree'-Nee' hears what she calls "The VOICE." It is a facet of the Divine. She doesn't feel that she works with Guides or a group of advisors, rather, she believes that she gleans information from the quantum realm.

To-Ree'-Nee' has read Tarot cards since the 1980s. She feels that the imagery on the cards sometimes triggers information and bypasses the rational mind. She doesn't need the cards to read for clients, but clients like to see the cards.

According to To-Ree'-Nee', psychics can give clients information so that they can make wise choices. A psychic reading is like a helpful counseling tool. She doesn't think that psychics can predict the future because the future is made up of all the minute choices people make in the moment. There might be four appointments in a lifetime which are predestined, but if a person chooses not to show up, they don't happen. The future is very flexible. The future which seems set in concrete, changes as soon as a person gets out of their car and decides to go a different way. A whole new time line opens up.

To-Ree'-Nee' believes that loves holds the universe together. People may think that love is a passive energy, but love is the most serious dynamic force on the planet. She believes that we are all connected. To-Ree'-Nee' remarked, "If we understood that we were profoundly connected by love . . . if we knew that a child who died in Zimbabwe was connected to the steel worker in middle America who was connected to the Inuit who was connected to the little girl in Bolivia, and that we were all in this together, the world would be very different."

She also believes that it is possible to accomplish work while asleep and in the dream world. Certain realms of dreaming access higher dimensions.

In addition to her work tracking energy, To-Ree'-Nee' is a professional artist. Her gifts and abilities work seamlessly together. She is an artist, a psychic and an intuitive all at the same time. These gifts are used to listen to clients and communities. She tries to make sure that everyone is heard, whether they state their opinions aloud or not.

10) Erik Assman - Empath, Reiki Master, Spiritual Counselor

Erik Assman is an empath. He actually feels what other people feel. He is also a Tarot card reader, a Reiki Master and a Spiritual Counselor. Although Erik can read Tarot cards for clients, he prefers to perform Reiki (energy work) because he believes Reiki helps people in broader ways than answering questions while reading cards.

When a client comes for Reiki treatments, the person lays on a table and Erik touches him or her lightly or floats his hands over the body. There may be incense or relaxing music. As Erik performs Reiki, he sees the body as an energy matrix and he tries to align it. He looks for places where things aren't right and sends energy in to re-align the matrix. Sometimes, he sees the beginning of disease manifesting in the body. Sometimes, he sees actual disease. Sometimes, after Reiki treatments, people experience a huge emotional outpouring.

Erik's psychic ability is connection. When he connects with someone, he "zones out." He hears things. He feels what the person is feeling and gets an idea of what they <u>want</u> to hear and what they <u>need</u> to hear.

When Erik works as a Spiritual Counselor, he listens to people and talks to them about their problems. He provides emotional counseling and helps them connect with their own spirit so that they are better prepared to deal with future problems. There is a spiritual aspect to each issue. According to Erik, "It is important to deal with emotional and mental problems, but some problems stem from a lack of connection with Spirit. People end up living on auto-pilot to such an extent that they may seem healthy emotionally and mentally, but they have lost meaning in life."

Erik remembers his past lives. There is a lineage of psychics in his family so his mother understood when, as a child, Erik talked about his past lives. He also dreams about his own past lives and the past lives of other people who are connected to him by genetic memory. Dreams about his ancestors are very different than dreams about his own past lives. He might be in a certain person's body, but he is just an observer. He can't always understand what they are thinking or talking about, but he recognizes people and sees events which happened long ago.

Erik also communicates with animals. This kind of communication is soft and gentle. Animals "don't have lives in their heads" so they can be easier to read than humans. Erik feels what animals feel.

11) Cherie Fraine - Psychic, Reiki Master

Cherie Fraine has been giving psychic readings since 1993. She also travels around the country leading Shamanic Journeys. On these journeys, Cherie takes people into a parallel universe where spirits live so that people can receive their own guidance.

Cherie began seeing auras when she was only seven years old. Because she has spoken with Spirit Guides all of her life, they were able to explain the auras to her. Cherie has always had a direct connection to the spirit realm.

When Cherie reads for people, she sees and hears information. In addition, her Spirit Guides tell her what is coming. She uses Tarot cards for the person she is reading because people feel comfortable when they can look at something. However, Cherie is also able to sit down and read people without using any tools. Clients can bring a person's name on a folded piece of paper, or bring a photograph, and Cherie can tell them about the person and the things that have happened in that person's life. She doesn't need to see the person or have the person nearby in order to do this work.

Cherie commented that one of the difficult things about doing readings is telling the difference between "spirit time" and "people time." Time doesn't exist on the other side, but it exists on Earth. In spirit time, "soon" could be anything from tomorrow until three months from now. She has worked out a system with her Guides to use Tarot cards to be precise about time.

Cherie is also a Reiki Master teacher and can help people heal.

Cherie believes that we are all connected. Every molecule is connected to every other molecule. It doesn't matter if it is a tabletop, a rock, or a dog; everything is connected. We all breath the same air. Cherie believes that all of our answers are available in the collective unconscious. If we know how to tap into it, we can ask questions and receive answers. On that subliminal level, we are all connected.

When it comes to the future, Cherie thinks it is very malleable. Readings can indicate that a certain situation will occur at a certain time and, if the person does nothing which affects that outcome, it will happen that way. But almost anything can affect timing. Nothing is carved in stone. People have freedom of choice and every choice lays the groundwork for a different outcome.

When it comes to 2012, Cherie believes:

> "People will either get things together, or they won't. People who get it together will survive and people who don't, won't. There is going to be a big house-cleaning. It won't be about survival in the sense of having five years worth of food in the house, it will have more to do with what a person is thinking and how they treat other people."

The universe is an abundant place and Cherie thinks that there will be a much more level playing field in the future.

12) Trish Silay - Intuitive, The *One Brain* System

Trish Silay doesn't think of herself as a psychic; however, she knew she had some psychic abilities as a child. She saw things like fairies, but she didn't know what they were. Her mother told her that it was "just her imagination," so she shut down that part of her brain. Also as a child, Trish picked up on other people's energy, but she didn't realize what was happening at the time. This situation overwhelmed her because she felt other people's feelings. As she matured, Trish learned to separate what she was feeling from what other people were feeling.

As a young adult, Trish thought she might be crazy. She felt that she didn't fit into this world. She began working with a system called *One Brain* and the system helped her integrate both sides of her brain. She felt better. It took a while, but she was able to return to what she had always known she was: intuitive. Then, the *One Brain* system opened her psychic abilities. According to Trish, the *One Brain* system is about empowerment. Once someone learns to tune into their Higher Self, their abilities surface.

Now, Trish uses the *One Brain* system to help clients. This system uses muscle testing to help people understand their personal belief systems and how those belief systems can block them from being fully who they are. Muscle testing provides bio-feedback from the body. Sometimes, the body remembers events and traumas better than the mind. Trish gently touches her client's arm to begin the bio-feedback process. By asking "yes" and "no" questions, bio-feedback allows Trish to gather information from the client so that she can help them clear their issues. Surprisingly, muscle testing works over the phone. Trish is able to test her own muscles as a surrogate for the client's muscles.

When clients come to Trish, they discuss the issue they want to resolve. Trish tunes in to each client's body and uses bio-feedback to access information. In addition, Trish may hear messages or see images relating to the client. In some cases, her body becomes a rod and she feels things. Then, she relays the information to the person. When she is open, she receives the total energy of the client. Trish connects to the person's physical, mental, emotional, or essence self. By sharing information with the client, the client better understands their issues and this process allows healing to begin.

According to Trish, the *One Brain* system helps people clear and diffuse their issues so that they are no longer confused. People begin to feel centered and integrated. They stop reacting to events in their lives and feel like they have choices.

In order to do this work, Trish connects with her Higher Self, universal intelligence and nature's intelligence. Spirit Guides surround her. When Trish is attuned to her Higher Self, she understands what needs to be done and how to help other people.

13) Laurie Hays - Spiritual Intuitive, Psychic

Laurie Hays has been doing psychic readings in Tucson for more than 20 years. She often works over the phone and finds that readings over the phone work very well because she isn't distracted by facial expressions or body language. In addition, Laurie volunteers as a Chaplain at a local hospital.

When Laurie was about 13 years old, she could close her eyes and see images. She told her mother about it, but her mother shushed her and told her that everyone could do that. She was raised Catholic and it was not something which was discussed. Her mother told her that reading Tarot cards and horoscopes meant she would burn in Hell.

It wasn't until Laurie was 26 or 27 that she found a mentor. She went for a psychic reading and the woman said, "You can do this as well as I can." Laurie knew she had a powerful gift, but she didn't know how it worked. Her mentor taught her how to use her psychic abilities.

Laurie is very visual and has a creative imagination. She <u>feels</u> through her imagination and also receives images this way.

According to Laurie, being psychic means that she is very sensitive to emotions. Joys are tremendous. When nice things happen, she feels like a happy little kid. The downside is that when she is hurt, she feels devastated. When she knows good things are going to happen, she is giddy. When she sees sad things, she suffers.

When Laurie gives readings, it is almost as if a part of her brain steps aside and another part comes through. The information comes to her as fast as thought. She gives the messages to clients at the speed they are received so her working brain doesn't have time to interfere and say, "Don't go there. That would be rude!" As she gives information, it picks up speed. Laurie says whatever Spirit tells her and sometimes she can't believe the things which come out of her mouth. She has asked to be "Divine loving truth." Her purpose is to help people. As she works, information flows through her. However, Laurie doesn't remember the messages in the readings.

In her personal spiritual work, Laurie communicates with Mother Mary, Kwan Yin, Buddha and Christ. These are her four pillars and they have permission to tell her everything. She knows that there are other positive entities out there, but she asks that all messages come through her four Guides. When working with clients, Laurie unites her Spirit Guides with the client's Spirit Guides.

According to Laurie, "Spirit" is not an individual entity. It is like a collective. "Spirit" is similar to a glass of water in that water is a bunch of drops, just like Spirit is a group of individuals. If one drop is taken away, it is still water. They could individualize, but it would reduce the intensity, clarity and power. When she asked Spirit for the names of her personal Spirit Guides, she was shown a group, like a circle, around Mother Earth and Laurie understood that it was the connectedness of all consciousness which provided information.

Laurie thinks that 2012 will bring a shift in thinking. After 2012, people will have a new perspective. There is going to be a shift, but it doesn't mean that people will be obliterated. This is the hippy/baby boomer generation. As rebels from the start, this generation will change the way people think about senior citizens and everything else.

14) Kat Riegel - Animal Communicator

When she was growing up, Kat Riegel had a few experiences which made her wonder about psychic phenomena. She was fascinated by information about being psychic and wanted to be psychic, but she realized that having a desire, and actually being able to do readings, were two different things.

As an adult, Kat had a cat who was acting up. Kat attended a class to learn about animal communication. People brought photos of their animals so that they could attempt readings for each other. As soon as Kat tried her first reading, she realized that she was able to get information from the photo of a dog. She discovered that she had a gift. Since then, Kat has taken several more animal communication classes. Sometimes she feel like a sponge; she wants to know everything!

According to Kat, there is an intuitive area near the solar plexus where emotions come through. She gets a sensation, almost like her stomach is flipping, when she has made a connection with an animal. In addition, when she gets "yes" answers, she feels that flip. For "no" answers, or if she is on the wrong track, there's no feeling at all. Kat also gets pictures in her mind and, sometimes, hears sentences. If she is on a topic an animal likes, she feels warm and good.

Kat connects directly with animals. She doesn't need to work through Spirit Guides. If the animal is alive, it is easy to establish a connection. If the animal has passed, she goes directly to their energy. The energy of a person or animal who has passed is very different; Kat feels "swirly" as if she has been spinning in circles, then trying to stand still.

When communicating with pets, Kat prefers to use a photo of the animal rather than having the animal present. When the animal is in the room, it is often distracted by Kat (and by the activities going on in the room) making it more difficult for Kat to communicate with the animal.

People come to Kat when they want to know how their pet is doing. Is the animal happy and healthy? Does the animal need something different in terms of care? Sometimes there are animals with an illness or injury and the people want to know what happened and if they are doing everything possible to help the animal. When an animal has passed, people often want to know how, and why, the animal died.

People also want to know if their deceased pet will come back as another animal. Kat has been told by animals that they want to come back, but it is not their time. She has had other readings where the animal had already come back. Contacting animals who have passed, and are now alive in a new body, can be confusing.

Kat suggests that when people want to communicate with their pets, they say what they are thinking out loud and think the picture in their mind. This is the easiest way to communicate.

In addition to pets, Kat also communicates with horses, iguanas, owls, chickens, cows, parrots, fish and ferrets.

15) Marta Taylor - Energy Sensitive

Marta Taylor has been interested in Tarot cards, Ouija Boards, palm reading, and psychic channeling since she was a child. Now, she works with the Akashic Records, practices Reiki and works with flower essences. Marta also reads cards. She prefers Mah Jongg cards because the Mah Jongg deck reflects the "here and now" and provides more-immediate information than Tarot cards.

When Marta works with the Mah Jongg cards, she sees the cards, gets ideas from the cards, and then things open up. She tells people what she sees. She also gets a feeling about certain topics, an atmosphere. She picks up the energy surrounding things. Marta sees images and thinks that just picking up a piece of someone's life, like an image, is enough for people to understand that there is more out there than just themselves.

She believes that everyone has intuition, but that the ability to see and connect to Spirit is a different kind of gift. To her, "psychic" is seeing, knowing or hearing something which is going to happen. Marta isn't sure whether or not she is psychic. She thinks she may be a "conduit" or an energy worker. She is very sensitive to energy. However, Marta's sister, son, daughter and grand-daughter are all psychic.

One of the reasons that Marta suspects she may be some sort of energy conduit is that she often feels the need to move from one home to another, sharing her energy connections. Instead of going on a vacation, she just packs up and moves. However, wherever she goes, she makes a community of friends. With every move, she finds someone who becomes a lifelong friend. She influences people. She often feels like a gypsy fortune teller, traveling around the country and positively-influencing friends and neighbors.

When working with clients, Marta can usually feel or see their Spirit Guides. Even when she can't see them, she can understand what they are communicating. The Guides provide the information which the person needs to know. According to Marta, clients will never get information during a psychic reading which is not meant for them to hear. A reading should be done with great love and there should be a feeling of relief and support afterwards. Marta added:

> "I feel like every message I give, I am also getting something. Just like when you teach, you learn. It's a great gift."

Marta has had several near-death experiences. These experiences have confused her because she has not had the classic experience of seeing the Light, then seeing deceased relatives. She was just in the blackness. Marta remarked:

> "I could have been dead and not known it. It didn't matter to me. If I had died, I would not have known. Life went on, I just would not have been a part of it. I felt no pain. I wasn't aware of anything. Every time I came back, I was just here. I didn't remember anything."

On the other hand, one time when Marta was ill, she had the experience of laying in her bed and feeling complete love. She commented:

> "It is true that G-d is love, no matter what term is used. It is all love. It was the most incredible thing I can remember – the pureness of being in that love."

Marta's life experiences are like a mosaic and she is working to see the complete picture.

16) Jeff Sonnenburg - Psychic, Financial Advisor, ChildFinders

Jeff Sonnenburg has many psychic talents. One of the things which sets him apart from other psychics is that Jeff is familiar with financial information and is very comfortable predicting the stock market. He predicts the financial markets every week. His predictions are based on both logic and intuition. He receives many kinds of traditional financial information (such as newsletters), then sifts through the information to recommend stocks. Interestingly, Jeff's Guides told him that if he did this work, he would not be allowed to invest in the stock market because it might skew his impressions.

Jeff had always known he had a gift, but it wasn't until he was in his late twenties that he met a mentor. She encouraged Jeff to do psychic readings on the street and in the subway station. She never wanted him to need any particular environmental setting in order to do readings. She didn't want him to need Tarot cards, pendulums or a quiet place to work. She wanted him to be able to do readings in places where he could easily have been distracted. Jeff learned to focus so that nothing could distract his intuition.

Now, Jeff meditates and gathers information on his clients before readings. He puts about an hour of preparation into an hour of reading. He does a kind of automatic writing to ensure that he has information on the client prior to the session. He usually comes to the meeting with 3-5 pages of information to verify that he can pick up on the client. In addition, Jeff receives intuitive information during the session.

Jeff receives information on three levels, depending on the issue being addressed. The most basic level of information/energy is like a personal consciousness. If he hears a voice which sounds coarse, grounded and practical, the information provides answers to practical and minor questions. This is the level where people have the greatest amount of free will. For example, people have choices about the kind of car they want to buy.

Jeff calls the second level of information "Sphere of Influence." If the voice sounds a bit different, like a conversation, the information is coming from this second level. It is as if the information came from a group consciousness. This level provides answers about relationships, health, finances and career. On this level, the person still has some choice over the future.

The highest level of information comes from the Holy Spirit. When Jeff connects to the Holy Spirit, the voice is extremely loud. This level of energy provides answers regarding life path and big decisions. When Jeff receives information without the client being present, it is most likely that he is getting Divine Will. The Divine Will predictions never change. They are certain.

Here is an example of how this works: According to Divine Will, the client may be destined for the experience of marriage. On the second level, there may be advice about the best spouse to select, but the person can choose from a few potential partners. On the first level, there are less-important choices, such as where to have the wedding ceremony. Jeff hears different voices giving advice on each of these levels.

In addition to private readings, Jeff has worked with the United Nations doing business, financial and political readings. He has also formed "ChildFinders," an organization of 200 psychics in eight countries who find missing children.

17) Rhonda Harford - Astrologer

"Starlady" Rhonda Harford is a gifted astrologer. Working with the dates and times of a client's complete birth information, Rhonda can compile an astrological chart and provide a wealth of information for her client. Rhonda's main tool is the astrological chart but, because she is gifted, additional thoughts may pop into her head. Rhonda doesn't consider herself psychic because the additional information is not always available. She feels like the knowledge comes in at the right time and goes out at the right time. She prefers the term "gifted."

Rhonda has been working with astrology since she was 17 years old. Her first teacher discovered that she was gifted. Originally, Rhonda wrote the charts by hand, but now they can be generated by a computer.

Before meeting with clients, Rhonda has them fill out a form which ask about their birth date and time, and the birth dates and times of the people who are related to them. Appointments are scheduled. Rhonda runs their charts and asks if there is anything which they want to talk about. She records the sessions. She asks clients if they want to hear everything she has to say, good and bad. Most people ask about their life purpose, career and health. Rhonda has a gift for helping people understand their health. She is here to help people heal. Rhonda's first session with a client takes two hours and twenty minutes.

While working, the image of a man often comes though Rhonda's walls. Originally, she could see him, but she didn't know who he was. At one point, she went to a conference and a woman handed her a piece of paper with his image on it and said, "I am supposed to give this to you to let you know that he works through you." Rhonda discovered that his name is Djwal Khul and that he is a Buddhist who lived thousands of years ago. Djwal Khul, an Ascended Master, provides information beyond the astrological charts.

According to Rhonda, astrology provides all of the technical answers for her clients. She looks at the technical charts then paints a picture. If she uses the charts alone, she is 100% accurate. There are days when she doesn't receive intuitive insights. However, when she does receive intuitive information, she can sometimes see or hear people from the other side. If she looks at the wall and sees Djwal Khul, she can hear his voice providing messages. If she doesn't receive that kind of communication, she just works off of the charts.

At this time in her life, Rhonda is very pleased with her abilities. That feeling comes from age and experience. When she was about 35, Rhonda was in a very serious car accident and she walked through the Light. She was in a coma for five days. Walking through the Light was like trying to stare into the sun. When she walked through that Light, she met a woman who told her that she was going to be fine. There was a beautiful, peaceful brook. At the end of the experience, she told Rhonda that it was not her time and that Rhonda had to make a choice. She could stay or go back. The woman told Rhonda that she had not yet done her greatest work. When Rhonda asked about the other people who had been in the car accident, she was immediately "whooshed" back into her body. When she came back she was paralyzed. She had to learn to do things all over again, but she thinks that her psychic/intuitive gift became stronger.

One of the unique things which Rhonda prepares is a Solar return birthday chart which is based on both the location of a client's birth and where they are living now. People can change their destiny for one year by changing the location in which they celebrate their birthday. They can't change what they created at birth, stop the planets from rotating around their chart, or stop eclipses from bringing things into their lives, but they can change their year, for one year, by being in a certain latitude, longitude and time zone. It takes a lot of time to prepare a birthday chart and to discover the best place for someone to celebrate their birthday, but it can influence an entire year. It can bring in wonderful adventures. Many books have been written about these birthday trips, but Rhonda has her own ideas and hopes to write a book which includes several secrets from the ancients which have been shared with her.

Rhonda enjoys being an astrologer because she is able to travel and to meet phenomenal people. She loves to help people understand their struggles and to provide them with guidance and choices.

18) Raquel Spencer - Spiritual Teacher, Multi-Dimensional Energy Specialist

Raquel Spencer is a Spiritual teacher, Multi-Dimensional Energy/Light Specialist and facilitator. She believes that spiritual awakening is both an energetic and a physical process which brings a person's awareness to a level where the person remembers that part of his or her self, the Higher Self, which is beyond this 3-D reality. Raquel works with clients' energetic and physical bodies to help them remember who they are -- Divine Beings of Light. She understands that the physical body is the vehicle for spiritual awakening. As light is infused into physical cells, spiritual awakening is enhanced.

Raquel's journey began in 1985 after waking from an unexplained medical trauma which left her in an unconscious state for more than five weeks. This experience, called a "soul braid," was the weaving together of many aspects of her Higher Self into this reality, preparing her for the spiritual work she was to complete in this lifetime. The process was so intense that her physical body nearly couldn't handle it. She was pronounced dead three times and she was revived three times. While in this expanded (yet unconscious) state, her physical and energetic bodies were encoded with information which she agreed to bring through to assist with the awakening of humanity.

As an adult, Raquel worked in the business community for many years. Eventually, she received the direction from Spirit to bring her work to the public. Like everyone else, Raquel had to learn to listen to promptings from Spirit, follow her intuition, and figure out how to live comfortably in the physical world while developing her spiritual connection. She has had many experiences which were considered paranormal or spiritual in nature, and often questioned if they were real. Because of these experiences, she understood what people went through when waking up to their true selves. She has experienced personal triumphs and challenges which have expanded her understanding and given her the ability to relate to the people with whom she works.

Raquel works directly with each person's energy system to clear, activate and upgrade the body so that the person is physically prepared to embody his or her Higher Self. Raquel communicates with a vast array of Light Beings, Spiritual Councils, Ascended Masters, angels and nature spirits, bringing through the most appropriate Light frequency/energy, information and wisdom for her clients.

As her journey of awakening continues, Raquel follows the promptings of Spirit to serve Gaia (the earth) and humanity. In doing so, she travels to sacred places around the world, including Bali, Peru, Ireland, Central America, the Caribbean, Hawaii, Europe, Australia, New Zealand, Bolivia and England. She also travels across the United States. During her travels, Raquel anchors Light and raises the frequency of the people and places she encounters.

Raquel is dedicated to being a Divine Instrument of Light.

19) Jan Class - Holy Spirit Communicator

Jan Class considered herself to be a normal teenager until she had a near-death experience (NDE) which opened things up. She had a near-fatal asthma attack and saw her grandfather, several angels and a group of people waiting for her. She was out of her body and could see the doctors and nurses, as well as her frantic parents. She was dying and it felt good to be out of her body and out of pain. She was very light-weight. Jan looked at all of the people who were waiting for her and wondered why it was taking so long to die; she was ready to go. Then she heard them say, "We just want to make sure you really want to do this." At that point, Jan heard her mother bawling and knew she couldn't go. She told them that she had to stay and she was immediately swept back into her body. It was extremely painful!

After the NDE, Jan began studying spirituality. Her mother and step-father were well-known spiritualist ministers and Mediums, and she had always known her mother was psychic. Jan attended spiritualist churches and enrolled in "unfoldment" classes. Before long, she was giving messages and doing hands-on healing. She believes that everyone has natural psychic abilities, but they have to take the time to develop these abilities.

Jan is also a Medium. She connects with the Holy Spirit and can connect with people who have passed on. She also talks to angels and masters [Spirit Guides]. When she connects to Spirit, she hears a little bitty voice, like a chipmunk or a bird. Other times, thoughts are infused into her brain or pictures appear. In addition, Jan reads past lives, uses a crystal ball, and interprets astrology charts. She also works with stones which people have carried or held.

Jan sees the past, present and future. Mainly, Jan focuses on the present because that is when problems arise and when decisions need to be made.

When Jan reads for clients, she often uses Tarot cards because the public likes the cards. She enjoys using a Moon Garden deck because these cards have fairies and unicorns. She shuffles the cards until Spirit tells her to stop shuffling. Then, she interprets the cards the way Spirit wants her to interpret them. She just listens. The cards help organize the readings and the thoughts.

In addition to her spiritual work, Jan teaches high school age "exceptional education" students. Her abilities help her understand the needs of these children and how to meet these needs.

Jan thinks that Tucson is a special place to live. Tucson is going to become a new "Mecca," a spiritual town. This is because many beliefs and faiths are already here and Tucson is very open to spiritualism.

20) Denise Singerline - Medium, Reiki Master, Chakra-Balancing Specialist

Denise Singerline has seen ghosts and spirits since childhood. She was born with sight and always knew what people were thinking and feeling. As a child, spirits visited Denise every night and stood at the edge of her bed. When she realized what was going on, Denise thought that she might be seeing ghosts because there was some sort of an energy vortex in her home. Later she realized that wherever she went, she saw ghosts. To her surprise, she discovered that she was a Medium.

Denise met her first spiritual teacher when she was 17. She went to a psychic fair, saw a reader across the room, and knew she had to talk with her. As soon as Denise sat down, the woman said, "You have very strong psychic powers and you are afraid of them. I could teach you how to use them to heal others and to help them in their lives." Denise started crying because she realized that she was not alone. She had never met anyone like herself and she had felt very lonely. Denise began taking classes from this woman.

Before Denise understood her capabilities, she would sometimes see evil things. She worried that bad things would appear when she fell asleep so she stayed up as late as she could. As soon as she fell asleep, entities showed up. Eventually, she learned to feel the difference between the good energies and the bad ones. If an entity was bad, she made it leave immediately. If it was good, she asked if there was a message for her. Denise learned how to control who showed up so that only positive energies came to her.

Now that she understands her gifts, Denise uses them in her healing work. Denise's specialty is chakra balancing. This work enables energy to flow easily through a client's body. As Denise works in a client's aura, she picks up 10 or 12 pieces of information, such as supplements the person needs, blocked energy, stuck emotions, or cords which need to be removed. Afterwards, there is a 30-minute consultation to review the information which Denise received.

Denise also provides Tarot card readings. She can use the cards but, because she is clairvoyant, she doesn't need to use them. Even when she uses the cards, she asks Spirit to help her step aside so that Guides can communicate through her. She asks her Spirit Guides and angels to talk to the client's Guides and angels so that she can help the client for his or her highest good. She holds the client's hands for a moment to feel their energy, then she looks at the cards and asks Spirit what the client needs to know. She steps out of the way, hears the messages, then tells the client whatever she hears. She likes to relay the messages before people ask their questions. After the reading, people are welcome to ask about their issues. Ninety-five percent of the time, their questions have already been answered.

When performing Reiki on clients, Denise asks Archangel Michael and his Angels of Protection to completely surround her with their wings and keep her safe. She asks for golden saucers on her hands. She asks that she be protected from any energy which is not hers, not of the Light, or related to a disease. After the healing work, she flushes out all of the negative energy and fills herself with Light.

Denise teaches classes on Reiki, Emotional Freedom Techniques, and essential oils. She also teaches a form of Tai Chi known as Tai Chi Chih. She loves teaching and she also loves taking classes. Each year, Denise strives to learn about a new aspect of energy work. She is very pleased with her growing abilities because she can use her gifts to train healers. She wakes people up. She sees people coming in with all of their drama and problems, then she sees them change. Their lives improve and they are able to help other people.

In addition to one-on-one work and group classes, Denise also facilitates a Universal Energy Circle which meets each month. The idea for an energy circle was inspired. Each session starts with a 20-minute guided meditation. Denise plays a crystal singing bowl during the meditation and the sound enhances the experience. After that, there are two 20-minute rounds of chair healings. Then, there is a prayer meditation and a global Earth meditation. The Circle has grown over the years. Half of the people are healers and half of the people come for healing. This is a safe place for participants to give and receive energy work.

According to Denise, as we approach 2012, G-d is calling all Light Workers: "It's time to turn on!" He is turning everyone on and people are becoming more and more aware.

21) Delphina Nova - Native American Dreamer and Wisdomkeeper, Spiritual Healer, Geo-Empath, Animal Messenger, Author

Delphina Nova is intuitive and works as a Spiritual Advisor. She sees and perceives what is happening with people, the environment and the world. She sees trends and events which are about to happen. According to Delphina, having his awareness is delicate. Sometimes when she feels something is going to happen, she wants to warn the person who is involved, but she can't warn them because it might disturb their life path. Everyone has free will and chooses their own destiny. Delphina realizes that she must respect each soul's path.

When clients come to Delphina, she may help them with spiritual counseling or hands-on healing. Either way, she tries to get to the root cause of the symptoms whether they are spiritual, emotional, mental or physical. Sessions with Delphina begin with a conversation. She determines what each person needs and the best way to meet that need. She sees herself as someone who gives clients a "jump start." When someone comes to her for healing, she reminds them that the healing is within them and that she is only there to assist them on their healing journey.

Sometimes Delphina hears a still, small, nurturing voice which guides her. She calls it her Higher Self, the Divine Voice of G-d, or the voice of the Divine Creator. She lives her life guided by this nurturing voice of unconditional love.

Delphina *intuits* changes before they happen. Intuition is different than sensing, feeling or understanding; it is a "knowing." She is not speculating, she knows.

During this lifetime, Delphina has had six near-death experiences (NDEs). In some cases, she has seen the Light, spoken with ancestors and been told that she needed to remain on Earth because she had not yet completed her work. After six NDEs, Delphina is ready to share these experiences so that people remember that they are not their bodies. People can become too attached to material things, jobs and who they think they are, but people are more than their possessions and professions.

Delphina feels that there is a continuum of life. She believes that she has never died because all of her lifetimes are occurring on a continuum. According to Delphina, "The 'I' in me has never died. If I have done healing work in the past, I still have that ability."

Delphina thinks that we are going through a period of planetary changes right now, but that we are not alone. She thinks that many people will be pleasantly surprised by helpers who assist in the Earth's transition. Entities exist outside of our dimension and they are here to help us. There is help from other galaxies and from unseen angels who surround this planet with love.

She believes that we are on the brink, we are at the 11th hour on this planet. We are at the point where we have a choice about how we are going to conduct our lives, how we are going to treat each other, and how we are going to take care of the environment. She believes that in the blink of an eye we will choose love. It is up to us.

According to Delphina, the current Earth changes are part of a birthing process and the end result will be a new paradigm. Delphina explains that the baby doesn't come out in one push. We make progress, then we go back, then we make progress again . . . and it hurts! Finally, the waters break and the baby is born. Right now, we are experiencing earthquakes, tsunamis and oil spills which are like birth pangs. We are living in a period where things fall apart. Things which need to go, go. Things are going to be shaken up. This shaking needs to happen so that we can enter a lengthy time of peace. We are going through this shaky period as Earth births herself because we are part of Earth. We need to go through the changes and release the things which no longer work in our own lives, such as relationships, music, and food. While we don't know exactly what the outcome will be, we have to let go and know that the changes which are occurring are for our highest good.

Delphina is the author of *Turtle's Dream* (Open Books Press, 2010) and *Heart of Gold* (Dolfyn Press, 2010), and is currently writing her memoir.

22) Marianne Patyk - Medium

Marianne Patyk is a Medium which means that she communicates with people who have died and crossed to the other side. She has seen spirits since she was about eight years old and she reports that all of her relatives have visited her after passing. During their visits, it feels like they are having a normal conversation.

Marianne has had brain seizures since birth. As a young teenager, Marianne had several seizures where she astral-traveled to the other side, then came back. She has seen Heaven. Marianne's brain has experienced trauma and she believes that she is psychic because of the trauma to her brain.

Even with all of her experiences seeing spirits and astral-traveling as a child, Marianne knows that her abilities as a Medium didn't really open up until after a traumatic event in her 40s. At that point, she started hearing things she had never heard before. Her experience was similar to what happened to Whoopi Goldberg's character in the movie *Ghost* (1990): suddenly she started hearing a lot of information from people who had crossed over.

When Marianne's gift as a Medium surfaced in her 40s, her abilities were more potent than when she was a child. She started smelling aromas which were not physically present and hearing messages. It was overwhelming. She had to determine which abilities and tools she had as a Medium. Then, she had to accept, embrace, and learn how to work with these gifts.

When clients comes to Marianne, she asks them what they want to know or if they have someone specific whom they would like to contact. If there is someone with whom they want to speak, Marianne asks for that person's name. She takes a quiet moment to see if she can contact the person. Then, she gets a vision or hears a voice. She connects directly to the person the client is asking about. However, she doesn't fully understand how all of this works and how she is able to make the connection. It just works.

Marianne is intuitive, empathic, clairvoyant (sees images) and clairaudient (hears messages). She also smells aromas (which are not physically present), provides pet readings, and performs automatic writing.

Most of Marianne's readings are done over the phone, but she also meets people in person.

When Marianne reads for people it can drain her energy and affect her emotionally and physically. Because she is empathic, she is open to people's emotions. Sometimes, clients are very intense and that is hard on her. She absorbs all of their emotions. Marianne finds that it is best to limit her readings so that she has time to relax and recover each evening. She tries to rest and live a stress-free life so that she can continue working as a Medium.

23) Jackie Chin - Professional Psychic Advisor

Jackie Chin is a Professional Psychic Advisor who mainly works over the Internet. She works in on-line open reading rooms on AOL and in other chat rooms. She has provided psychic readings since 1987.

Working as a psychic allows Jackie to counsel people through very difficult times in their lives. When she is able to give information to people who are hurting and seeking answers, it makes her feel terrific. While she knows that she is not the source of the answers (the answers come from a greater consciousness which she is able to tap into), it gives her peace to be of assistance. Jackie has found that clients often contact her after they have repeatedly tried, and failed, to get answers from other people.

When clients contact Jackie, she has them think about specific questions which are immediately affecting their lives. Usually those concerns have a lot of energy behind them. It is as if they have a high energy or a spark to them; like a lit match. Once the question is asked, Jackie goes backwards in time to examine the initial spark of energy. Everything has a beginning and an end. People know their past and their situation. They also know that Jackie doesn't know anything about them so once she gets information about what initially occurred, they relax and Jackie can move into their current energy and retrieve their answers.

Jackie doesn't hear voices. She "knows." This knowing is different from seeing images because when she gets a "knowing" message, she doesn't see an image attached to it. However, images sometimes do appear during readings. She may see the people who clients are talking about, places where they have been or places where they are going.

Jackie loves working with skeptics. These people have questions which they think Jackie can't answer. Once they discover that she can do the reading, their attitudes change and Jackie feels wonderful. Skeptics help her keep doing what she loves doing.

During her life, Jackie has seen many deaths, helped people cross over with Reiki, and counseled clients about these issues. She knows that there is life after death, but she believes that each person has their own idea about what death will be like and this influences their experience of the afterlife.

In fact, Jackie's family often has house guests who are not biologically alive. As long as they are not frightening anyone, they are welcome to stay. Sometimes the family allows them to join events and makes a space for them at the table. Her family has decided not to turn them away unless there is a reason to do so. At some point, the ghosts may decide to go into the Light and be with their own families. However, if they left Jackie's family, she feels that a part of her family dynamic would be forever changed.

Each time Jackie gives a reading and hears from someone on the other side, she is pleasantly surprised. She is mystified that we can actually talk to those who have crossed over. They are still very involved with our lives.

Jackie believes that people who are in touch with spiritual energies already understand that there are many Earth changes which are affecting their personal lives and the life of this planet. If people continue to worry and not take action, things will get much worse. She thinks that the people who are aware of this situation should form groups and teach others how to connect to the life source by prayer, meditation, and energy healing. As long as these people are doing positive spiritual work, it will magnify for the good of the planet. Each color, thought, and living thing has a healthy vibration. It is up to those who understand this concept to teach others how to build up their vibrations and heal themselves. Once they have learned how to do that, they can give back to the planet.

24) Gigi Sample - Psychic Counselor

For a long time, Gigi Sample thought that she was perfectly normal. She didn't think she was psychic at all. Of course, she had experienced things as a child which she couldn't quite explain, but she thought that everyone was that way. She just knew things. As a child, Gigi played with Tarot cards, read palms and worked with astrology.

It wasn't until Gigi was in college that she had her first overpowering experience which led her to believe that she might be different from other people. She was sitting in a stairwell in London and she was very upset. She received an overwhelming message that she was holding herself back because she didn't want to be a prominent psychic in the limelight. She had been hiding from her gifts because the idea of being psychic and having an important role to play in life had been too much for her to grasp. She just wasn't ready at that time.

After Gigi graduated from college with degrees in Fashion Design and Business, she moved to Los Angeles and managed a fabric store. She married and had a daughter. While she was married, Gigi enjoyed her psychic abilities, but didn't work with them publicly.

After Gigi's divorce in 2000, being psychic became a larger part of her life. Many people "woke up" between 2000 and 2002. According to Gigi, we are in the Aquarian Age and it is about the waking up of humanity. This is the lifetime we have all been waiting for. People are waking up and shifting. The teachers have to figure things out first so that when waves of people wake up, the teachers are ready and in the right places. Gigi thinks that everybody is psychic, but that each person has a different role to play in this shift. People might not think that they are psychic, but they are just playing a different role than that of a practicing psychic.

When Gigi works with clients, she starts with an "open reading." This means that people don't ask their questions before the reading. According to Gigi, Spirit Guides know what clients want to know and, nine times out of ten, their questions are answered during the open reading. After the Guides' messages have been delivered, clients are welcome to ask questions.

Gigi also reads Tarot cards. People like to see the pictures on the cards and hear a story. She gives her messages and the cards validate what she is saying. She feels things and hears thoughts, then double-checks the ideas in the cards. When she is correct, she gets goose-bumps. She thinks that any method a person uses to communicate with their Guides, the Guides will know how to relay messages to them. For example, if she decided to read tea leaves or work with numerology, her Guides would know how to provide insights using the new method. According to Gigi, "They know us better than we know ourselves."

As a matter-of-fact, Spirit Guides know what people should be doing with their lives. They communicate with Gigi so that she can see a client's future and deliver the messages. However, people have free will and can choose to go against all of their Guide's suggestions. Gigi can see future possibilities when someone is listening to his or her Guides. She can see what the Guides would like them to do, but the Guides can't make people do anything. People make their own choices. People can say "no" to their Guides and that is what changes the outcome of readings.

Gigi's specialty is answering questions about life purpose and relationships. Most of the people who come to her are teachers and healers, such as psychologists and nurses. These people want to learn about spirituality so that they can do their jobs in a better way. In some cases, these wonderful people are not in romantic relationships because their Guides don't want them to be deterred by dysfunctional relationships which keep them from their life purpose. Of course, people have free will and can do what they want but at this time, with all of the shifts, it's best to be in a supportive relationship if a person is here to do spiritual work. If not, it is easy to get sidetracked.

Gigi believes that 2010 was the year when people moved to wherever they needed to be for the upcoming shifts. In 2010, teachers figured out their life purpose so that they could be ready for 2012 when the masses will wake up.

According to Gigi:

> "This lifetime is very different. I don't know how I know that, but I just know it. It is very different from other lifetimes. I am not concerned about the Mayan calendar. I just know we are in the Aquarian Age and the Aquarian Age is about consciousness shifting, humanitarianism and unconditional love. In the 1960s we were testing the waters, now we are going to see changes. Our planet is the farthest it has ever been from the Milky Way Galaxy. Now it is turning back towards the Light. As dark as we have gotten, now we will move back towards the Light. We have been testing the waters. Now is the time for change."

My perspective on the interviews

The interviews were amazing. People were willing to share their true, personal stories and I felt honored that they chose to share their stories with me. I learned so much! Looking back, it seems as if each interview introduced new concepts which built upon previous interviews. The ideas grew organically from the basics, to the more intricate, to the inspirational. I found myself asking: "How can this be true? Is this real? Really?" Psychics live between the seen and unseen worlds, in a world of wonder.

In addition, each psychic told me about myself, this Project, and my place in the world. Having my own mini-readings was an eye-opening bonus. I walked away from each session glowing. There is a saying about having "an embarrassment of riches." That's how I felt after each interview. I was glowing, ecstatic and slightly embarrassed to tell people how wonderful each interview had been; how much my life had been enhanced.

People always ask me, "Who is your favorite psychic?" My answer is, "The last one I interviewed." I spent so much time thinking about what each person had said, and I so fully-enjoyed our time together, that they were my favorite . . . until the next interview which brought the same level of delight.

Thank you to all the incredible participants in this Project!

Section II

Life as a Psychic

Chapter 4 - Figuring things Out

What it is like to be psychic? What is like to be a child who knows they are different from other children, but doesn't understand that they are psychic? How do people figure out that they have a gift? Where does their gift come from? Are there pros and cons to being psychic? Really, are there cons? This Section explains what it is like to have a strong psychic gift. The psychics discuss what they tap into and reveal how they can tell the difference between information coming from their imagination and information coming from an outside source. They talk about G-d, near-death experiences, and the limits to psychic ability. They discuss marriage, parenting, and employment. If you have ever wondered what it is like to be psychic, this information is for you.

Are you psychic too? Compare your reality to the reality of these 26 PRISMS and see if their personal histories help explain your life experiences.

What is it like to be a psychic child?

When people with intuitive abilities are born, they are "just kids" and are completely accepting of whatever life has to offer. They don't realize that other kids can't see spirits, feel what other people feel or know what other people think. At some young age, they discover that they are different from other children and that if they don't hide it, the other children will make fun of them. Hiding their abilities makes them feel separate from other people. Society tells them that they are odd and there usually isn't an adult in their family who understands what is happening and can help the children see that they are not crazy. They have difficult childhoods and painful young-adulthoods. Eventually, someone helps them understand that they are not crazy, they are intuitive. Then . . . they blossom into their authentic selves.

Alternatively, a few psychics were born into this lifetime knowing exactly which gifts they had and what they were here to accomplish. They remembered their past lives and the contracts they had negotiated before agreeing to be born. These psychics had slightly easier childhoods than the psychics who had to figure out why they were different; however, they faced their own issues. For example, a few psychics remembered being part of World War II in Europe and had flashbacks whenever this period was discussed in school.

Interestingly, several people revealed that they were very smart and that their intelligence helped them navigate this world while exploring the non-physical world. This was particularly important when figuring out how to fit in, and how to cope, at school. To-Ree'-Nee' Wolf was reading at a college level when she was 7; Leah Taylor was considered a genius at 4; and Rhonda Harford was born with a photographic memory.

Eventually, Intuitives figure out and accept that they are different from other people and that they have a gift which allows them to tap into energy and information which can help other people. They realize that one reason they are here on Earth is to help others. A second reason PRISMS are here is to learn their own life lessons. They believe that every soul is here to experience life, to grow and to evolve.

How did people figure out that they were psychic?

Of the 26 people I interviewed, four were born knowing they were psychic, eighteen knew they were different from other children but had to figure out that they were psychic, and four were "normal" children who developed their gift later in life. Most of the "Psychic Snapshots" in the previous chapter mentioned how individual people discovered that they had a gift. The answer to this question pulls the information together to provide a more-complete picture.

The four people who came to Earth knowing that they were psychic either remembered their past lives and how the Universe worked, or remembered making an agreement (before being born) to come to Earth and help people. They had experiences in childhood which reinforced their "knowing." One psychic told me that when her class learned about World War II in second grade, she remembered the whole thing and couldn't get out of bed for a week.

Two psychics who were born knowing about their roles said:

> ☼ I was born remembering past lives . . . People often forget things which happened before they were born, but my mother helped me to remember these things. There is a lineage of psychics in my family . . . The most powerful ability I had as a child was empathy and it wasn't until I was in fifth grade that I discovered that other people didn't have that. It blew my mind; it really traumatized me to find out that other people didn't feel the same way that I did. *(Erik Assman)*

> ☼ I was psychic from childhood. I knew what other people felt and thought and what was going on with them. My Mom said that I was only about a year old when I began showing empathy. I was very precocious as a child and I think it is because I remember a lot of my past lives . . . I came in knowing what I had. *(Leah Taylor)*

Eighteen psychics knew they were different from other children, but had to discover that they had psychic abilities. What made them different from other children? They saw fairies, astral traveled, talked with spirits, or knew things about other people which they had no logical way of knowing. At eight years old, one psychic told his mom that a neighbor was pregnant before there were any indications that this was the case. Also at eight years old, another psychic started seeing people's auras. At five years of age, a third psychic had an out-of-body experience. When these children talked about their experiences, they found that other people didn't see the things which they saw. These eighteen children knew that there was something different about them, but it took a while to put the pieces together.

How did they figure things out? Of the eighteen people who knew they were different, but had to find out what was happening:

- 5 people talked to a spiritual teacher who explained their situation;
- 4 people explored metaphysics on their own and discovered that they had gifts;
- 1 person had Spirit Guides who explained what was going on;
- 5 people either had a near-death experience, a medical issue or an emotional trauma which opened their abilities; and
- 3 people had abilities which unfolded naturally as they matured.

Here are several examples from people who knew they were different as children and later discovered that they were PRISMS.

<u>People who talked to a psychic and discovered that they were gifted</u>

☼ I knew I had an ability, but I didn't know what it was called until I was 18 and met someone who explained it to me. When I was younger, my family lived in France and I had déjà vü all the time. I always knew exactly where I was; there were no surprises. It was a very strange feeling. I didn't know that I was different from other people until they looked at me like I had two heads and I thought maybe they didn't know what I knew.

When I was 18, I moved to Nebraska and met a palm reader. She looked at my hand and said, "You should be reading mine!" Then she looked in my eyes and said, "I've been waiting a long time to meet you." She had been told that I was coming to her. She explained to me what I am and she taught me everything she knew about hands. Then, I taught her what I knew. The hands would open up and tell stories. She became a mentor for me. I talked to her quite a bit and we became very good friends. *(Cecilia Nemmers)*

☼ As a child, I knew something was going on, but I couldn't figure it out. I had a lot of déjà vü, but I didn't know how to deal with it so I shut myself out of the world for most of my life. As a child, I lived in my bedroom because that was where I could deal with the realms and the spirits who came to visit. They were my friends and I hung out with them. At night I astral-traveled and it was fine. I couldn't share this information with anyone. I went to school and functioned, then immediately went home and hid in my room. I thought I was crazy. I grew up thinking I was nuts. I was happy. No one knew what to do with me.

It was very fortunate that, as an adult, I had my brother and my other teacher to show me things. My brother and I were close as children, but we never talked about these things. He, and my teacher, helped me to understand what was going on. *(Gina Stanfill)*

☼ I was about 13 years old when I could close my eyes and see things. I told my mom and she shushed me and told me that everyone could do that. We were raised Catholic and it was not something which was discussed. However, she must have had her own impressions because my Dad used to call her a witch. She would say, "I have to sleep on things." She was the witch and I was the little witch. My other sister wasn't called a witch. My mother wouldn't talk about this at all. As a matter-of-fact, she told me that reading Tarot cards and reading horoscopes meant you would burn in Hell. This is how I was raised: just read the Bible. To this day, members of my family ridicule me for being a psychic. To this day, my sister says I will be the nicest person burning in Hell.

I didn't have a mentor at home. The first mentor I had was when I was 26 or 27 and going through a divorce. Reverend Julie Anne Kreig was an amazing mentor. I went to her for a reading and she said, "You can do this as well as I can." I told her that I was afraid of it because I didn't know the rules and the laws. I knew it was powerful, but I didn't know how it worked. She offered to teach me. I respected her so much because she was very normal. I would tell her what I saw and she would help me to understand what it meant. I am very visual and I have a very creative imagination. I feel through my imagination. I receive pictures through my imagination. *(Laurie Hays)*

☼ I was born this way and I thought everyone was like me. As I grew older, I realized that other people were not like me and that some people were afraid of me when I told them things. I started keeping things to myself. As a child, I didn't have anyone to tell me what was going on.

I was born with sight and I always knew what people were thinking and feeling. I could walk into a room and feel the energy. As a child, I had spirits come to me every night and stand at the edge of my bed. I would wake up in the middle of the night in the process of astral traveling, but I didn't know what it was. I felt like I was sinking down into the bed as my spirit was lifting. As I woke up in the middle of it, I would see a spirit standing in the doorway beckoning me to follow.

I met my first spiritual teacher when I was 17. I went to a psychic fair and the minute I sat down in front of one of the psychics she said, "You have very strong psychic powers and you are afraid of them. I could teach you how to use them to heal others and to help them in their lives." I started crying as I realized that I was not alone. I had never met anyone else like me. I had always felt so alone and it had been scarey. I had needed to keep things hidden. I started taking her meditation classes. *(Denise Singerline)*

<u>People who researched, studied, and discovered they were psychic</u>

☼ About 10 years ago, after moving to this house near Tucson, I had a job which was about an hour drive away. I started listening to recorded material in my car while commuting to and from work. I listened to everything regarding spirituality that I could absorb. I didn't have a mentor, but I listened to the tapes.

I have always known that I had psychic abilities, I just didn't understand the context for it. I have always known that I knew things that other people didn't know, but I thought it was because I could see the larger context of things, instead of just reacting to what was going on. I was always able to separate myself from my ego, see things as they were, and know what was going to happen. Other people tended to be so involved in their ego responses that they did not have that same overall view. I didn't consider it a special gift, I just knew that I was able to separate out from that part of me that was caught in the mix. It was interesting because I have always known that I had this ability, but I didn't classify it as "psychic" or "intuitive." *(Beth Hays)*

☼ I have used psychic abilities most of my life, but I didn't know what they were. I probably didn't realize what it was until high school. That's when I started dabbling in it to see, but it wasn't until later that I realized that this wasn't normal.

After my first husband passed away, I wanted to know why, and no one could give me the answer. I went to someone who did an astrological reading and I started taking lessons. Then I started learning about numerology and it was like a glove; it just fit. I spent my first couple of years dealing with astrology, then I fell in love with numerology, so I do several things. As far as mentoring the "abilities," I never really thought of them as abilities, I just thought of them as "one of those things." *(Patricia Kirkman)*

<u>People who experienced a trauma which opened their gifts</u>

☼ I have always been intuitive. As a child, I talked to the angels at night. I said my prayers, asked questions, and mentally knew the answers. For example, I lost tickets and was told where to find them. I just knew things. It's not like hearing something, or having someone whisper in my ear; it's a knowing. However, around six or seven years of age, I started to lose that connection. I didn't really get it back until after I had a medical issue.

When I was about 20 years old, I slipped into an unconscious state. Five and a half weeks later, I woke up. I was pronounced dead three times and I came back three times. There was no medical reason, no accident, which caused this event. When I woke up, I was fine. Now, I understand what happened while I was unconscious: I was being "re-wired" for spiritual work.

Several years later, I started to become spiritually aware. My interests, curiosity and knowledge started to come on-line. At that point, I started on the path of spiritual exploration. I am very good at following my inner promptings, following Spirit. When I get an intuitive message to go somewhere or to read a book and I follow those instincts, I run into the right people and into the right contacts; new doors and understandings open up.

I was introduced to a woman who was on the cutting edge in the spiritual world. She was a channel of Metatron [an angel]. I went to see her, not really knowing what a channel was, and she said, "I have been expecting you. Where have you been? You are behind schedule." I was surprised and I had no idea what she was talking about. She did a reading for me and introduced me to new concepts, such as "light body" and "ascension." I was reeling after that discussion as all of the information tried to settle in. Three or four months later, I followed Spirit and went to northern California for a three-day intensive workshop on etheric surgery with a woman named Tachi-Ren. Someone told me about it and I just went. That weekend, she activated me, bringing in my knowledge and wisdom about my work. I started to remember things. It was a "remembering" from the part of me which was not in physical form. I remembered my Higher Consciousness, what I came here to do, and what my work was all about. That is where it all began. *(Raquel Spencer)*

☼ I think I was about five years old when friends in the neighborhood used to line up and come see me. It was like a game. They would come and see me because I would do healings or I would know what was going on with them. This was very innocent. I knew from a very young age that I wasn't playing. I knew when things were going on with a person's family, or if they needed a healing. I sensed it.

I have prophetic dreams. One of them was what happened on September 11. I had that dream when I was 11 years old. The towers hadn't even been built at that time. It was a futuristic dream . . . I ran into my parent's room and I told my parents that something terrible was going to happen. They asked what was going to happen and I told them that many people were going to die. I saw the towers in flames. I felt that I had to find a way to prepare people for this event. It shocked me out of my childhood innocence. It was a shift for me. When I was younger and playing doctor, I was innocent. When I was 11, I had this prophetic dream which shifted everything for me. *(Delphina Nova)*

☼ The State of Arizona removed my daughter from my care and sent her to live with my parents. This created great trauma in my life and the trauma brought forward my abilities as a Medium. I started hearing things I had never heard before from people who had crossed over. I started smelling aromas and hearing things. It was an overload. I had to learn how to control it and work with it.

It's almost like wishful thinking. You want to see your loved ones after they have crossed over, but it doesn't happen . . . then it begins to happen. I had to learn how to manage it. I had to figure out what abilities I had as a Medium and which tools I had. I looked on-line to see what I had. Then I had to accept and embrace it. *(Marianne Patyk)*

<u>People who had abilities which unfolded as they matured</u>

☼ I was always different from other people because I knew things that they didn't know. I always knew who was good for me and who was bad for me. I never tried to use this ability as a child, but I just knew things. Many people asked me for advice about things and it surprised me because I was so young, maybe 15 or 16. *(Shirli Millmond)*

☼ Now that I know, I can look back and see that I had abilities as long as I can remember. I didn't think of it that way at the time. As a child, I spent a lot of time alone. I knew things. I thought that everybody felt like this.

When I was around 10 years old, I heard my mother calling me in her unique accent. I asked her what she wanted and she told me that she had not been calling me. Turns out it was my Grandmother Virginia calling my name. She had lived in our house and had recently passed. At the time, I didn't quite figure it out.

When I was in college, I was sitting in a stairwell and I was very upset about things. I received a huge, overwhelming message that I was holding back because I didn't want to be a big psychic in the limelight. I had insecurities. It was like: what if I really was the person I was here to be? It was too much for me to grasp; I was hiding from it. I get goose bumps even saying it. I remember sitting in that stairwell, crying, and thinking, "I have all of this stuff to do for the planet!" I wasn't ready to do it. *(Gigi Sample)*

☼ I had an idea that something was different about me when I was 11 years old. I had a friend who I used to hang out with at my middle school. Before school, we would take a deck of cards and guess the color, suit and number of each card. Eventually we were able to go beyond that and do other things. We were very connected. Also, I knew that there was something odd in the house we lived in and I began to learn about how energy can be transferred by using my hands to touch items. It seemed that the more I practiced feeling energy, the more I could do it effectively. *(Jackie Chin)*

The remaining four people had normal childhoods. They didn't know they were gifted as children. They developed their abilities as teens or adults. One of these people had a near-death experience (NDE) which opened her abilities and, afterwards, she began studying spirituality. The other three explored spirituality on their own. They played with Ouija Boards or Tarot cards, or took classes, and were able to develop their skills.

Two people who had normal childhoods and whose gifts opened later in life said:

☼ I figured it out on my own. The more I learned about anything metaphysical, the more I understood the possibilities. In 1970, I started a study group in Wisconsin to understand metaphysics and I had a very powerful experience during an automatic writing session. We were all sitting in my studio and the teacher explained what automatic writing was. I had just returned from a trip to Sedona and had found out that the mother of a good friend of mine had passed away while I was gone. The woman who had passed away was named Hannah. In the past, every time I had gone to lunch with Hannah she had said, "Thank you for being my friend." In addition, whenever she talked about her son she would say, "Oh, Ron will be Ron." Back to the automatic writing session. We did a guided meditation and we each had a pen and paper. The teacher said that if nothing was happening, just to write our names. I started to write my name and my arm started shaking. I opened my eyes in disbelief and I wrote, "Sad." I wasn't crying, but suddenly tears were running out of my eyes. Then I wrote, "Thank you for being my friend," and I realized it was Hannah. My hand moved down the paper and my hand wrote, "Ron will be . . . " I put the pen down and I was completely freaked out. It was the first time I had had that kind of a mind-boggling experience. That was when I realized that there was a lot out there which I didn't understand and it increased my interest in finding out more. *(Nancy)*

☼ When I was a teenager, I had a near-death experience which opened things up. I had a near-fatal asthma attack and I saw my grandfather, several angels and a group of people. I was out of my body and I could see the doctors and nurses, as well as my frantic parents. I was dying and it was nice to be out of my body and out of pain. I was very light-weight. I was looking at all of these people and wondering why it was taking so long to die; I was ready to go. I heard them say, "We just want to make sure you really want to do this." Then I heard my mother bawling and I looked down at her and I said I couldn't go. I was only 16. I told them that I had to stay and immediately, as soon as I said it, I was back in my body. It was extremely painful! No wonder babies cry when they are being born. If their souls are coming in while they are being born, it hurts!

After I came back into my body, I wanted to know more about what had happened. My parents started taking me to spiritualist churches. I enrolled in "unfoldment" classes. Before long I was giving messages, maybe in my early twenties. I could also do hands-on healing. *(Jan Class)*

Where does their gift come from?

I asked the PRISMS where their gift comes from. Is it a happy, random accident, or is there more to it?

There are two common answers to this question. The first answer is, "It is a gift from G-d." Most psychics believe that intuition is a natural G-d-given talent which helps people navigate this world. They believe that everyone can develop their intuition up to a certain level.

The second answer is related to family. Many of the psychics were raised in families where other members were also psychic. It seems that there is either a genetic predisposition to be strongly psychic, the psychics were raised in families where their natural gift was accepted and nurtured, or the psychics actually <u>chose</u> to be born into the kinds of families where psychic abilities were accepted. Keep in mind that these are not people with a "normal" amount of intuition. These people have a strong gift, making it easier to see how things work.

If you are interested in the numbers, here are the answers to the question, "Does psychic ability run in your family?"

Of the 26 people interviewed, 22 saw the gift in other family members:

12 said their mother had intuitive abilities;
2 said they were not certain, but that they thought their mother had abilities;
1 said her dad was gifted;
1 said her father might be gifted; and
6 said that they didn't see it in their parents, but they saw it elsewhere in their family, for example, one of their grandparents was intuitive.

Four psychics reported that they were the only people in their family with psychic abilities. Of these four, only one was born with the gift and the other three developed it later in life.

What about brothers and sisters?

11 psychics saw the talent in a brother or sister;
5 psychics did not see the talent in a brother or sister; and
10 psychics did not comment on their siblings.

What about the psychics' children?

19 psychics had children; and
7 psychics did not have children.

Of the 19 psychics with children,

15 saw the talent in at least one child;
3 did not see this gift in their children; and
1 did not comment on her children's abilities.

Can we draw any conclusions from these answers?

I always have to start with the fact that I only interviewed 26 people so my information wouldn't stand up to scientific testing. And, as my grad-student daughter keeps reminding me, "Correlation is not causation." With that said, it sure seems like there is a genetic component to psychic ability, especially in the kind of people who have strong gifts. Everyone can develop a certain amount of intuition but to be really good at it, most people had to have been born with the gift, been born into a gifted family, or had a traumatic experience. There seems to be an especially strong tie to having a mother with psychic abilities. Does psychic ability come down the mother's line? Perhaps.

Why would genetics have anything to do with psychic ability? One of the psychics surmised that she was gifted because her brain was wired a bit differently from other people. In her family, her mother, brother, aunt and child were all psychic. In this case, there seemed to be a strong genetic component to her psychic ability. However, she was also one of the people who was born knowing she was psychic. This just gets more complicated! One theory is that she knew before she was born that she was here to assist people with her psychic gifts so she chose to be born into a family where this gift would be accepted, understood and nurtured. The mosaic pieces seem to fit together nicely, but beg the question: What is most important? The person's natural talent, the family genetics or the family environment? Ah, more questions than answers . . .

Can PRISMS turn their abilities on and off, or are they on all of the time?

This answer depends on the person and their gift. In most cases, psychic abilities are on at a low level all of the time and PRISMS learn to turn the volume up or down, as needed. However, people who are empathetic need to turn their abilities off during their daily routines so they can lead normal lives. They find it very distracting to pick up other people's emotions when they are out in public.

Most people are aware that their abilities are always on because they receive intuitive impressions as they go about their daily life. Psychics usually enjoy having her abilities on because they feel surrounded and protected by friends. However, they sometimes become disillusioned with their gifts and choose to turn them off completely.

It takes time for psychics to learn how to handle their abilities and how to turn their volume up, down, and off. Each phase of a psychic's life may require a different level of openness.

<u>The Learning Phase</u>

Several PRISMS had trouble regulating their connection when they were young and learning to use their abilities. As they matured, they learned to control the messages. Here are a few examples:

☼ I was not able to turn them off in the beginning. Most people who are born with it, can't turn it off. For the first year or two of learning about your intuition, you need to learn boundary issues and how to turn it on and off. If you are born with it, you really can't turn it off, but you can make it minimal so you are not really listening to it. You can keep yourself open and you will only be bothered by something if it is critical that you know about it. It's like a radio on low volume which gets louder if there is an emergency. *(Jeff Sonnenburg)*

☼ When I was young, in my teens and early twenties, it was on all the time and I was exhausted. I had to learn to open and close that third eye if I didn't want to be drained. Otherwise, there were spirits all over the grocery store who wanted me to communicate. I didn't know who they were. When I went to a big box store, I saw what was going on with all the people who I passed. I had to learn to close that third eye, to turn it off and on. *(Jan Class)*

☼ I channel a group and when I was younger they would all talk to me at once. Finally, I told them to stop it and to decide on a single spokesperson . . . I just let the group give me information as they want to talk. Early on, they were my closest friends. There's no explaining who I am and there's no acting like someone else. It's comfortable now. *(Cecilia Nemmers)*

Daily Life

As adults, most psychics have their abilities on all of the time, but turn the volume up and down. They explained how this works:

☼ It feels like they are on all the time. They can be dampened, but they are still on. I don't know if I made a choice to leave them on all the time to have the connection, or if that is just how it works. When I turn them off and go into "everyday" stuff, I miss them too much. *(George)*

☼ I can delay it, but if something needs to come through, it will come through. If I am not listening when I am awake, it may come through in my dreams. It will keep pushing. I can limit it, put it on a lower level, but I can't turn it off. *(Shirli Millmond)*

☼ It is on all of the time, but I don't always have to consciously connect to it. I am continuously working, but my attention doesn't always have to be on it. Most of the time, I am "on" and I am doing planetary service. I go to certain places to anchor light and to anchor energy. I will walk into a room and if there are people who are aware, they will react to me being in that room. *(Raquel Spencer)*

Other psychics are able to turn their abilities completely off for limited periods of time. One psychic told me that she gets so much information that it would be very distracting if it were on all the time. She wouldn't be able to drive a car unless she could turn it off. Here are other examples:

☼ I turn it off normally. I don't read every person who walks by. However, sometimes Spirit is protecting and warning me and I receive messages. One day I had my toddler son in a store trying on shoes. All of the sudden I felt every hair on the back of my neck stand up and I knew I had to leave. I grabbed the kids and we left quickly. On the way out, we passed a man who had just walked in who I knew spelled trouble. I had not been alert and looking around, but Spirit had let me know something was wrong. It must always be on at some background level, but I turn it up when I do readings. I am beginning to understand how much I use it all the time. *(Laurie Hays)*

☼ They are not on all of the time. Sometimes, I get thoughts, but I don't read people's minds unless they ask me to. Who would want to go around reading people's minds all the time?! *(Gigi Sample)*

☼ I have to take control of my abilities or I could not have a normal life. They are on low all the time, but I can negotiate with them not to hear them all the time. There are things that I don't need to know. I try to filter things out. *(Richard Schickel)*

<u>Turning it off Completely</u>

Three psychics made conscious decisions to turn off their abilities earlier in their lives. They explained:

☼ We all have free will and can ask Spirit, Source, to make it stop. I did that for a number of years after I had a terrifying vision in 1984. I know that it can be shut down. When I felt that it was okay to start up again, things went back to my "normal." *(Jackie Chin)*

☼ I turned a good chunk of it off when I was a child. I saw things walking through walls and it became very disconcerting. If I am going to be here and work with the dynamics of this realm, I don't want to see things walking through the walls. I get very confused and distracted. I can dampen it down. However, I am always looking to fine-tune it and sometimes that means paying attention to small things and listening to them. I am on call for a certain amount of work and for certain kinds of work. I don't want to see anything scary – I don't want to see "tentacle-head!" *(To-Ree'-Nee' Wolf)*

☼ The only time I told my psychic abilities to go away was when I saw my divorce coming in my first marriage. I loved him. When I saw the turmoil which was coming up, I didn't want to know things anymore. When my abilities went away, it was like living in a black hole. I realized how much I used this gift for the simplest of things. I begged Spirit to have it back and it returned slowly, in increments, so that I learned to value it. Now it is sacred to me. I won't let it go again.

When all my psychic abilities went away, I didn't even know what to wear! Something calls you to put on certain clothes; I didn't have that. We are guided more than we know and I found that out when I said, "No more." I won't ever say that again! *(Laurie Hays)*

A fourth psychic reported that someone else had tried to limit her connection:

☼ My crown chakra is open and one time an awful person threw a psychic net over my head and I felt like I was suffocating. I nearly died because I had no connection; I felt alone. It was like a tree that didn't get any sun. Another psychic friend removed that netting and instantly a light force started coming through the chakra and I was fine. I could center and be okay. It was an awful experience. I don't know how people go through life not having a connection. I think everyone must be connected, they are just not aware of it. *(Cecilia Nemmers)*

<u>During Readings</u>

In order to do readings, psychics can focus and increase their ability to connect to information. They tune into the Universe and connect completely.

Chapter 5 - Working with Invisible Partners

In order to bring information from the unseen world into this world, psychics need to communicate with invisible partners. This chapter discusses non-physical information sources and the workings of inter-realm communication.

What do psychics tap into?

This is a big question! What is out there? Is there really something more than life on Earth? Can we know what is out there?

Twenty-three psychics said that they accessed information from one or more of these sources:

Spirit Guides (their Guides and/or the client's Guides)
Angels
Archangels
The Creator by any name (G-d, Universal Energy, Universal Intelligence, etc.)
The Holy Spirit
The Higher Realms (Guides, angels, G-d by any name)
Their Higher Self and/or the client's Higher Self (the non-physical part of the soul/spirit)
A group which seems like a spiritual family
A collective unconscious
A cosmic library of images and information

Akashic Records (the energetic record of each soul's development)
A personal consciousness
A global consciousness
Ascended Masters such as Mother Mary, Kwan Yin (the Oriental Goddess of Compassion), Buddha, Christ and Djwal Khul
The White Brotherhood of Light ("White" refers to the color of the aura, not to race)
The Emissaries of Light
The VOICE (a facet of the Divine)
The quantum field
The spirit of a person or animal who has crossed over
The client's personal energy field
Nature's Intelligence (e.g., fairies)
Devas of the plants (Devas are flower angels and there is a Deva for each type of plant)

The information source accessed by each psychic is often linked to their specialty. For example, Mediums connect directly to the deceased person's spirit. The woman who works with flower essences communicates with the Devas of the plants. The gentleman who carves masks accesses a cosmic library of images and the woman who works with Light energy communicates with the Emissaries of Light.

Most psychics know with whom they are communicating. However, three psychics don't know what they tap into, but have learned to trust the quality of the information they receive. I asked one of these psychics, Gina Stanfill, if she was curious about where the information came from and she responded:

> "No, I just thank them. They are always there; they have always been there. I have been walking with them all my life . . . To me, it doesn't matter if information comes from plant spirits or a distant planet, it makes no difference. For me, it serves no purpose to know. If my ego wants to be in there, then my ego will tell you it came from a certain place. One of my lessons is to trust it."

Which sources are used when reading for clients?

When psychics read for clients, they are likely to communicate with Spirit Guides, their Higher Selves, angels, Universal Energy, the Holy Spirit and people who have crossed over (their spirit). Spirit Guides have lived on Earth, crossed to the other side and chosen to stay there to guide people on this side. The Higher Self is the part of each person which resides in the non-physical world and knows why the person has come to Earth and the lessons which he or she needs to learn. Angels are G-d's messengers. Universal Energy and the Holy Spirit are some of many terms similar to the title "G-d."

Here are a variety of thoughts from the psychics about their information source:

☼ I often work with Spirit Guides. I think we all have them. Because I have done a lot of meditating for myself, I can connect with Spirit Guides. When I am working with other people, I feel like I can feel or see their Guides. If I don't see the Guides, I can still see what the Guides are communicating because that is what they feel that this person needs to know. *(Marta Taylor)*

☼ I usually communicate with a group of Guides: a hippie from California, St. John the Baptist, a Tibetan Priest, a Chinese Priest, a Chinese doctor, a female Indian Shaman, and a Lakota Indian healer. The Lakota healer, the Chinese doctor and the Chinese Priest actually do the healings with me. They come in at different times for different people. They tell me what I need to know when I need to know it for a particular case that I am working on; the person I am working on that day. *(Richard Schickel)*

☼ I communicate with a group. My understanding is that there are seven groups and we all come from one of these groups. It's like a family group. There are groups of healers, teachers, adventurers, musicians, etc. We all have those abilities, but the groups we come from influence our abilities. *(Cecilia Nemmers)*

☼ When I have asked Spirit for the names of my personal Spirit Guides, they showed me a group, like a circle, around Mother Earth and I understood that it was the connectedness of all consciousness which gave me the information. I call them, "The Guys." *(Laurie Hays)*

☼ I am connected with the Spirit Guide and Angelic Realms. I have my own Spirit Guides and angels. In addition, each person I work with also has their own Guides and angels. *(Beth Hays)*

☼ One of my Guides looks like a wizard and I think he is a protector of the planet; one is a part of myself that I came in with who looks like a priestess. They both work with me on the healings. Sometimes I will walk away during the healings and the Guides will keep working on the person. The person tells me that it feels like there are hands all over their body. I have another Guide who recently came in. I have a Guide who showed himself to me when I was listening to drumming. I was thinking about different gods and he came up and he was an African water god. I talked to him and he told me that he was a spirit who had been known traditionally on other continents. He was not embodied, but he came to people who did healing and that is what I do; I heal. *(Leah Taylor)*

☼ I have many Guides around me and I know who they are so I am always connecting to one or two of them. There are some who are always around me and there are others who come and go. When I call on my Native-American medicine person, she is always there, but I think she is just another aspect of myself. I used to think that she was separate, but then I recognized she was part of me, another aspect of me, perhaps that I had lived in another lifetime. *(Trish Silay)*

☼ I connect with Spirit Guides and the Creator, by whatever name you want to give that. We are all creations of the Creator and we are all connected. Every molecule is connected to every other molecule. It doesn't matter if it is the tabletop or the rocks outside or the dog, everything is connected. We all breath the same air. I think Jung calls it the collective unconscious. All the answers are there. All you have to know is how to tap into it. You have to tap into the collective unconscious, ask your questions, and the answers will be there. It just is. On that subliminal unconscious level, we are all connected. *(Cherie Fraine)*

☼ I think I am attuned to my Higher Self and my Higher Self knows what I need to do and that gets me connected. When I am connected to my own spirit, I know that I can help others. *(Trish Silay)*

☼ A great deal of what you are connecting with is your Higher Self. It is your connection to the energy of the Universe. Part of that comes from training in hypnotherapy: you realize that you have to get into the subconscious. The subconscious is there to protect you and when you get to the other side of it, you learn things. When you can get past your own walls and get to that place of freedom where all information is stored, there is a connection to Spirit. *(Nancy)*

☼ There are people who have Guides with names. I have never had anyone show up and tell me that they were my Guide. I hear what I call "The VOICE." I know it's a facet of the Divine . . . There are beings out there, but I have never felt like there were individual beings bringing the information to me. When I have tapped into relatives on the other side, it has been specific information from certain relatives. I don't have Guides or a group of advisors. Another psychic told me that I have a whole Indian village which steps up to help. I don't have a recognition of that at all. *(To-Ree'-Nee' Wolf)*

☼ I call it the Higher Spirits. I am afraid to call it G-d because I am afraid to say that I am speaking for G-d, but I think that it is the energy of G-d. *(Richard Schickel)*

☼ When you give the entities who are providing information a name or a label of any sort you narrow down the information and the opportunity to get information. If you only call on Archangel Michael, then that's all you are going to get. I take whomever is out there and wants to give information. *(Cynthia Rae)*

☼ I connect with the Higher Realms. I connect into the higher frequencies and that is where I do my work. I go into a certain "space" where I connect with clients energetically in the Higher Realms on the higher frequencies (energy vibrating at a faster pace). I connect to the client's Higher Self. My Higher Self works with their Higher Self then it comes down into physical reality. *(Raquel Spencer)*

☼ For me, the highest level of information comes from the Holy Spirit. If I get information without the client being there, it is most likely that I am getting Divine Will. This level of energy provides answers regarding life path and other big decisions. *(Jeff Sonnenburg)*

Additional information on communication sources can be found in Chapter 13, "All About Readings."

What is it like to work with Spirit Guides?

Some PRISMS communicate with individual Spirit Guides while others communicate with a group of Spirit Guides. The psychics have a conversation in their mind so that they can hear, see, or know what to tell clients. They hear voices and/or see images *in their imagination.* It is like an inner voice or a third eye.

What does it feel like to connect to a Spirit Guide? It feels like receiving information with a unique kind of energy.

Gigi Sample works closely with her Guides. During our interview, she provided the following insights:

☼ Some people know the names of their Spirit Guides and other people ask me to tell them the names of their Guides. The Guides may not provide a name because they have had different names in different lifetimes. The name is not as important as just recognizing their presence and their energy.

☼ One of the things I have been thinking lately is that our Guides might be us in a different lifetime, or a different realm. Maybe my Guide is a different version of me.

☼ Some Spirit Guides work with individual people, but some may work with a bunch of people who are meant to work together.

☼ I can bring messages from Guides. However, people can choose to go against everything their Guides are guiding them to do. They have the choice. I can see the future possibilities when someone is listening to their Guides. I can see what their Guides would like them to do. Our Guides can't make us do anything. We make our own choices. We can say "no" to our Guides and that is what can change the outcome of readings.

Neither Spirit Guides nor psychics can make decisions for people. People must make their own decisions and take responsibility for their own lives. However, Guides can gently whisper their suggestions in someone's ear and help them stay on course.

Where are Spirit Guides located?

When I asked one psychic where his Guides were located he thought that they were right next to us, but at a higher vibrational level. People were at a lower vibration because of their bodies. Unencumbered by bodies, entities were at a higher, free-er level of spirit.

Another man who communicates with a group of Guides says that there is no way to explain where they are located. The easiest-to-understand concept is that the astral plane is the closest plane to us. Guides are located in the highest stratosphere of the astral plane. In order to communicate, we need to lift our vibration to connect to them and they need to lower their vibration to communicate with us.

How can psychics tell if information is coming from an outside source, or from their own imagination?

Through practice and feedback, psychics learn to discern which information is coming from their own minds and which information is coming from outside sources. One of the major ways of confirming outside information is having other people receive the same information. Raquel Spencer explained:

> "I have had many experiences in the physical realm which have validated my work. I have had people be able to see and know what I am seeing and knowing simultaneously. If someone else is experiencing what I am experiencing at the same time, it can't be my imagination."

Another way to confirm that information is coming from an outside source is to have clients corroborate information. Often, psychics don't understand the messages which come through, but clients understand the messages. During readings, Laurie Hays receives pictures and stories which don't make sense to her but, when she relays them to clients, the clients know exactly what the messages mean. The clients leave happy and at peace.

Receiving messages can baffle the psychics. Gigi Sample remarked:

> "You know things, but you don't know if you really know them or if you are just thinking them and you get into a mind loop. I have an analytical mind and I have worked diligently over the years <u>not</u> to listen to that while I am doing readings. The analyzing and worrying have to be removed from the reading. When I remove my analyzing and worrying, and just tell people what I hear, I am usually correct. People keep coming back to see me and referring me, so I have learned to trust that I am hearing and feeling it right."

Jackie Chin works with energy and commented:

> "When I do a reading I ask the client to give me a specific question then I work backwards to the point in time where the issue began; that initial energy point. There is no way that I could personally know about them, or about that specific situation. That is the barometer I use to know that I am getting information from an outside source. Also, before I do the reading I know full well that it's not me doing the reading, it's the energy that created me allowing me to tap into the energy stream and gather needed information to create peace in that client's life."

Denise Singerline explained that it is all about trust:

> "Over the years, I have wondered if I was imagining information, but I would write it down and share it with people and I would get feedback that the information was correct. People confirmed the things which I told them. Finally, I started trusting the information. Sometimes I give a person a message and I tell them that I don't know what it means. Spirit told me that I don't have to understand the information, the client will know what it means."

At least three psychics mentioned that they have transmitted messages in languages which they didn't know. These languages were understood by the client, but not by the psychic. This was a pretty good indicator that the information was coming from an outside source.

To-Ree'-Nee' Wolf recalled:

> "I once did a reading in the Navajo language. I have a good friend who plays the bass and I was with him when I heard words in my head. I asked if he knew what the words meant and he told me that they were Navajo. I told him that someone wanted to talk to him and I asked if he was open for the information. He was. I conducted the whole message in Navajo and his eyes got really big. I asked if he understood the message and he told me that he understood all of it. I had no idea what I was saying. This happens once in a great while. I didn't need to know the information; it wasn't my business."

Similarly, Richard Schickel found himself praying in Lakota, but didn't know what he was saying. After this happened a few times, he learned to have faith that he was providing positive messages.

Several psychics remarked that they know they are getting outside information when they hear a particular voice in their head. Jeff Sonnenburg clearly hears voices. If the level of intuition is pretty basic and is applicable to daily life, the voice sounds similar to his own voice. If the information deals with relationships and health, the voice sounds like a conversation. When the information concerns life purpose, it comes from the Holy Spirit and the voice is extremely loud and <u>not</u> his voice. Information which comes from an outside source feels completely different than information which comes from his imagination. He can always discern the difference. However, he acknowledges that when he teaches other people how to use their gifts, this can be a stumbling block. They need to learn discernment.

In contrast to the loud voice Jeff Sonnenburg hears, Delphina Nova hears a calm, still, nurturing voice of unconditional love and Jan Class hears a small "chirping" voice, a little bitty voice, like a chipmunk or a bird. To-Ree'-Nee' Wolf just calls it "The VOICE."

Laurie Hays knows she is receiving information from a Higher Source when she hears information during readings which she just couldn't imagine. It is not how she thinks. In addition, she receives surprising information during her daily activities. For example she and her husband might go to a restaurant and, as soon as they sit down, she gets the urgent feeling that they need to leave. They had been looking forward to dinner, but need to leave immediately. She added, "Sometimes the messages don't make sense, but they are so strong that you know it is not your imagination."

In addition, when Laurie glimpses her own future, she isn't always ready to acknowledge that the information could be correct. She may not want to see the future which she sees; however, time proves that the messages are correct.

Marta Taylor, who thinks of herself as an energy conduit, mentioned that intuitive information comes on its own, unexpectedly. Her imagination feels like a thought, like she is looking for something, or forcing something. If she steps back and just sees what pops up, intuitive information comes by itself. Through experimentation, she has learned to step back. It comes with practice. She said that there are exercises which have been developed over centuries to help people get over emotion and imagination, and move to the next step which is real information coming from something beyond their own desires, expectations and hopes. Pure information.

Nancy, an energy worker, recounted a past-life regression which had brought in "outside" information. She was under hypnosis and went to the year 1876. She was able to describe things which she had not seen in her present life. For example, she described the Native American boots she was wearing, along with particular weaving patterns which she had never seen. She continually questioned herself and wondered if she was making up the information. Sometime later, she found the weaving patterns in a book.

In the process of doing her energy work, Nancy also receives intuitive insights. She says that receiving information feels different than using her imagination and it is easy to tell the difference. In the past, she has worked in stained glass, weaving and watercolors so she knows what it feels like to use internal energy to do creative and imaginative work. When she receives messages from an outside source, it feels different. This information is very concise and informed. It is information which she could not have known on her own.

Trish Silay observes that when people begin using all of their faculties, and they are integrated, they learn to trust that they are getting the information from a Higher Source. The key is not to have ego involved. Ego and personality can reshape the messages because people add in an intention about what they think is right. Information has to come from pure energy.

Finally, Jan Class advises, "Your abilities, and your ability to unfold, start with your imagination."

Do readers think G-d is involved in their work?

Some people are wary of psychics because they fear that psychics are connecting with negative energies or are dabbling in areas where they shouldn't be dabbling. Interestingly, many of these people are religious and while they pray and nurture their own personal relationship with G-d, they have been taught that psychics are not working with the same G-d energy. I asked the psychics straight-out, "Do you think G-d is involved in your work?"

The answer is "Yes." All of the psychics believe that some form of G-d is involved in their work although they don't always use the term "G-d." They work with a high level of energy and each of the psychics has their own concept of G-d. They don't feel like He is a man sitting on a throne. G-d is an energy which is around us and is a part of us. They connect with a G-d-force energy.

Some of the PRISMS are reluctant to use the word "G-d" because the term is too closely aligned with organized religion and they feel that religion and spirituality are not always the same thing. They refer to this energy as the Supreme Creator of the Universe, the Holy Spirit, a Higher Power, a Universal Energy, a Universal Consciousness, a Universal Intelligence, a Divine Source, "The Force," and "Source" – what all creation comes from.

Richard Schickel has received messages that G-d doesn't want us to confine Him or name Him. A strong message came to him saying, "Quit trying to name me. Quit trying to tell me that I am Mohamed, Elijah, or Buddha – I am all these things. Simply . . . I am!"

Richard added that he sometimes calls this energy "The Higher Spirit." He is reluctant to call it G-d because he is afraid to say that he speaks for G-d, although he thinks that he connects with the energy of G-d. He feels that Jesus may have spoken to him several times, but he notes that this is Jesus as a prophet, like Isaiah or Elijah. It is the energy of these people. These are the Ascended Masters or the highest spirits. In fact, several readers work with Ascended Masters to bring information into this dimension.

Denise Singerline believes that this universal energy is in another dimension which exists along side of ours:

> "It's all Divine. I don't think G-d is one single entity, I think it is more like a consciousness. It's an energy. I am tapping into that Universal Divine Energy."

Cecilia Nemmers commented on humanity's relationship with G-d:

> "We are all connected to G-d. We are all energetically connected. G-d is a creator; He doesn't get overly involved. He creates and whatever we do with it, it's up to us to fix. We need to figure out solutions to the problems we create. However, there are groups of Spirit Guides, angels and people who have gone before us who help us fix things."

In contrast to this vast concept of G-d, a few psychics hear a more-personal voice of love which conveys information to them. They believe that this is the voice of G-d.

Several of the psychics believe in multiple gods. However, when they read for a client, they try to use terms which the client will understand so they generally refer to a singular G-d.

To-Ree'-Nee' Wolf explained:

> "I think G-d is love. Ultimately, G-d and G-ddess are love. The thing that holds the Universe together is love. People think that love is a passive energy. Love is the most serious dynamic force on the planet . . . "

Patricia Kirkman noted that she absolutely worked with the power of G-d. She asked, "Without the G-d force putting me together as I am today, what would I have to offer?"

Chapter 6 - Pros and Cons of Psychic Ability

When I asked the PRISMS about the pros and cons of being psychic and working as a psychic, I received a glimpse into their lives. Being psychic is a mixed bag of blessings.

What are the pluses and minuses of being psychic? of working as a psychic?

The most common response on the "plus" side was that it was very rewarding to help people. It felt very purposeful. Readers had the sense that helping people was why they were here on Earth and that anything they could do to help someone else make their road in life easier was a blessing. In addition, they were able to travel, meet phenomenal people, and make a living doing a type of work which they truly loved.

Here are some paraphrased **"plus perspectives"** from the psychics:

> ☼ You are so sensitive, the joys are tremendous. Even with little things, you're like a happy little kid. The downside is the opposite. When you are hurt . . . it's devastating. When I know good things are going to happen in our lives, I am giddy. When I see sad things, I suffer because I see them coming, I suffer if I try to stop them and no one listens, and I suffer afterward because I know that they could have been prevented. *(Laurie Hays)*
>
> ☼ I want to know things. I want to know everything. Being psychic gives me the tools to do that. *(Erik Assman)*

☼ It can be very gratifying when a matter which has gone unsolved comes to light. Working as a psychic, I am able to counsel people through very difficult times in their lives by showing them a different path. It is rewarding to get out there and do the right thing when someone else may have already failed. I know that I am being allowed by Spirit to do these things and when someone finds me it is usually because they have exhausted all other means for direct answers. *(Jackie Chin)*

☼ These abilities save wear and tear in that there are times when I have been able to save my own life by knowing about things like where to drive, or where not to drive, to avoid an accident. *(To-Ree'-Nee' Wolf)*

☼ It is a gift to give to people. It feels so good when people want a reading or a consultation. I feel like every message I give, I am also getting something. Just like when you teach, you learn. It's a great gift. *(Marta Taylor)*

☼ One plus is the way that I can talk about things when I am going through changes. In the past, I could talk to anyone in a superficial way, but now I ask different questions and I feel things in a different way. I feel more alive now. I wouldn't change it for anything. *(George)*

☼ In some cases, the plus and the minus is the same thing; for example, knowing what is in other people's hearts. Sometimes, you don't want what you see to be true and other times it is a blessing to see what is going on with someone. *(Leah Taylor)*

☼ When someone has broken your heart, you can go to the Universe and say, "I am feeling so sad, it would really help to have a shooting star come by," and the stars show up. *(To-Ree'-Nee' Wolf)*

☼ It gives a sense of meaning and direction to life. I enjoy being in touch with possibilities. I like that it opens more possibilities than, "What you see is what you get." *(Leah Taylor)*

☼ It enlarges my world. There is always the element of synchronicity. I have never felt lonely because I have always felt as if I am a beloved of the Universe. I am one of the Universe's favorite children and so is every other child of the Universe. Most of us just don't know that. I have a hugely intimate connection with the Universe and with the Divine. Some schools of thought say that the Universe is impersonal, but that is not how I experience it. The Universe responds to my needs very delightfully. *(To-Ree'-Nee' Wolf)*

In addition to the joys of being psychic, some readers understand that there are **challenges** to being psychic. One main issue is that there is a stigma attached to this work. Some people discount people with psychic abilities. PRISMS have to accept that some people are going to think they are crazy. Being psychic isn't yet a scientifically-measurable talent. It is similar to being good at art. In addition, psychics have to understand that they are different from other people and they have to accept the fact that some people won't like them.

Another issue, mentioned by several psychics, is that it can be difficult to know things about people and upcoming events, and not be able to share the information. When they see someone going through hard times, they can't just tell them what is going on because it might upset the person or circumvent the person's life lessons. It can be painful when the psychic knows something personal and can't do anything to help. Along these same lines, it can be frustrating when a psychic does share difficult information with a client, and the client refuses to do anything about it. On a larger scale, it can be punishing to see terrible world events coming, knowing that nothing can be done to stop them.

Here are several perspectives on the difficulties of being psychic:

☼ As a child, I picked up other people's information, but I didn't know that. I couldn't tell the difference between what was mine and what was somebody else's. It overwhelmed me because I was always feeling other people's feelings. Your greatest gift becomes a challenge until you realize what it is. As I got older, I was able to separate what I was feeling from what other people were feeling. I could tune it in and out. *(Several psychics)*

☼ Sometimes you get information, such as an upcoming death, that you can't do anything about. That's hard. *(Richard Schickel)*

☼ I am a fairly emotional person so I have to work not to let readings depress me. I hear a lot of sad stories. I work not to let them affect me. *(Gigi Sample)*

☼ In some cases, there is a fine line between insanity and psychic ability. Being empathic can be difficult. I don't like being around too many people's emotions at one time. When I am in that situation, I'm not even sure what I am thinking anymore. *(Erik Assman)*

☼ It can be very lonely, especially when you would like to have a partner. You are different from "normal" people. *(George)*

☼ People want to know why I can't come up with lottery numbers. Well, it is not for their highest good. When it's their time to win, they will win! *(Kat Riegel)*

☼ One minus is not having a meter to say if you are right or wrong. It can be hard to trust yourself when everything in society says that you are totally insane. *(Leah Taylor)*

☼ I am often asked for quick answers, instead of being asked to do formal readings. People want to know "just one thing." I want the communication to be more relaxed and thoughtful. *(Kat Riegel)*

☼ Sometimes it is too hard. How can you tell people what they need to know? How can you take care of people after giving them difficult messages? *(Shirli Millmond)*

☼ Sometimes we get overloaded. There are people who gravitate toward us only because of what we do, and I call them "psychic vampires." The psychic vampire wants to know everything and can suck your energy dry. That's their purpose for calling you. I have people who call me every day for information and, after a while, I stop taking their calls. *(Patricia Kirkman)*

☼ Being psychic is really, really hard work. You need to continually learn and use new information. *(Richard Schickel)*

Many psychics feel that amazing things have happened in their lives. There isn't a separation between the good and bad aspects of being psychic. It is simply who they are.

The Challenge of Honoring your Intuition

Jeff Sonnenburg provides two examples of the pros and cons of using psychic insights. The first example demonstrates how we need to follow our intuition even if we don't receive validation. The second example shows how following our intuition may make us appear rude or arrogant. Still, it's best to follow our intuition.

Jeff's first example: If you were coming home from work, your intuition might tell you to take a different route. What you don't want to ask is, "Why?" If you got home and found out that there had been an accident on the street you were to have taken, your intuition would have been confirmed and you would know why you needed to take a different route home. If there was no accident, you would have no way of knowing if you might have been the car which had avoided the accident. Even though there was no confirmation, your insight probably led you to the correct choice; that's a good thing.

Jeff's second example: You meet someone and you get a strong sense that you should not associate with this person because they have bad or negative intent. Or maybe they just have a cold. If you honor your feeling, you should not want something to happen to confirm your intuition. You don't want to wait until you get hurt and then say, "Oh, I knew I should have stayed away." The better action to take is to move away before reality confirms your intuition. Unfortunately, some people may think you are rude or a snob because you are following your intuition before the person has done anything wrong. You have to accept that there may not be evidence in your reality that you were correct.

It can be difficult to follow intuition when reality doesn't always confirm the messages.

Even with all of the pros and cons, are psychics generally pleased to have these abilities or are they a burden?

Personally, I think it would be cool to be strongly psychic, to have a glimpse of the Universe and a clue about the future. I was surprised to find that while most psychics felt that way today, they didn't always feel that way. Psychic ability comes to people in three ways and the way that it arrives has a big impact on how psychics feel about their abilities.

First, some psychics are born knowing their gifts and understanding that they are here on Earth to use those gifts. For these people, there is an adjustment period to life on Earth. They need to learn to walk and talk and use their physical bodies. They need to figure out how to manage their abilities so that they are not overwhelmed by messages and impressions. They need to find the place where they fit in. After the adjustment period, they are very happy to have their gifts and to share them.

Second, some psychics are born with gifts, but don't know what they have. They just feel like they don't fit in on Earth. These people often find that their abilities are a burden until they figure out that they are gifted, not crazy, and that their special abilities can assist other people. Once they realize what is happening, they become very pleased with their gifts.

For example, Beth Hays commented that as a young person, she felt that her gifts were a burden because she couldn't understand why other people didn't know what she knew. It didn't make sense. Eventually, she realized that it didn't matter what other people understood. She stood up for herself and began living her authentic life.

Delphina Nova explained how her thoughts about her abilities had shifted as she matured:

> "As a young child, I felt my abilities were more of a curse than a gift. For example, when dating, I knew what people were thinking . . . . Now, I think it is a blessing. I claimed it for myself when I realized that I am supposed to have this blessing and that it is okay. I said 'Yes' to the Creator who made me how I am. I realized that I have this gift so that I can help people. There is nothing to fear. I will just deal with whatever comes up and, hopefully, I can help."

Trish Silay commented that she loves her abilities because they make her more fun!

Denise Singerline pointed out that once she understood what was happening, she was very pleased with her abilities because she could use them to create healers. She teaches classes and trains people. She wakes people up. They come to her with drama and problems, then they change. Their lives improve and they are able to help other people. It is very rewarding.

Third, some psychics were not born with extraordinary abilities, but developed them later in life. Most of these people worked hard to develop their abilities and were very happy to have them. One psychic whose gifts opened up late in her teens told me that she was very pleased. She considered her abilities to be a gift from G-d and she loved making the most of them.

But what if you didn't work to develop them and they just showed up? Marianne Patyk became a Medium in her 40s. She had to overcome her surprise, figure out what was happening, and become comfortable receiving messages from non-physical entities. Once she had worked through this adjustment period, she was pleased to have her gifts.

Do PRISMS have easy lives?

When I started this project, I thought that PRISMS had easy lives. After all, they could glimpse the future so they could prepare for whatever was coming. They could read people's energy so they could know who was nice and who was nasty. They could recognize their soul mate so they didn't have to go through the same crazy dating dance as the rest of us. They could make sound financial decisions because they knew which jobs were right for them and how to get those jobs. Maybe they could even foresee lottery numbers and the direction of the stock market?

What I discovered was that most psychics had difficult lives. Even though they tapped into unseen information sources, they still had to flourish on Earth. They still had to have incomes, form relationships and/or raise children. While they might have had some insights which made their decision-making easier than the rest of us, they also had insights which made decision-making harder (for example, knowing it was in their best interest <u>not</u> to date someone and still being attracted to that person). In addition, psychics often had to hide their gifts in order to fit in at work, or with people who might not accept them.

So, why don't PRISMS have easy lives? This relates back to the "cons" of being psychic. Each individual deals with different issues. Some psychics tell me that they are simply messengers while others tell me that they know too much!

Here are a few ways that being psychic complicates life:

<u>Some psychics are simply messengers who are here to learn their own life lessons</u>

In many cases, psychics are simply messengers. They tap into an information stream which allows them to bring messages through for clients. They are not any wiser than the rest of us when it comes to their personal lives. Psychics come to Earth to have their own experiences and learn their own lessons. They have the same challenges as the rest of us.

I talked to several psychics who had been married multiple times. I wondered why they didn't get it right the first time. Didn't they know who they should marry? They reminded me that psychics needed to learn relationship lessons just like everyone else. A person can't know true love, unless they have also known pain. In addition, even though the marriages didn't last, the psychics understood that the marriages provided life-lesson-learning opportunities.

People put pressure on psychics to keep proving their abilities

No one wants to live life under scrutiny. Some people expect psychics to know everything and if they don't know everything, these people doubt the psychics' abilities. They expect the psychics to be lucky and win the lottery. The PRISMS explained that they don't know lottery numbers unless winning is for their highest and best good; just like the rest of us. When it is anyone's time to win, they will win.

Some psychics live double-lives

Psychics often have to be quiet about what they know so that they can fit in, especially in the work place. For example, they can't discuss their impressions when business isn't going well. They may know too much. As a second example, one psychic always knew what needed to be done at work, but when she did it without her boss' direction, her boss felt threatened. He wanted to retain his power by making all of the decisions.

Even outside of the work place, psychics can't tell everyone about their abilities because many people are wary of psychic gifts. People can be skeptical or hostile. They don't want to hear ideas which don't align with their personal or religious beliefs. A few PRISMS remarked that this work is still considered taboo. Psychics have to be very cautious sharing what they know.

Sometimes psychics know more about people than they want to know

If a psychic can read someone's energy just by looking at them, they might feel great when they meet someone wonderful. On the other hand, they can feel terrible when they see evil in someone's heart or mind. Most psychics won't read other people's energy without their permission, but sometimes the energy is too clear to avoid.

When it comes to dating and marriage, problems can arise when the psychic knows that their partner is unfaithful. PRISMS often know when the other person is cheating on the relationship.

Many psychics are too sensitive to energy to mix with other people

Empathic psychics experience other people's emotions. This makes it difficult to go to places where people congregate such as shopping malls, airports, hospitals and clubs. They are overwhelmed by other people's emotions and need to shield themselves. Similarly, some psychics are very emotional because they are so open to impressions.

It can be difficult to have personal relationships

In several cases, psychics commented that this lifetime they were here to help people and this work did not leave time for marriage and/or children. They needed to focus on their assignments. If they chose to be in a relationship, they had to find someone on the same spiritual path. In some cases, so much healing energy came with this work that only very strong partners could manage to be with healers and seers. In other cases, PRISMS had trouble forming relationships because the non-psychic partner could not understand what the psychic experienced. It was too "out there."

Many psychics struggle financially

Working as a psychic reader or healer takes time and energy. It is difficult to focus on this work and also find time to bring in income. Several people commented that they worked regular jobs, but their hearts were in their healing work. They hoped to retire one day and completely focus on their spiritual work.

Some psychics are prone to illness and mental illness

A psychic allows a lot of outside energy into his or her body to do this work. This extra energy can cause problems with internal organs, and can complicate pregnancy. Some psychics suffer miscarriages because they are not grounded enough to carry a baby. They can also become prone to illness and, if they are already sick, they can become more ill than if they had been in a more-balanced state.

Other psychics walk a fine line between sanity and insanity. They must be able to control voices and advice from non-physical entities.

Some psychics have a hard time adjusting to life on Earth

People who remember other realms often have a hard time adjusting to life on Earth. They remember other lives and other abilities and find Earth daunting. For example, they often remember the ease of telepathic communication and find verbal communication cumbersome.

An empath answers: Would you prefer <u>not</u> to be psychic?

Erik Assman feels that his empathic abilities are sometimes an emotional burden. However, this isn't the first lifetime he has been psychic. He would like to be a little more balanced and wise about the information which comes to him. For example, sometimes he perceives what is going to happen, but he mixes up the way that he thinks about it.

When I asked if he would prefer not be psychic, he had a visceral response, "I would be terrified and broken if that were to happen! It would ruin me to the core." He is very pleased to have his abilities even though coping with them can sometimes be difficult.

Erik's response illustrates how many psychics feel. While some aspects of being psychic are difficult, it still has so many rewards and highlights that people willing accept their gifts. They put themselves out to help other people. They live amazing lives.

Chapter 7 - Being Psychic

This chapter answers a variety of often-asked questions about being psychic. PRISMS have an assortment of opinions, experiences and dreams for the future.

Do most psychics think the same way or does each psychic have a different perspective?

Each psychic is unique and has a unique working style. However, they have some things in common and some things on which they disagree. The more psychics I know, the more I see that they are just like the rest of us in that they have differing viewpoints and personal perspectives on being psychic. Just as people don't fit into one simple "non-psychic" group, PRISMS don't fit into a simple "psychic" group. Here are a few ways that their perspectives differ:

<u>Cultivating vs. concealing talents</u>

Some psychics are born fully aware of their abilities. They understand what they tap into and know from the beginning that they are here to help people. Even as children, they shine brightly. They cultivate their talent. Other psychics realize at a young age that they are unlike other children because they know things that other people don't know. This makes the children feel "different" so they try to conceal their gifts and just fit in. They often have difficult lives until they accept who they are and begin living authentically.

General information vs. targeted problem solving

All of the professional psychics are happy to help people. They seem to fit into one of two groups regarding how they help people. The first group provides intuitive insights to clients. They strive to provide the best, most accurate information on a wide variety of topics. People come for general readings, or to ask specific questions, then use the information however they see fit. Once the client leaves, it is up to the client to use the information to create his or her own future.

The second group of psychics is very goal oriented. Their primary motivation is to help clients achieve the specific goals which the clients identify. For example, one psychic is a life coach. She helps clients identify specific goals or problems, then helps them achieve these goals or solve these problems through life coaching. Her psychic ability provides an extra tool to help people craft their solutions. She sees multiple futures and helps clients select the future which is right for them. Her passion is to help people achieve their dreams.

Similarly, another psychic uses flower essences to help her clients achieve their goals and solve their problems, including goals such as "good health." According to this reader, flower essences vibrate at different frequencies. If a person has a specific problem, such as a digestive problem, he or she can use a flower essence which vibrates at the frequency of a person being able to digest well and eliminate well. This psychic uses her intuitive abilities to determine which essences to provide to each client. In addition, she makes the essences herself intuitively knowing the properties each plant will provide to the user. Very solutions-oriented.

Wanting to know more vs. not wanting to know more

Some psychics know where their information comes from and some don't know. Many psychics communicate with specific Spirit Guides and entities who can be named. Other psychics don't know where the information comes from and don't want to know where it comes from. They don't ask about the information source because they feel it would be overwhelming to know too much. One reader felt that the more she knew, the more she would want to know. She didn't ask too many questions because she wanted to thrive in this world and not wander too far into the spiritual world. Another reader remarked that it didn't matter where the information came from as long as it was useful. A third reader commented that she didn't want to overanalyze anything. Overanalyzing limited her ability to give a clean reading.

Focusing on questions vs. an open reading

During readings, most psychics want their clients to give them a clue as to where to look for answers. For example, they like to know if they should focus on love, finances or health. They are happy to have clients show up with a list of questions. Other readers prefer "open readings." In open readings, the client sits quietly while the reader asks Spirit for whatever information the client needs to know. The reader shares all of this information then, after the open part of the reading, encourages the client to ask questions. In most cases, the questions have already been answered.

The future can be predicted vs. the future is fluid

Some PRISMS believe that the future is firm enough to predict. However, most readers explain that the choices people make each moment influence their future. Even one of the readers who feels he can accurately predict the future remarked that he can only predict the things which have already been decided. In many cases, clients have not yet decided their future.

Religion vs. Spirituality

Many of the psychics were raised in particular religions and some of them still participate in those religions. Other psychics have found that religious traditions are too restrictive and prefer to take a more-spiritual approach to life. PRISMS agree that people can be both religious and spiritual.

Do psychics feel safer, or more vulnerable, when they know things that other people don't know?

Because psychics draw information from the non-physical world, they often have hints about the future. Does knowing what might happen in the future make the psychics feel safer because they can prepare for the event **or** does it make them feel more vulnerable because they know what is coming and may not be able to stop it?

In their own lives, most PRISMS feel safer when they know things which other people don't know; they like having a clue as to what is coming so that they can be prepared. Information helps them avoid unpleasant situations. Several psychics mentioned that they always feel safe because they work with the non-physical world to co-create their protection.

One psychic acknowledges that her feeling of safety is the baseline for her sense of personal survival. She finds that whenever something happens which might make her question her security, she always has a higher perspective. This higher perspective helps her feel safe.

Some PRISMS commented that they can either feel safer, or more-vulnerable, depending on the information. One of these psychics mentioned that there were times when he had been upset by what he knew because he couldn't do anything about it. This made him feel vulnerable. Other times, he knew that something unpleasant was going to happen and he knew that he needed to leave the area before the incident occurred. This made him feel safe.

Another psychic who said it "depended on what she knew" elaborated that sometimes she knew certain things, for example, whether or not money would be coming her way. She felt safer when she knew money was coming, but more vulnerable when she knew it was not coming. Either way, the knowledge helped her plan ahead. She always felt protected and cared for so she was not often scared. She felt like she created her future and was able to manifest whatever she needed. Knowing what was coming helped her know what she needed to create. She added that she can feel the direction the energy is flowing and she can feel when it shifts. She told me that people can work with the flow of the universe to get what they want; they can ride it like a wave.

Only one psychic disclosed that he feels more vulnerable when he knows what is coming. He doesn't understand why he needs to know the things that he knows about other people. He tries to see the positive in everyone, but sometimes his intuition warns him that not everyone is trustworthy and that makes him feel vulnerable.

Delphina Nova provided a unique perspective on the question of safety vs. vulnerability:

> "I think feeling vulnerable makes me feel safer. I know I am in a place of safety. When I am feeling vulnerable, I am feeling love. When a person is open, they are able to give and receive love. If a person is closed, it is hard to be a vessel of love."

She clarified:

> "It makes me feel vulnerable, but I also feel safe. How I see the situation depends on my connection to my spirituality. I can't control what is going to happen in the future, all I can do is take care of my own inner environment. If I am in a space of love, no matter what is happening around me, I am not going to be affected. If there is chaos, or

a nuclear attack on Tucson, it won't affect me if I am in the right spiritual space. Am I going to wait until that happens, or am I going to be here in a place of love, nourishing my relationships with G-d and my family? Whatever happens, happens. On my way out, I want to make sure I am in the place of being vulnerable which allows G-d in."

Finally, several psychics said that it is difficult to see their personal future. They can see information for other people, but need to have readings from other psychics in order to see their own lives.

Do many psychics have near-death experiences?

Seven of the twenty-six people I interviewed have had at least one near-death experience (NDE). In addition, another person described an NDE, but called it "astral planing." I didn't directly ask people if they had NDEs. These were just things which came up during our interviews. It's possible that additional psychics have had NDEs, but these events didn't come up during our conversations. To me, seven (or eight) out of twenty-six people (27 - 31%) having NDEs seems like a high percentage compared to the general population.

Of the seven psychics who have had near-death experiences:

2 people have had a single NDE;
1 person has had 2 NDEs;
2 people have had 3 NDEs;
1 person has had 4 NDEs; and
1 person has had 6 NDEs.

At the moment of death, there are different experiences. Often, there is a life review. In some cases, if the body is not damaged beyond repair, people may be given the choice to go to the other side or to stay on Earth. If it's their time, they stay on the other side. If it's not their time to go, they come back.

In some cases, NDEs lead to enhanced abilities, but not always. Some people have NDEs complete with the tunnel, the Light and the choice to stay or to go. Other people are clinically dead and are revived, with no memory of the event. It's a "Near Death," but without the "Experience."

Cynthia Rae remarked, "I believe that when you have a death experience you come back with a level of gifts that people don't understand. I am in an NDE support group and every person reports that their life is different than before they had the experience."

Delphina Nova has had six NDEs. She feels that these experiences have prepared her for the work she is here to do on Earth. She knows that she is more than just a person in a body.

Nearly every psychic mentioned that they were not afraid of death. They were concerned that the circumstances of their death might be painful or frightening, but they were comfortable with the idea of being dead. Their overall attitude was that they had been dead before, and they would be dead again. It's what they did in between that counted.

Chapter 17 has additional information on the psychics' NDEs, their attitudes towards death and how NDEs have shaped their lives.

How do psychics improve their skills?

I asked several PRISMS if they tried to improve their psychic abilities. Did they take classes or read books? Most of them answered that they improved their abilities through classes, reading, or personal meditation.

One of the psychics commented that she maintains her openness by taking an hour-long morning walk. Her walk is like a daily meditation which helps information come to her quickly and clearly.

Another psychic echoed that sentiment, stating that she takes time to listen to her inner guidance. She feels that the quieter she gets, the more she can hear. Similarly, several psychics stressed the importance of maintaining a quiet, calm, centered state. If they are not centered, their readings may not be as good as they could have been.

A third psychic does yoga, attends sweat lodges, spends time in solitude, prays, and goes to the canyons and desert by herself.

Shirli Millmond explained that the best way for her to improve her abilities was to lay back and let go a little bit. She is the kind of person who pressures herself to be perfect. Sometimes she just needs to relax and take care of herself. She said, "The more tired I am, the more I let go, and the more I lose control of the situation, the more information comes to me. Sometimes when you let go, great things happen."

Some psychics work with mentors and several psychics talk with other psychics. They help each other. Even psychics need occasional sounding boards, especially when it is difficult to foresee their own futures.

Many of the psychics either read books, or have books fall off of the shelf and magically open to just what the psychic needs to read at that moment.

Rhonda Harford, the Astrologer, commented that, "We are losing a lot of our older astrologers so I like to buy their books while they are still available. I can lay a book beside me, meditate, and it is like I have already read the book."

However, a few of the psychics did not read books or take classes because they did not want to be influenced by other people's ideas or techniques. Raquel Spencer clarified:

> "I have been directed to keep my energy as undiluted as possible. I am not reading a lot of books or trying to learn other people's way of doing things. I am here to do what I am here to do and that is the purity of who I am. I have probably read 10 spirituality books in the last 10 years. If I get an intuitive hit that there is something I need to read, I read it."

In order to receive pure information, Raquel travels to sacred sites around the world where she receives information downloads. She is continually upgrading her body and her knowledge.

Some of the psychics attend conferences while others take, or teach, classes and workshops. They are very happy to attend workshops and trainings put on by other psychics.

In addition, some of the psychics work with formal systems, such as the *One Brain* system, which require them to attend continuing education seminars in order to remain certified to teach classes.

People who do energy work have been trained in those techniques. For example, PRISMS who practice Reiki have received Reiki training. Denise Singerline tries to obtain a different certification each year. In the last few years, she has studied Emotional Freedom Techniques (EFT), Karuna Reiki, and new variations of Tai Chi. She thinks that all of the tools use energy and provide a starting point which she builds upon when doing her work.

Some of the psychics test and improve their skills by playing games. For example, they will have a friend read a name from the Sunday obituaries, then the psychic will contact the deceased person and tell the friend what was in the obituary. Others try to determine who is calling on the phone before they answer the call. More simply, they try to predict when the phone will ring.

Several of the psychics look for synchronicities in life. Then, they back track and double-check their insights to fine-tune their skills.

What feelings do psychics pick up from other psychics when they meet?

Most psychics recognize strong psychic abilities in other people. While they agree that everyone has intuition, it is apparent to them when someone has particularly strong gifts. Recognizing other psychics' expertise has played an important role in some PRISMS lives. In fact, several people said that they didn't realize that they were psychic until they saw a reader who recognized their gifts. These people went for readings and the psychic said something like, "You can do this just as well as I can!" They had known something was going on, but had never thought that it was psychic ability. The seasoned readers immediately recognized the novice's psychic potential.

When psychics meet, there is often a feeling of friendship or familiarity. Sometimes psychics resonate with each other. Other times, they can tell when they are not going to align with each other for a reading. However, most of the psychics do not regularly socialize with other psychics. They often feel that the only thing they have in common is that they are working in the same field.

One person suggested that when psychics interact, it increases the energy field. This explains why psychic fairs hum with energy.

However, psychics can also tell when other people are mis-using their gifts. Just because someone is psychic, doesn't mean that they have integrity or are looking out for a client's best interest. Some people are just born with an intuitive talent. Denise Singerline remarked:

> "When I meet other psychics, I can tell if they are coming from ego and self-gain, or coming from their heart. I can tell if they are trying to manipulate or cord people. I can tell if they are coming from love, light, and understanding and if they want to help others. Our purpose is to be of service: to help others, train others and teach others. It's not about ego. I try to stay away from psychics with egos."

Another reader says that she has met fake psychics. Sometimes she can see in their aura if they are psychic or if they are imposters who are taking advantage of clients.

Are there limits to what psychics can do?

Yes, there are limits to what psychics can do. Here are a few:

<u>Psychics are only able to do what their gifts allow them to do</u>

Each reader has a personal set of skills. For example, some psychics can talk to the dead and other psychics can't talk to the dead. Some psychics see the future while other psychics see the emotions around a current issue or talk to animals. The information they obtain depends on their gifts.

<u>Psychics can't read for people without the person's permission</u>

Reading someone without their permission is a violation of that person's privacy. When a client asks about a friend or a relative, the psychic doesn't usually access the friend's information. Instead, the psychic can see the energy relationship between the client and the friend and is able to use that connection to answer the client's questions.

<u>Psychics are not allowed to tell everything they know</u>

Psychics often know information which they are not allowed to share and this can be very difficult for them. The information cannot be shared either because the clients are not ready to hear the information or the clients need to go through personal adversity so they can learn and grow. Psychics cannot interfere with another soul's destiny. In addition, most psychics are not allowed to predict death. PRISMS often wonder why they are permitted to know things which they cannot share.

Not surprisingly, some clients say that they only want to hear good news, not bad, and this also limits what psychics can share.

<u>It is difficult to understand the time frames for future events</u>

Cherie Fraine explained that one of the difficult things about a reading is telling the difference between "spirit time" and "people time." Time is an artificial construct. There is no time on the other side. In spirit time, "soon" could be anything from tomorrow until three months from now.

She has worked out a system with her Spirit Guides and the Universe to use Tarot cards to be precise about time. She had to work with her Guides for quite a while to get everyone organized so they could provide information in the specified time frames.

<u>Psychics can't read clearly for themselves, close family members or friends</u>

Psychics usually can't read clearly for themselves. They receive some personal hints, messages for other people, and broad-scope messages (about the world), but they generally cannot see their future. They have to talk to other psychics to make sure that they are on their own right path.

Raquel Spencer, a Light Worker, commented:

> "I can't even see my own life past the next three months! I never know what is coming. I have never been able to see my future. I think this is comfortable for me. If I knew what was coming, I might fight it. I might get in my own way. I have been trained to be okay with not knowing what was coming. If anyone had told me that I would have gone to Ireland, Maui, the Carribean, through the Panama Canal, and to Cost Rica in a three-month period, I would have told them that they were out of their mind! I would have blocked myself from being able to do it."

Furthermore, PRISMS often feel that messages for close friends and relatives could be colored by their own thoughts about the issues. Once they love somebody, it can be difficult to think logically and get straight answers.

Jackie Chin explained the information balance in her personal experience:

> "Most readers cannot read for themselves or their immediate family members. I think this is because everyone has a right to their privacy. However, if there is an emergency, or something that is going to fully unbalance the family, then I do get information concerning the event. It may not be complete, but it will alert me to call, or do whatever I need to do, to see who is in trouble."

<u>Psychics can't heal family members or friends</u>

Some psychics work on family members and friends while others are reluctant to do so. Delphina Nova provided this perspective on why she doesn't work on the people she is close to, "It is almost like when someone is an authority figure, a minister, a priest, or a doctor; it's easy to abuse the power because we are human, so I have taken an oath not to work on family or friends."

Can psychics be jerks?

Yes. Being psychic is a talent. Some people can paint, some can play music and some can access unseen sources of information. Psychics can be jerks who were born with an intuitive talent. These people are immature and are not on a spiritual path. Their psychic skills might be admired, but they can't back them up with a spiritual understanding or with compassion for others. There is more to being a professional psychic than obtaining information. What a psychic says, and how they say it, is critically important.

On the other hand, some people can be highly evolved, but not recognize any psychic ability at all.

When psychics think about their abilities, what do they see as their future?

When the time is right, most PRISMS hope to expand their businesses. They are interested in teaching classes, writing books, leading tours to metaphysical locations and/or working with the police department. The psychics who are still working at "day jobs," hope to retire and spend more time on their metaphysical work.

After retirement, Richard Schickel would like to be a full-time psychic. He explains:

> "I would like to be able to work with more people than I can work with now. I want to explain to them that it is not "un-Godly" to explore relationships. Don't be afraid. People should be more afraid of the mind-control of organized religion. I often suggest that people pray, which is just talking to G-d. People should also meditate; then they should just listen. The problem is that people are trying to connect, but they don't listen. People choose not to hear messages because they don't trust the answers. The answer might be what a person doesn't want to hear, so they ignore the answer. People think G-d isn't sending the answer, but actually people aren't listening.
>
> "I have been told that this is my mission on Earth. I need to wake people up, and I need to plant seeds. I have had 'normal' lives before, but this one is different."

Similarly, Jackie Chin would like to teach others how to develop their spiritual birthright. She believes that people are part of a greater consciousness and they should be encouraged to develop their minds, bodies and souls to the fullest extent. When this occurs, people will come up with solutions to heal disease and will make better decisions for healing the planet. The first step in this process is understanding that there is something greater than our physical reality.

Kat Riegel, the Animal Communicator, would like to offer her services at veterinary clinics. She does not want to diagnose illnesses, but would like to ease each animal's mind. In addition, she would like to open a no-kill animal shelter.

Another psychic would like to have a call-in radio show where she could help listeners.

Raquel Spencer, a multi-dimensional energy specialist, understands that her work on Earth is to enlighten people and help with humanity's ascension to a higher level. Raquel remarked:

> "I see it all expanding. I kept getting the message that people were not ready until 12/12/09. Since then, my work has become more well-known. People are finding me. I have had numerous classes and workshops and people have shown up. I think that this is the beginning for me. I have dabbled in this work, I have done workshops, but my work has been limited because it wasn't time for me to do more until this year. There is truth in Divine timing. I think I am ready and I think that there are people who are ready for me."

When I asked if she thought she would continue doing one-on-one work and teaching workshops, she answered:

> "I want to do it all. I think the one-on-one sessions are very important. I think that the intensive workshops shift people beyond belief. I do a 2½ day intensive workshop and all of the participants report that they have come out changed. I can see myself talking to large groups in an auditorium. One thing that I saw when I was 17 was me standing and speaking in a huge auditorium. I now know exactly what I am going to be doing with that. I don't know how I am going to get from here to there, but I can foresee myself doing the energy work for thousands of people at one time. I don't think I will have the time to do one-on-ones with everyone, but I can see myself working with huge groups. One of the best things for me right now is the teleconference format. I can do energetic tune-ups and angelic healings as teleconferences. I am a good speaker and a good teacher, but my true gift is the energy work. I would like to be able to reach a lot of people at one time."

Gigi Sample would also like to work with large audiences and teach people about their intuition. She would also like to educate children. A few years ago, she started Indigo Teen Clubs in Oregon and Arizona, but she ended up spending so much time traveling that she didn't have time to focus on these clubs. Indigo Teen Clubs meet monthly to explore metaphysical topics. Teens socialize and learn about matters like astrology, palm reading, angels and Tarot cards. Sometimes there are guest speakers or field trips. Eventually, Gigi would like to start clubs all over the United States.

Each psychic is using his or her special gifts to create their unique impact on Earth. Me too.

Chapter 8 - The Personal Lives of Psychics

Now that we've discussed what it is like to be psychic in general, let's learn more about the personal lives of psychics. The PRISMS answered questions about dating, marriage, parenting, and family relationships.

How does being psychic affect dating?

When I think about dating, I remember it as a time of exhilaration and anxiety. Who would ask me out? How would it go? What would happen? It seemed to me that dating would be so much easier if I knew the answers in advance! If only I could know who was worth dating, who was a dud, and whether or not things would work out. If only I were psychic . . .

So, what do PRISMS think? Do they know in advance how things will work out? Is dating easier when a person is psychic?

Here are some anecdotes illustrating how being psychic can help when searching for a mate:

One psychic recounted that as a teenager she worked with a Ouija Board and asked, "Who will I marry?" She was told that she would marry a man named "Bob." She hated that name but, years later, she married a man named "Rob." Very close; both short for Robert.

A second psychic mentioned that while in high school she was consistently able to picture her boyfriend in her mind, picture a telephone with the boyfriend, and motivate him to call her!

A third psychic mentioned that when she met her current boyfriend, they held hands across a table and she could feel his energy rushing through her. She knew she was in trouble. Good trouble.

A fourth psychic remarked that she had looked at a man's palm and known that they were destined for marriage. They barely knew each other at the time. She wasn't particularly interested in marrying him and found it very eerie to see herself in someone else's hand.

A fifth psychic, unsure of the relationship she was in, tried automatic writing and Spirit told her, "This is your beloved. This is the one you have prayed for and waited for." She had made a list of the qualities she had sought in a man and he had met most of the qualifications. Even so, she had endured other difficult relationships and she needed to have Spirit re-assure her that this was the right man for her. Today, they are happily married.

Finally, one psychic met her intuitive future husband at a barbeque when they were both teenagers. When they met, the future husband had a profound sense of knowing her, but he didn't feel like it was a magical thing. He was just sure that they knew each other. Maybe they had been friends in kindergarten? It was love at first sight, but it wasn't puppy love; it was a deep feeling of familiarity. He kept trying to figure things out. Eventually, they discovered that they had lived previous lifetimes together and that they really had known each other. Now, both of them remember their past lives together.

On the other hand, being psychic can sometimes be a barrier to finding a mate. Several PRISMS reported that being psychic can be an issue because people don't feel comfortable dating psychics. In some cases, people don't like to date PRISMS because they don't believe in psychic ability or don't like the idea of someone dabbling in the unknown. Other people worry that the psychic partner will know their secrets. And, sometimes, psychics are emotionally-sensitive or have other issues which make dating difficult. For example, many psychics pick up other people's emotions and don't like to be in crowded movie theaters or restaurants. The non-psychic partner may not understand why the psychic doesn't want to go on these kinds of traditional dates.

Here are some anecdotes illustrating how being psychic can make dating difficult:

One reader, "Starlady" Rhonda Harford, commented that she was not easy to date. When she was with a man, she picked up on his health issues. It was difficult for her to be with someone who drank too much or had other addictions. With one partner, she kept feeling like he was going to have a heart attack. When he eventually developed health problems, she also began having health problems because she was empathic and absorbed his illnesses.

A second Intuitive observed:

> "It makes it easier to date because you can flesh out the bullsh*t. It also makes it harder because you can't play games. It's about integrity. I want to come from the clearest space I can. I want to be able to tell people who I am and what I do." *(George)*

Delphina Nova explained a different aspect of dating:

> "I never know if someone wants to date me for me, or if they are more interested in what I do. I dated one guy for a week or two when I realized that what he really needed was healing. He didn't know that that was why we were dating, but I knew. I had to stop that relationship. I have to walk with incredible integrity because it is easy to become interested in someone, but I don't want to do that when I know it can't work out."

A fourth psychic mentioned that his partner wanted readings and the psychic was reluctant to read for this person because if the truth was not what the person wanted to hear, it might affect the relationship. It can be awkward to read for the people who psychics date.

A fifth psychic admitted that she always went with her intuition even when she understood things were not going to work out in the long run. She knew there were reasons to be with the people she was with, for them and for her. Even if she knew the relationship wasn't going to last forever, she knew there were lessons to be learned.

On the other hand, a sixth psychic disclosed that she often went <u>against</u> her intuition. When she was attracted to someone who she knew she shouldn't date, she dated him anyway. It always ended badly.

Here is another way in which being psychic can be a barrier to dating and relationships: some psychics understand that they are here to help people and that their work requires that they move around the country. One psychic told me that she moved too often to form lasting romantic relationships.

In addition, not all psychics are able to read well for themselves. In these cases, being intuitive has no affect on dating because these people don't know how dating will work out.

<u>What about psychics who date other psychics?</u>

Two couples pointed out that they knew immediately that they were destined to be together. They recognized each other and had a feeling that they already knew each other. Pretty quickly they realized that they had formed relationships in other lifetimes. However, one psychic who knew that he and his partner had experienced troubled relationships in other lifetimes, felt a different kind of dynamic where he wanted to scream, "Not again! I'm sick of this person!"

How does being psychic affect marriage?

When one person taps into universal knowledge and the other person doesn't, how does this affect their marriage? The psychics have a wide variety of experience with marriage. Some are married, some are single and some are divorced. I interviewed 26 PRISMS of various ages and life stages. Of these 26 people,

6 are in their first marriage;
1 is widowed and re-married;
1 is divorced and re-married;
2 are divorced twice and re-married;
1 is separated;
9 are divorced once and not married;
1 is divorced twice and not married;
1 is divorced three times and not married; and
4 are single and have never married.

Some psychics find that their partner is amused by their intuitive gifts. One psychic remembers that her former husband had been fascinated whenever she picked up the telephone and knew it was him just by the way the phone rang.

Another psychic reports that she and her husband are both gifted and that they have a lot of fun. Being intuitive deepens their marriage. They share insights and tell each other what to look out for. Sometimes they think the same things or answer each other's questions before the questions have been asked. In addition, they enter each other's dreams and work together while dreaming.

One psychic often asks her husband to go to a grocery store to pick up a specific item. However, she can intuitively see the grocery store shelf and tell if they are out of the item so, when they are out of that item, she sends him to a different grocery store. The husband gets irritated by her micro-management and likes to go to the first grocery store just to see if she is correct. She is… He moves on to the second store.

In addition to amusing each other, some spouses have benefitted from marrying a psychic who can help them work through their personal issues and challenges. One psychic has been married for more than 20 years and has helped her husband clear mental and emotional blockages. Her husband had been an adopted child and had carried a lot of anger when they met. She was able to help him work through his anger and become a bright, caring person.

However, some psychics realize that they have to be cautious and try not to let what they know negatively impact their marriage. For example, one psychic recognizes that she needs to be careful not to dismiss her partner's ideas just because she has psychic insights on certain matters. When they have a difference of opinion, she has to make sure she doesn't allow herself to feel wiser than her husband just because she has intuitive answers.

Other spouses are put off by what their psychic partner knows. They feel that they can't get away with anything because the psychic partner knows what is going on.

I interviewed four people who had been divorced at least twice. Some had remarried and some had remained single. Why would psychics be divorced multiple times? Didn't they know who they should, and should not, marry? The psychics provided the same kinds of reasons for failed marriages as everyone else. For example, one psychic knew she wasn't supposed to marry her first husband, but she was young and her mother made her marry him. In other cases, spouses started cheating or the couple grew apart.

Cynthia Rae has been married and divorced three times. During her second marriage, her husband had an affair and he didn't appreciate the fact that she knew about the affair because she was intuitive. Neither of them could handle the reality that she knew what he was doing. She commented, "Everybody who is in our life is a soul mate of a sort. At the time, my marriages were choices I made in order to have growth-producing experiences." She reminded me that, in some cases, psychics were simply messengers for information; they had lessons to learn just like everyone else.

Laurie Hays has been divorced twice. Her story illustrates the intricacies of psychic dating and marriage. Laurie is in the regular font and my questions are in *Italics*. She began:

I am married because I am psychic. He and I worked together in the court system. We did spiritual work with a group during lunch. We discovered that we had shared energy in a past life. In this life, he was my boss so it was hard for me to talk to him about private matters. When we discussed a past life which we had shared, he told me, "You were in the pyramid and I was on one knee, and I am never going to let you go again." We had a spiritual connection. If it wasn't for him I wouldn't be doing readings. I kept my abilities quiet and he kept telling people I was a wonderful psychic.

When you met your current husband, did you know right away that he was the one for you?

No. Not only didn't I know right away, but a psychic had told me that I was going to marry a man who I already knew from work who had a lot of "eeees" in his name and we were going to live on an orange grove. I thought she was nuts. First, I thought that if there had been some guy at work who I was going to marry, I would have felt something. Second, I thought about every guy and I couldn't think of anyone with a bunch of "eeees" in his name. Turns out his name is Eugene. Our first address was on Orange Grove Road. Finally, this was my third marriage and I didn't know if I would marry for a third time.

How did it happen that you were married twice before?

The first time I was married I was 18 years old . . . That marriage had anger issues and violence on his behalf, but I loved him. If he had not cheated on me I would probably still be married. Cheating was the one thing I couldn't handle.

My second husband was a University of Arizona professor. It didn't feel right, but he was good at taking care of me and my children. When I told him it didn't feel right, he told me that I had just never had anyone love me like he did. We were married on a cruise ship and, on the honeymoon, he yelled at me. I just wanted to jump ship. When we got back, I went to counseling and was told to get him out of the house as fast as I could. I was divorced within 10 weeks of marriage.

I don't understand . . .

How could I marry someone when it didn't feel right? I was trying to be logical not sensory. Logically, he was taking care of the kids and he was a good provider. We dated for a year and I never saw the negative side of him. To me, he was nice. At that time my children were around 12 and 16. After that relationship . . . it threw me. I kept asking myself how I could be psychic and end up in that situation. It took a wonderful, wonderful man and another mentor who took me under his wing for me to move on. The mentor explained to me that the second marriage had been Karmic. My ex-husband had been a Roman soldier who had killed me in a previous life and I had hated him. This life, he had to be kind enough to me to get me to care for him to the point where I would marry him in order to clear that Karma. I wasn't meant to live with him. I was just meant to get to that point and then move on.

How did it clear the Karma when you ended up divorcing him?

It cleared the Karma when I married him.

After that marriage, I doubted everything and I was single for a long time. I dated one guy for several years. He felt right, but he wouldn't commit. When he was finally ready to commit, I said, "No," because I felt that I didn't want to marry him if he wasn't certain. So I cried on the Judge's shoulder and the Judge fell in love with me. I asked him how he could fall in love with me when he knew I was pining for the other guy. He said he fell in love with my vulnerability.

Complicated.

In some cases, psychics feel that their marriage is not impacted by their abilities because their spouse is not interested in intuitive information. If partners don't want to be read, the psychics don't read them. The psychics either keep their insights to themselves or they don't apply their gifts to their marriages.

One reader conceded that being psychic had hurt his marriage. Spirits were coming in and out of the couple's bedroom all night long, so his wife never slept well. They began sleeping in separate bedrooms and they eventually separated.

Another reader also observed that being intuitive had made her marriage difficult. After her divorce, she realized that she had to be in a relationship with someone who was on a similar spiritual path. They had to connect on a spiritual level. Until she meets that kind of man, she won't get involved with anyone. The work comes first.

In many places in the world, Shamans are single women because men can't handle being in a relationship with a woman who is a healer or a seer. So much healing energy comes with this work that only very strong men can manage to be with these women. As a matter-of-fact, it can be difficult to have any sort of a personal life when doing this work.

Gigi Sample runs into this same kind of situation when clients ask about their life purpose and relationships. She works with teachers and healers and some of them are not in relationships. They are terrific women and men who are wondering about their partners. According to Gigi, we are in a time when Spiritual Guides don't want people to be deterred by dysfunctional relationships which keep them from their life purpose. People need to be with supportive partners or they get off-track. Of course, people have free will and can do whatever they choose, but their Guides prefer to have them wait for supportive relationships.

Being married to a psychic is similar to any other marriage. Each partner brings their gifts and talents and people either learn to appreciate the unique characteristics of their spouse or they resent those characteristics and the marriage suffers. When the partner is psychic, these particular gifts can be used to amuse each other and reinforce the marriage, or they can become a source of irritation and an excuse for distance between spouses.

How does being psychic affect parenting? What if the children are psychic too?

Of the 26 people interviewed, 19 had children and 7 were not parents. Of the 19 psychics with children, 15 saw intuitive talent in their children, 3 did not, and 1 did not comment on her children's abilities. A couple of psychics mentioned that this was not the lifetime for them to have children. They were here to do spiritual work.

Three psychics shared amusing stories about raising psychic children.

One PRISM recounted that when psychic children become teenagers, it's a real test. She told me, "My daughter thought she could outsmart me. She came to me when she was 16 and said, 'You don't know half the things I have done,' and I said, 'Unfortunately, I do. I just don't want to!'" Now that they are both adults, they tease each other with their psychic abilities. However, the daughter thinks that because the Mom is psychic, she doesn't have to tell her things. Wrong. Everyone wants to hear from their kids!

A second psychic had a more serious recollection. She had a child when she was still a teenager and her parents helped raise this child. Her son was very psychic and was able to manifest (create by thought) whatever he wanted. According to the Mom, the problem was that the boy never developed a proper conscience. It was very difficult to discipline this child because he could have anything he wanted whenever he wanted it. She wasn't able to set limits for him and, consequently, he didn't develop a good sense of right and wrong.

She believes that her second son is also intuitive, but he calls it "common sense." She can never surprise him with a gift. Whatever she gives him, and however the wrapping is disguised, he knows what the gift is because it is just "common sense." If he's not intuitive, how could he guess correctly every time?

The third psychic had a seven-year old daughter who was psychic. The daughter remembered being in her mother's stomach and, when she was about three years old, she asked her Mom, "Do you remember when I was in your tummy? It got really tight in there. At first, I was swimming and that was fun." Later the child asked, "Do you remember when I went down the egg waterfall?" In addition, the child was able to describe what happened when she was born, who was in the room, and that her grandmother was crying.

At one point the little girl asked, "Remember when I was in your tummy and we painted Easter eggs?" Her Mom responded that they were Jewish and that they didn't color eggs to celebrate Easter. Later, the Mom remembered that when she was about eight months pregnant, she had colored Easter eggs with a friend.

This Mom also recollected that when her daughter was two years old, she touched a friend's cat's belly and said, "There are babies in there." The cat had just been in heat and was pregnant, but no one knew at the time.

From what I have seen and read, it seems difficult for non-psychic parents to raise psychically-gifted children because the parents don't understand what is happening with the child. The parents don't know what is real and what is coming from the child's imagination. In the case of psychics who are raising psychic children, things seem a bit easier because the parents can help the children understand their abilities and challenges.

How does being psychic affect extended family relationships?

Some psychics come from families with other psychic members and some psychics are the only gifted people in their family or in their generation. In some cases, non-psychic family members are interested in the information which the Intuitive can provide but, in other cases, they are not comfortable with the psychic's work. I asked the PRISMS how being psychic affected their extended family relationships. There isn't a consistent answer to this question, but the answers helped me to understand what it is like to live as a psychic.

Here are some paraphrased comments on how being psychic has positively influenced family relationships:

☼ It's all been positive. It opened up our communications. My parents were very open to ideas. *(Marta Taylor)*

☼ It has connected us and made us inter-dependent on each other rather than co-dependent. We respect each other. *(Trish Silay)*

☼ It makes it easier to deal with my family because I know that things will all work out in the end. I am just not sure how things will work out right now. It's a quiet knowing that what is happening is supposed to be happening. *(Richard Schickel)*

Here are some comments from psychics who say that being psychic has not had much of an impact on their family relationships:

☼ There was no impact on my family relationships, except that they knew not to bother me when I was doing a reading. *(Cherie Fraine)*

☼ No impact that I can perceive. My mother is psychic and, before I was born, she expected me to be psychic. *(Erik Assman)*

☼ They think I'm nuts! [lol] They think I make things up, but then they listen to me, and they see what happens. *(Cecilia Nemmers)*

☼ My parents look the other way. One brother doesn't mention it. My sister loves me no matter what I believe in. She says I am going to be the nicest person burning in Hell. My husband is very proud of it. *(Laurie Hays)*

☼ I don't talk about it with my family members who don't understand it. One brother is very Christian and I remind him that I work with Jesus and he can understand that. I can talk about it with my youngest brother because he is very much like me. My mother may not understand it, but she accepts it. She's a little psychic too. I don't talk about it unless they ask. *(Denise Singerline)*

Two psychics mentioned that being psychic could be hard on family relationships:

☼ It is very stressful. I don't see them or talk to them anymore. They think I am crazy, which is not true. *(Marianne Patyk)*

☼ I would like to say that being psychic has always had a positive effect on my family, but there were some points where I would have loved to stop it all together. I have had people call me because they want my intuitive assistance, but they give nothing in return, not even kindness. When this happens over and over, it makes it difficult to continue offering assistance. It is like being the doctor in the family and having people constantly talking to you about their health issues. They stop seeing you as a person and only see you as someone who is useful to them. At one point, this situation became more than I could handle so I told one of my relatives that I would rather eat glass than tell them one more thing. *(Jackie Chin)*

Here are a few more glimpses into the world of psychics and extended families.

Kat Riegel provided an example of how she was able to help her family understand her gift:

"My dad was in the Air Force and he is a guy who wants hard facts. However, when I visited him he was fascinated by my abilities and began asking me about what I do. It gave us a better connection. He told me that he and his wife had bought their house from a gentleman who had passed away. I didn't want to hear anything else, except the man's name. I went through the house and gathered information on the previous owner. I was able to give them information which they already knew about the man, confirming my answers."

Shirli Millmond commented that being a psychic had helped her family, but was hard on her:

> "As a kid, I didn't really get to be a kid. I had hard decisions to make. I have always been the psychologist in my family. I had to listen to people's problems and give advice. People asked me for help. If I couldn't have provided the advice, they wouldn't have asked, but I was able to do it."

Delphina Nova pointed out that she felt things which were going on in her family, but her parents tried to protect her by not sharing information. This created an awkward situation. She said:

> "There are certain things my family doesn't want me to know, but I have bodily sensations and I can tell when something is going on. I knew something was going on with my father and it turned out that he had cancer. No one wanted to let me know about it. They were trying to protect me. Maybe they thought it would affect me too much. When they called to tell me that my father was cancer free, they mentioned that my mom had undergone an operation a couple of weeks prior to that phone call. I am affected anyway, I might as well know exactly what is going on."

My original thought was that being psychic would make life easier. Now, I see that being psychic just changes the way things work. In some ways, life is easier but, in other ways, it is harder. It all balances out.

Chapter 9 - Psychics in the Workplace

Do most PRISMS have "day jobs"? How does being psychic affect their jobs? Does this ability make a person a better artist? a better accountant? a computer whizz?

In addition to being psychics, energy workers, spouses and parents, some people have "day jobs." When I asked about this topic, I really wanted to know two things: (1) were psychics working regular jobs and hidden among us without us realizing that the perfectly "normal" person next to us was psychic, and (2) does being psychic make a person better at their job?

The psychics, intuitives and energy workers who are part of this Project are at many life stages: some are young, some are working professionals and some are retired. They are currently employed in professions such as home health care provider, bookkeeper, teacher, tax collector, artist, medical assistant, financial analyst, life coach, computer programmer, sales consultant, advertising and marketing consultant, and administrative assistant.

Other interviewees had moved on from jobs such as electrical engineer, bailiff, artist, computer professional, United Nations consultant, human resources professional, bartender and marketing professional.

You just never know if the person next to you at work has strong intuitive insights.

Here are some of the ways in which intuition affects work life:

One psychic, Beth Hays, used to work as an **electrical engineer** and now works with plant essences and energies. Working as an electrical engineer helped her understand the flow of energy. I asked her if being intuitive had helped her when she was an engineer and she replied:

> "Being psychic made me better at my job. I had always been a high achiever and my psychic abilities helped me to know what a client might like, or how best to present information. It often happened without me realizing I was using it. It just came through me. I would say things without thinking what was coming out of my mouth and it was often the exact right thing to say."

Another psychic had been a **bailiff** for 15 years. She noted that being psychic had helped her with her job because she was able to anticipate what the judges needed. Her only difficulty was that she knew who was innocent and who was guilty, and she couldn't do anything about it. One time she knew that a defendant was guilty, but the judge set him free. She asked the judge about the case and he told her that it was the State's responsibility to prove the case in a court of law and that the State had not done its job. Being a bailiff became very stressful and she eventually had to leave her job.

One psychic who is particularly well-suited to her current line of work is a **home health care provider.** She uses her psychic abilities to help people either to heal, or to make their peace, depending on their desires. If the patient wants to get well, she helps them take responsibility for their sickness, cleans energetic blockages, and cleans their aura. She can clear a patient's energy system so that the patient can heal. This work fills the patient with Divine love. If the patient is very ill or elderly and doesn't want to live any longer, the two of them talk and she helps the person prepare for what might come. She asks them if they believe in an afterlife and she tells them what she has heard; what might be possible. She helps them find comfort in the unknown.

One of the Intuitives has been a self-employed **bookkeeper** for more than 13 years. At first, she tried to keep her intuitive work separate from her bookkeeping work. After a while, she discovered that she could use her intuition to assist everyone with whom she did bookkeeping. She found that while she was working on their financial information, clients asked questions and she answered them. In some cases, she spent more time talking to the clients about their lives than doing their books . . . . and that is what the clients wanted. Once she realized that she was living in two worlds (spiritual and accounting) and that they were really one world, she was able to merge these realms and evolve into her authentic self.

Many psychics go into "helping" professions. One woman works as a high school special ed **teacher**. Her psychic insights improve her job performance because she understands how to help her students.

Another woman works as a **substitute English teacher**. In the classroom, her abilities help her see which children need additional attention. She also uses her Reiki and intuitive abilities to defuse dense energy in the classroom before students arrive. Many times regular teachers who enter the room remark that the room seems different. She responds, "Yes, isn't it nice?"

Also using his psychic talents is a **tax collector**. Being psychic helps him to know whether people are telling the truth or lying when he is negotiating with them. He knows when they are hiding assets.

One woman is a retired **artist** who has always liked bold colors, shapes and sizes. The benefit of being psychic was that, when she was painting a series of patterns, her psychic abilities helped her understand what the patterns meant. Without psychic insights, she would have created the same images, but being psychic added a depth of meaning to her painting process.

According to one current **artist,** being psychic makes her better at her job. When To-Ree'-Nee' Wolf works with a client, she can see what they are seeking. She said, "It gives me another sense of how to hear people, and I know how to listen to people deeply. I hear what they say and I hear what they don't say." She added that all of her gifts and abilities work seamlessly together. She is an artist, a psychic and an intuitive. All of these gifts are used to listen to clients and communities. She tries to make sure that everyone is heard whether they state their opinions aloud or not.

I also interviewed an artist who makes gourd masks. He used to be a **computer professional** with a "rational, linear brain," but after a series of health issues and life-changing events, he began producing gourd artwork. His artwork was inspired by his connection to an etheric library of images. While he couldn't say exactly where the images came from, he told me that once he had completed a mask design, he could see that it depicted alien images, portrayed deep spiritual messages, or provided images from ancient Atlantis.

One of the Intuitives is a **medical assistant/receptionist/co-office manager** for a doctor who practices preventative and alternative medicine. She uses her intuition if the doctor "gets stuck." She can provide an insight to the doctor which prompts his intuition and helps him to help the patient. Prior to this job, she had worked as a medical assistant with a different group of doctors.

At that time, she knew that she had intuitive gifts and that she could share those gifts, but the doctors would not listen to her. In order to work one-on-one with patients, she went to massage therapy school. There, she received hands-on training and found that she was able to feel things through clients. She had the opportunity to lay hands on clients and help them heal themselves. She worked hard to receive medical training then go to massage therapy school to get the license she needed to lay hands on people and use her medical intuition for their healing.

Here is another fascinating story: One of the psychics worked at the United Nations (UN) for three years doing business, financial and political readings. He didn't do personal readings at the UN. Because he was able to predict world events, the UN invited him to give presentations for larger and larger audiences. Eventually, he became a consultant for the Executive Staffing Council which provided information to UN diplomats. His title was **"Intuitive Consultant**."

After completing his work with the UN, he began doing **financial and economic predictions**. Now, he predicts the financial markets every week. His predictions are based on both logic and intuition and he has done exceedingly well. Interestingly, his Spirit Guides told him that he could do this work, but that he was not allowed to profit directly from his stock recommendations. He was not allowed to own stocks because ownership might influence his predictions. Fortunately, he is well-paid by the corporations which he advises.

Another psychic is a **life coach**. She earned a Business degree and started a life coaching company so that she would have the skills to help people and to give them a push. She doesn't want people to be dependent on her psychic readings, she wants them to be self-reliant. Her intuition is a unique tool which helps her to serve other people. She notes that every life coach has a different niche and a different background. Some life coaches know more about finance, health care, or acting. Her specialty is intuition. Clients enjoy coming to her because she has the extra ability to do Tarot card readings.

One of the empaths used to be a **computer programmer**. He felt that being a psychic didn't influence being a programmer, but being a programmer influenced being a psychic because it made him think about things in a different way. Moving into a different mind set helped with the psychic aspect of his work. The computer work provided structured and logical thought which he didn't generally experience as an empath. He noted that there were many faculties of the mind and when people integrated these faculties, they increased their ability to connect.

One intuitive woman has retired from a job in **Human Resources** with Honeywell. Her abilities made her better at her job because she could see who would be a good employee and she could understand how to resolve workplace conflicts. Unfortunately, her abilities irritated certain employees because these employees didn't feel that intuition belonged in the workplace. However, it was part of who she was and her intuition helped many of the managers.

One psychic works as a **sales consultant** for a high tech company. She is very good at her job because she can talk to clients over the phone and know exactly what they need. She works quickly and efficiently to solve their problems.

Another psychic has earned degrees in Business and Design, and also has a Real Estate License. Several years ago, she was a **store manager** at House of Fabrics in Los Angeles. This job combined her skills in design and business. However, she discovered that she liked working with people more than she liked working in a business setting. Now, she is putting all of her time and energy into her spiritual work.

Some psychics think that their intuitive work and their "day jobs" are completely separate. One energy worker owns a small business. She is an **advertising and marketing consultant** who feels that her energy work and her marketing work are two separate worlds.

Similarly, I talked with an **administrative assistant** who used to work for a telecom company. She revealed that she often knew when things were going to happen at the office, but kept quiet about what she knew because what she knew in advance was often negative.

A couple of people mentioned that being psychic made their day jobs more difficult. They couldn't tell their bosses why they knew things. For example, one supervisor didn't like it when the employee did things without being told to do them. The employee intuitively knew what needed to done, but the supervisor felt like he was being undermined. Another supervisor didn't like it when the employee knew about medical conditions without going through the proper testing sequence to discover the issues. Even when the employee was correct, the employee was told that protocols must be followed.

Do the most-successful people use intuitive abilities in a business setting?

The next set of questions comes to mind:

> Are people who are successful in business using intuitive abilities which they may, or may not, be aware of?
>
> Do people who are very good at their jobs have high levels of intuition?
>
> Where do inventor's ideas come from? Do they gather ideas from the ethers?
>
> Does Bill Gates have psychic insights?
>
> Does Warren Buffet have strong intuition about stocks and companies?
>
> What about Oprah Winfrey? She often mentions listening to an inner voice.

I think that this would be a fascinating topic for further study. I would like to ask highly-successful people about their intuitive abilities.

• • •

Now that we understand what it is like to be psychic, let's find out how PRISMS are able to provide readings, energy work and healings, and how people can benefit from their expertise.

Section III

Readings, Healings and Energy Work

Chapter 10 - Thinking about a Psychic Reading

People with psychic abilities tell me that anyone can learn to make this connection on their own. However, people who don't think that they have a clear connection might enjoy having a session with a professional psychic reader. If you have not yet learned how to connect to information sources yourself, you can ask someone to bring the information to you. Psychics are ready to assist. Chapters in this Section will help you to get your best psychic reading.

Is a Reading a Good Idea?

Why do people go to psychic readers? What are the benefits?

Many people seek a greater understanding of their life and the direction that their life is going. A psychic reading can provide fresh insights, a new way of looking at issues, or a second opinion. Some readers can tell people what signs to look for in the future so that people can make their best possible decisions. It's like talking to a wise friend. People are evolving and fresh information can help them change their perspective, enlarge their world view and become a point of light (a positive voice) in this world. Readings provide an opportunity for people to discover who they are, why they are here, and what their destiny holds.

Some people go to psychic readers just because readings are fun!

What do clients expect when they come for readings?

Clients talk with psychics for many reasons. Some people want hard facts about the present time or are curious about the future, and some people want evidence that there is an unseen universe of information and energy. Many clients want a validation of the intuitive messages which they have already received. Other people want to know about their health and their relationships, while some people just want to know that, even though they are going through a rough patch right now, things will improve. Similarly, people who feel "stuck" want to know the best way to move forward on their life path.

Everyone who talks to a psychic expects to be treated with dignity. No one wants to be embarrassed or belittled during a reading. People want a reader who provides information, insights and reassurance, not a reader who makes them fear the future. People want a reader who treats them with respect, supports their empowerment, and is able to answer their questions.

What <u>should</u> clients expect when they come for readings?

When clients talk to professional psychics, they should expect to be treated with integrity. They should expect the readers to be honest. Clients should expect the psychics to give the clearest information which comes to them, and they should expect to hear all of the information which is being sent to them for their benefit. They should also expect the reader to remove their ego from the reading, allowing the information to come through as cleanly as possible.

Here are some summarized, paraphrased, thoughts from the PRISMS about what clients should expect when they come for readings:

☼ Clients should expect that we will act in a professional manner. They will be treated with integrity. *(Richard Schickel)*

☼ They should expect a really amazing and interesting experience, depending on the information which needs to come to them. *(To-Ree'-Nee' Wolf)*

☼ They should expect a safe place. They should also expect confidentiality and trust. *(Delphina Nova)*

☼ Some people expect me to give them answers. What I do is confirm, or not-confirm, their feelings. Sometimes they are correct and sometimes they are not. Sometimes people think they need to do something, but I see that they are acting out of fear and I point that out to them. By the time they leave, they may have decided to change their own course. They may think that I told them what to do, but they decided for themselves. They have free will. If someone tells you what to do, it's still your decision to do it. But if you've made the decision and it feels right to you, that's the course you will take. *(Cecilia Nemmers)*

☼ People want to know what is going to happen. They want an outline for how their life is moving. I think that "outline" is the operative word. The cards will give them the outline but what I feel off the cards, and how the cards connect with other cards around them, will all shade that outline and provide more-expanded connections. People want to be pointed in a direction. I won't tell anyone what to do with their life, but I will say that a particular situation is coming up, and that there are things which can be done with it. If a client wants a straight out "yes" or "no" answer, I can do that. It is like providing guideposts from Point A to Point B. People want to know if they are going in the right direction. *(Cherie Fraine)*

☼ Clients should expect my intuitive perspective on things. I am able to contact loved ones and look at medical conditions. They should expect to have an experience with my intuitive perspective and to open themselves up to feelings. A lot of clients cry when they sit down. My Guides connect them to their soul and there can be tears. *(Leah Taylor)*

☼ People should expect to be treated with integrity, to receive what I call "a road map of their life" that they can take with them when they leave so they can do their own work. I am a guide. I'll show someone around their life, but it is their choice if they want to take the detours. I can tell people about their options and their potential lessons as they move through life. People internally know that there are certain lessons that they need to learn, but they don't always recognize them until they are in the middle of them. Sometimes people repeat patterns and it helps to have someone point out what is going on. Then, it's up to the client to make the changes. *(Patricia Kirkman)*

☼ I ask clients to focus on their situation so that I can work with the past energy surrounding that issue and give them hard information that they can use right now. I make them aware of dates, times and events. I offer tangible information which they can use so that when the [future] event occurs, they have direct signs. That is what people really want when they go to a reader. They want to know what signs to look for in order to make the best possible decisions. *(Jackie Chin)*

☼ Clients should realize that I am not going to see anything that they don't want me to see. Some people think I am like a confessional and that I can see everything they have done wrong. It's not like that. I want them to know that they are safe and that this is only for their highest and best good. If the information doesn't ring true, they should disregard it. The things I say should fortify in them what they have already thought. I never want them to substitute their wisdom for someone else's wisdom. Their gut is never going to lie to them. *(Laurie Hays)*

☼ They should expect to get tools and abilities to deal with their problems. They will get more clarity about their life and the things that they want to achieve. It's an "Aha" moment for them. It's also a relief for them to know that they are not alone. They understand that someone knows them. *(Shirli Millmond)*

☼ Everybody will be different and they are coming for a myriad of things. They are either in pain, have some sort of disease, or have some other problem. After they tell me what their issue is, I tune into their body and access information. What they get from this is surprise, self-discovery, and access to information. *(Trish Silay)*

Now, doesn't that make you want to run out and have a reading?

Finding a Reader

How can someone find the best person to read for them?

The most effective way to find a good-quality psychic reader is to ask a friend for a recommendation. People may be surprised to discover how many of their friends have had a reading or have had their own psychic moments. Try to find a reader with a genuine gift who knows how to use it wisely. Look for someone who gives information cleanly (not filtered through their own perspective, ego or religious ideas). The information should be presented in an understandable way, using empowering words which help people clearly see situations so they can make their best life choices. A person looking for pure energy may find a magical connection.

Each reader has a unique working style and personality. It is important to find someone who can convey messages in a way which works for the client. For example, I have had several readers point out personal issues on which I need to work. Sometimes the message feels like a loving suggestion coming from a friend, and sometimes it feels like a criticism. A reader will say, "You need to work on this issue . . ." and I will bristle because it feels like they are criticizing me and pointing out my flaws. Yet, another reader can point out the same issue in a way which makes me feel like I need to love myself and help myself move along my path. Both readers are accurate and are pointing out the same issue. For me, the kinder reader works. Everyone reacts in their own way. It is very important to find the reader who is best-suited for each person.

There are two basic situations where a person might be interested in selecting a psychic: (1) at a psychic fair where the short readings are a sample of the psychic's work; and (2) when seeking a full personal reading.

In the first situation, the psychic fair, it's best to select the kind of fair where the readers are prescreened for capability. Someone who runs the fair should have tested each psychic to ensure that they are competent. If it's a place where just anyone can set up a table, people need to be a little more cautious about the readers.

Once the psychic fair has been selected, the customer should look around the room and see if they are immediately drawn to anyone. If not, they should look at the list of psychics and see if anyone sparks their interest. Every psychic has unique gifts and talents. If the client wants to connect with a dead relative, they should look for a psychic who is a Medium. If the client is interested in information on past lives, they should look for a psychic who specializes in past-life regressions. Then, if there are choices of Mediums or regressionists, they should base their decision on how they feel about the person. If they feel aligned with the reader, they will probably get a good reading.

Similarly, if they want to know what their future might hold, they should look for a psychic who can see the future. Again, if there is a choice, they should talk to several readers for a moment and see where they feel the most comfortable.

If a client is interested in a certain type of tool, they should look for a reader who uses that tool. For example, if they want a reading based on numerology, they should look for a numerologist. If they are interested in a Tarot card reading, they should go to a card reader. However, the tool which is used is often not as important as the reader's ability to connect to unseen information sources.

If a person walks into a psychic fair and doesn't know which reader to select, they should calm themselves down to their center and say, "Whoever feels right, pull me in that direction," and their Spirit Guide will pull them in the right direction. They should select someone who they like, who they feel they can talk to, and who has their best interest at heart. The client should look for an affirmation in their solar plexus indicating that they have selected the correct reader. They should pick someone who helps them feel comfortable.

Patricia Kirkman suggested that a person may have to circle the room a couple of times until they find the psychic who resonates with them. It could be as simple as a reader looking up, smiling and making them feel relaxed. Or, it could be someone leaving a reading saying excitedly, "I can't believe what I heard," that makes a new client want to select that reader.

If a person doesn't feel drawn to anyone, they don't have to pick a reader that day.

If someone would like a full psychic reading and is seeking a psychic they have never met, there are several tips for finding a good reader:

1) Ask for a recommendation from a friend who has had a good experience with a reader.

2) Interview several psychics over the phone to see if there is a connection. The reader should talk about their credibility and mention their return rate. The way a person feels when they talk to a reader is important. A client should pick someone they like and respect.

3) Walk away the moment a reader gets bossy, rude, or judgmental, or if the there is some sort of ego involved. Walk away if the psychic asks too many questions. Some psychics ask leading questions and do cold readings; that is a waste of money. If they try to sell something, run!

4) If the first reader isn't great, find someone else. There are many good readers and once a person finds someone they like, they can receive a world of information.

When searching for a reader who works over the Internet, Jackie Chin commented:

> "The best way to select a reader is through word of mouth. There are many psychics on the Internet and not all of them provide a reading that is sound and useful. The reader should be able to provide references, articles and other information based on their way of reading so that the individual has the ability to make a sound choice. Most importantly,

> a reader needs to offer a money back guarantee on all their readings. Someone who has a good reputation will not have any problem making sure the client has exactly what they need before they leave a reading."

Are there ways for a potential client to tell if a psychic is legitimate?

According to the PRISMS, it's hard for a client to tell if an unknown psychic is legitimate before having a reading. Some people say they are psychic, but are only interested in making money doing readings. The best ways to ensure that a psychic is legitimate are to ask a friend for a recommendation and to make sure that there is a good feeling of connection in the solar plexus when talking to the psychic. Before a client signs up for a private reading, they should call the psychic and make sure they feel good about the connection. Then, just try it. If the psychic isn't the right one, not much has been lost and it may have been an adventure. Next time, the client should ask different friends for recommendations and try someone new.

Jackie Chin suggested stricter guidelines for deciding if a psychic was legitimate after having had the reading. She said that it is important for the psychic to be able to tell the details of the answer to a person's question, as well as specific details about what led to the question. She added, "A person knows their past and if the psychic can't give them those details, they need to find someone who can." She suggested that the first time a client works with a psychic, they only pay for a short reading. If they like what they hear, and it makes sense immediately, they can schedule a longer reading.

However, clients should remember that PRISMS have different working styles and receive different kinds of information; not everyone receives detailed information about specific events. Some psychics only communicate with people who have crossed over, while other Intuitives only receive emotional information or have an empathic connection. Some psychics only receive messages about medical conditions. It's unrealistic to expect every psychic to provide a high level of detailed information about the past and the future.

On a stronger note, To-Ree'-Nee' Wolf warned:

> "If someone says vague things, or you have to fill in information, be cautious. Some people do cold readings. Also, if people scare the sh*t out of you during a reading and say things like, 'Oh, there's negative energy around you. There are Devil forces around you, but I can make them go away, but it will cost you big money' – that's bullsh*t. People who charge large amounts of money to take the scarey things away? I don't buy that."

Do readings work over the phone?

Yes, psychic readings work over the phone. This is as effective, if not more effective, than doing readings in person. Why? In person, the psychic might be distracted by a person's facial expressions or body language. It can be hard not to be influenced by a client who is shaking their head, "No. No. No." Even though these clients often discover (at a later date) that the information made sense, it can be difficult to work with them face-to-face.

How long does a reading take?

Before a client meets with a reader or an energy worker, he or she should ask how long the session will last. Sessions generally take about an hour, but many psychics leave extra time open because they don't want to stop if they are in the middle of a thought when the hour is up. A few readers commented that a session will take as long as necessary for the client to feel that they have accomplished what they need to accomplish. Other readers do 45 or 60-minute readings and add another 20 minutes of energy healing at the end of the session. One of the psychics commented that a normal reading takes an hour. If there is also a healing or a past-life regression, the session can take 2 - 2½ hours.

Many readers provide multiple options and clients can choose the option which they prefer. For example, some psychics provide 15-minute, 30-minute, or 60-minute readings. Similarly, Tarot card readers may have several different card spreads which go into varying levels of detail. If people want in-depth information, or information stretching into the future, a reading may take more than two hours.

One of the energy workers said that her Reiki sessions usually last about an hour, then there is an additional 30-minute consultation to discuss all of the things which she found while doing Reiki.

The astrologer reported that her initial session with a client takes two hours and twenty minutes. Before the appointment, she prepares the client's astrological chart. When the client arrives, it takes more than two hours to share the information.

Apprehension and Skepticism

Why doesn't everyone seek a psychic reading? Some people just aren't interested. Other people want to forge their own destinies and make their own decisions without seeking outside intuitive information. Some people don't want to spend the money to talk with a psychic while other people have their own intuition and don't need to discuss their questions with readers.

On the other hand, many people are curious about psychic abilities, but are reluctant to consult with readers because they are afraid of what they might find out. They think that a reading is scarey. Some people may be afraid that the reader is working with a dark energy. Other people are curious about psychic readings, but are skeptical. They just don't think that it is possible to connect with unseen information sources. The following questions and answers may help people gain a new understanding of how readings work and help them overcome their resistance.

Are there tips for people who are too scared to have a reading?

When I asked the readers if they had tips for people who were too scared to have a psychic reading, three of the psychics answered that people who were scared of a reading shouldn't have one. No one needed to have a reading. It was just another tool for people who thought they might benefit from it. Marta Taylor emphasized:

> "You will never get anything which is not meant for you to hear. A reading should be done with great love and there should be a feeling of relief and support afterwards. If they have fear, they aren't ready to hear what is to be said, or they are not talking to the right reader."

Here are some of the reasons why people might be scared to have a reading, along with responses from the psychics:

<u>People have secrets</u>

People might be afraid that psychics will know everything about them, not just the things which the clients want to discuss. Clients might be interested in seeking information on one part of their life without having to expose all parts of their life. Some psychics explained that they won't see all of the information, they will only receive the information which needs to come through. Other PRISMS explained that clients had to provide permission for psychics to access their different streams of energy. For example, clients might allow them to access the information regarding life purpose, but the not information regarding marriage. The clients controlled this access through the questions which they asked. The questions opened the energy allowing the psychics to obtain answers.

Other psychics contradicted this position and said that they could see everything about clients. One psychic reported that she knows if clients are cheating on their partners, doing drugs, or drinking. However, this does not mean that she will discuss these delicate areas. Just because a person goes to a psychic doesn't mean that the psychic will tell them everything about their life. If a client doesn't want the reader to know certain things, like information about extramarital affairs, that's not something the reader will discuss. And, even if some information does come through during the reading, the psychics don't care about the secrets. Whatever information comes through is for the client; most psychics won't even remember the discussion.

<u>No one likes to be judged</u>

People might be scared that the psychic will judge them and their actions. The PRISMS pointed out that good readers are not judgmental so there is nothing to fear. Psychics are conduits. The information flows through the psychics to the people who are asking for guidance. There is no judgement and there shouldn't be anything to fear. Clients guide readings.

<u>Fear of being told they are on the wrong path</u>

Even people who know themselves well can fear that a psychic will tell them something which throws off their sense of self. What if a psychic tells them that they are on the wrong path, that what they know is not accurate, or that they are looking at things the wrong way? It could undermine a person's self esteem. However, if a client goes to a reputable reader, the reader is most likely to help the person understand the path they are already on, not tell them that they are on the wrong path. Everyone is working on their lessons.

<u>Fear of dark energy</u>

Some people are scared that PRISMS work with the Devil and they don't want anything to do with this kind of work. All of the psychics told me that they work with G-d and the Higher Realms. Psychics are here to help people access information for their highest good.

People who are afraid this work is connected to the Devil should choose a reader who works with the Light, not with dark magic. Part of this fear comes from religion. Certain religions suggest that spiritual contact can only happen through a church. People are discouraged from exploring their own connection. Congregants have been told not to talk to psychics. However, psychic readings are really just about relaying helpful suggestions which are coming from the non-physical realm.

Looking for specific answers

Some people don't want the answers to their questions unless they are the answers they want to hear. These clients need to understand that psychics can look at the past, present and future, but they can't create or influence the future. Each person creates his or her own life through the choices he or she makes. Psychics just report what they see, hear or know. It is up to the client to forge their future and create the answers they seek. However, if they don't want to know the most-probable answers, they may not be ready for a reading.

Fear of bad news

People are afraid of getting bad news. One psychic remarked that she has had people write to her in advance and tell her that if anything bad comes up, they don't want to hear it. She reminds them that anything which comes up can be used as a tool. If they get a warning about the future, they can work to change that future. Psychics share information so that clients can make wise choices.

Reluctance to deal with difficult issues

People may be afraid that readings will bring up difficult issues. Clients should remind themselves that difficult issues are often why they are going to a reader. They want insights into their lives. One psychic reminds people that things are always changing and that they shouldn't be afraid of change. Developing a new perspective on a difficult issue could be very helpful.

How can someone put aside their fear?

Even though someone might initially be afraid to have a psychic reading, most of the time, no matter what happens, it's an interesting experience. It is either fun, enlightening, or both. One reader suggested that people stop by their local psychic fair and see what kind of energy they feel in the room. They can watch other people receive readings, but they don't need to do anything. Just come for a "Girls/Guys Day Out." Many people who think readings are scary have never had a reading. Once a person has experienced a reading, they can judge for themselves if it was a worthwhile experience. Try it just for fun.

Do psychic readings work even if someone doesn't believe they are possible?

Yes. It's like gravity. It works whether or not people believe it works. However, it is difficult for psychics to read people who intentionally close off their energy to prove that they cannot be read. Even if someone doesn't believe that readings are possible, they should try to keep an open mind so that they can see what happens.

Are there tips for people who are skeptical?

Some people don't believe that psychics can access information. Other people are afraid to believe that a reading is possible. They want to believe it, but if readings were possible, they would have to re-think their belief systems. Similarly, some skeptics have trust issues. They secretly want readings to be possible, but fear that someone will take advantage of them or make them look foolish. I asked the readers if they had tips for people who were too skeptical to have a reading.

Most psychics felt that it was okay to be skeptical. People should be skeptical until they had a reading and understood the possibilities. However, it was best to be skeptical with an open mind, rather than cynical. Skepticism was considered a wonderful, healthy tool as long as people used skepticism to think critically and analyze a situation. However, if the skepticism came from a belief which had been taught, instead of coming from a bad experience, it might be worthwhile to think about why a person felt the way they felt. Thinking about beliefs can provide an opportunity for beliefs to evolve.

One psychic noted that some things need to be experienced. Until some people had their own experience of psychic phenomena, they weren't going to believe someone else. She commented that if most people thought about their own lives, they would be surprised at how many things had happened to them which they couldn't rationally explain. She suggested that skeptics try a reading just for the fun of it. They might enjoy it. It didn't make sense to judge something they had never experienced.

Several psychics commented that if they can give a skeptical person information from their life that the psychic shouldn't be able to know, they can break through the skepticism. From this kind of direct experience, skeptics can discover that it is possible to access information.

A few of the psychics told me that they can read skeptics so it doesn't bother them when skeptical people show up for readings. Cherie Fraine remarked:

> "I don't have to prove myself to them. I know I have this ability. I have been doing it all my life. It works whether they believe it or not. I tell them, 'Don't knock it 'til you've tried it.' If you think I can't read you, that is fine; I'll read you anyway. Then we will talk. Just because you can't do it, you may not think it happens, but there are definitely people out there who can do it."

Other psychics revealed that they don't especially enjoy reading for skeptical people because they have nothing to prove and it can be tedious to read for someone who is putting up resistance. The psychics understand their own abilities and if someone is too skeptical to have a reading, they shouldn't have one. Psychics don't recruit people. The people who are becoming aware are the people with whom they want to talk.

In addition, some of the readers don't like to read for people who are negative and closed down because they don't want to absorb the negative energy. Other PRISMS are empathic and don't like the feelings which come through when they read for people who are skeptical.

One psychic commented that it's not worth arguing about psychic ability and spirituality because people will know in the end that it is valid. They will know if there is a G-d, or Heaven, or if they did the right thing. If they are not getting this understanding through organized religion, talking to a reader is another avenue for people to learn about spirituality.

Psychics hope that by sharing their gifts they can help people expand their knowledge to include the realities of energetic connections, life lessons, and life and death. They strive to improve each client's life experience and lessen their fear of death. However, readers don't think it is their job to convince clients to believe something which they are not ready to believe. All they can do is open the door and spark the person's curiosity so that they do their own research.

To-Ree'-Nee' Wolf feels that skeptical people who are looking for proof might actually find proof; then, find a way to dismiss it.

Finally, two readers told me that they loved skeptics. As soon as skeptics figured out that there was something to this, they became big believers. The psychics told me that a breakthrough with a skeptic was a wonderful feeling. Converts became their biggest advertisers!

Chapter 11 - Preparing for a Reading

PRISMS and clients often ask how other people prepare for readings. Are there meditative rituals? Are there things which they should be doing which they don't know about? What should a client bring to a reading? Preparation is the key to most successful activities.

How do psychics prepare for readings?

Prior to a reading, most psychics have a special preparation routine, but not all of them. Preparation times can range from just a few minutes, to 45 minutes, to days. Here are some paraphrased examples of what the psychics do prior to a reading, from the simplest to the most complex:

☼ I just begin with the person. They have to be willing. If they are willing, I am ready to work with them. *(Trish Silay)*

☼ Sometimes the phone rings and a client needs an emergency reading. I have no time to prepare and that is just fine. I am ready to read whenever the client calls. *(Gigi Sample)*

☼ Before people come over, I pull out the card table and put a cloth on it. I bring out my cards and my forms for the different readings. I don't need to meditate or light candles or incense. The information is always accessible to me. *(Cherie Fraine)*

☼ I try not to prepare. I will "clear" before I start my day and at the end of the day. I release all that is around me for the good of the Higher Being. Sometimes I sage my office, or I spritz it with different oils or herbs. Sometimes I just open the door and let nature do its thing. Then I do a few blessings and prayers. None of us can do any of this without help. *(Patricia Kirkman)*

☼ I don't really prepare for a reading. I just ask my Guides to come in and hang out with me. I try to make it pretty for the people who are going to be here. I make sure that I have my supplies, such as crystals. *(Leah Taylor)*

☼ I surround myself with the white light of Christ for protection and ask for the Highest and Best to come through. Then, I start listening to Spirit. *(Jan Class)*

☼ I ask for help to remove my ego from the situation. I never want to filter someone else's experiences through mine. We do that sometimes as a frame of reference. *(Cecilia Nemmers)*

☼ A long time ago, when I realized this was part of my life, I said to the Universe, "If you want me to do this, you will have to keep me safe." I don't get up every morning and meditate or surround myself in the Light. This is part of our contract. Because I don't turn it off, when the client comes to me and puts their hands in mine, the information comes to me. I ask to be given the information I need for this soul. *(Cynthia Rae)*

☼ When I do readings or use Reiki, I calm and center myself so that I am more able to help people. I try to focus my mind. *(Erik Assman)*

☼ I spend time in prayer and solitude. I connect to nature. I meditate. I align myself with Creator's will for that particular person or situation and the healing for that person's highest good. I purify my own self. I eat very lightly and I drink lots of water. Then I put that person's highest intention up and I ask to be used as a vessel of healing. *(Delphina Nova)*

☼ I usually cleanse my cards and center myself. It is just who I am, I don't need to turn it on or off. I start my day centered so it is already there. I don't have to do anything special. To cleanse the cards, I shuffle them four times, tap on them, and they are ready to go. I do that between every reading. *(Gina Stanfill)*

☼ I like to have a candle. I like to have the atmosphere as clean as possible so it is pure for the person who is coming to see me. If I am doing a phone reading, I still light a candle. *(Marta Taylor)*

☼ I light a candle and wash my hands. I ask for help to be the pipe to give information to the client. Then I take a deep breath and I receive messages. *(Shirli Millmond)*

☼ I have a small alter to Kwan Yin, a Buddhist Bodhisattva, where I have a glass holder that contains a tea light. I always have a candle lit because it brings helpful energy towards the reading. Like a flashlight in the dark, it shines light where it's needed. *(Jackie Chin)*

☼ I meditate, then I connect with my Higher Self, their Higher Self and all the Emissaries of Light (those higher frequency Beings of Light who are working with us). *(Raquel Spencer)*

☼ I meditate for five to ten minutes before I do a reading. I have lots of crystals and stones which I like to carry with me and I use tools which help me to maintain a clear energy field. Meditation, preparation, and crystals help me to open up without judgement and with clear intentions. If I am going to do a phone reading, I create a very sacred space before making the phone call. In that sacred space, and on the phone, I create an energetic environment where, as the Guides speak to me, I hear and see things. *(Beth Hays)*

☼ For a scheduled appointment at my home, I take a half hour before the client arrives to sage and smudge my house. I sit and pray for the client. I hold them in love, light and clarity. I want them to feel that I have held a sacred spot for them. I want them to feel cherished. I put out a tape recorder, notepads, and Kleenex.

When I am going to the Psychic Fair, I pray the night before for guidance and illumination. I have stage fright. I am always worried that I won't have anything to tell people. However, when the time comes, I sit down and the words are there. I am always afraid that it might not work. I can't "make" it work, all I can do is "allow" it to work. *(Laurie Hays)*

☼ I meditate. I say my prayers. I try to say prayers every morning. The Bible says you are supposed to pray unceasingly, so I pray while I am doing my morning routine. My Higher Self is praying all day. *(Richard Schickel)*

☼ If I am going to do a reading in person, I don't go online to do readings during the day. I try to focus and save my energy. It takes a lot of energy to do this work, especially if someone who has passed comes to me and starts communicating with me. It drains a person. I guess I meditate in my own way. *(Marianne Patyk)*

☼ Before a reading, I meditate and gather information on the client. I put about an hour of preparation into an hour of reading. For three nights before the reading, for 15 minutes each night, I go into the five major areas of their life: career, finance, relationships, health and spirituality. I have never known how this works, I just have it. I have a sheet of paper and I do a kind of automatic writing. After I have done the work, I have to decide how I am going to present the information to the client. I also have intuition during the readings. In the beginning, I tried to prepare in advance for the readings because I was afraid that I wouldn't get the information during the sessions. Now, I know that it always works, even during the sessions. I usually come to the reading with 3-5 pages of information on the client to verify that I can pick up on them. *(Jeff Sonnenburg)*

☼ I begin to prepare as soon as I hear the client's voice. I usually receive a telephone call and the energy opens up when I hear their voice. I simply make myself attentive to the images, thoughts and feelings which come to me. I say prayers and ask that I be of the highest and best use, and be able to give them the information which they seek. Before they come to my home, I sit on the porch and see who shows up. I also interact with the nature realm. I work with ravens, hawks, and nature folk. I look for unusual synchronicities. I make myself available for whatever information shows up.

If they book a week ahead, there is a week when that energy is open. I pray right before they come. I bless and clear my home and then I allow myself time in a meditative, waiting, state. *(To-Ree'-Nee' Wolf)*

The next two psychics are a bit different. One communicates with animals and the other one is an Astrologer. These kinds of work require different kinds of preparation:

☼ Animal Communicator: I ask people to bring photographs of their animals or to e-mail them to me prior to the reading. Before they arrive, I protect myself, ground myself, and activate my abilities. I ask the Universe to let the animal know that I might be talking to it later. When I get ready to do the reading, I look at the photograph, ask where the animal lives, the animal's name, and if the animal is alive or dead. Then, I put out a call to the animal. I introduce myself and let the animal know that I am sitting here with the client and that we want to ask a few questions. *(Kat Riegel)*

☼ Astrologer: I prepare the astrological chart before the client arrives. I have the client's chart ready so I don't need to refer to the computer while they are here. I say a prayer. I bring in my Spiritual Guides. I ask for High Protection to bring in all of the good and all of the information which the client is truly seeking so that I might be allowed to give that information to them. *(Rhonda Harford)*

Do psychics protect themselves when they do readings?

The people with whom I spoke all work with the higher light energies and wouldn't normally attract negative energy or "bad" spirits. However, psychics need to be protected from any negative energy which a client might bring to a reading or an energy session. Psychic work is all about energy and when psychics tap into a client's energy, they can pick up negative issues. If a client is nervous or agitated, the psychic may feel jittery. If the client is hiding less-than-honorable activities, the psychic may feel these impressions. Even though the energy exchange is invisible, there can be a transference of the client's problems to the psychic.

PRISMS report that they either live in a protective bubble all the time or that they do certain things to increase their level of protection prior to readings. In addition, some psychics also increase their protection levels when they go out in public.

Most PRISMS have set limits on what they are willing to see or experience. They don't want to see things which might scare them, such as murder scenes or dismembered body parts. Many psychics won't allow any sort of entity to enter their body to channel messages using their voice. They will happily relay messages from entities, but the entities are not allowed to enter their bodies.

This is how they protect themselves:

<u>Prior to a reading</u>

☼ Before a reading, I surround myself with the white light of Christ for protection and I ask for the Highest and Best to come through. Then I start listening to Spirit. I surround myself with the white light because I can become so sensitive that I need a shield around myself to keep negativity away. A reader shouldn't just invite anybody in for communication. *(Jan Class)*

☼ My protection is prayer. I do not see myself as a healer. I am only the vessel. The healing comes from the Universe. Because of that, I am in alignment with Creator's will. That is my protection. *(Delphina Nova)*

☼ I was trained to Protect, Ground, and Activate myself before each reading. I protect myself by asking the white light to come down and protect me from anything which could cause me harm mentally, physically, spiritually, emotionally, socially or psychically. I ground myself by connecting to Mother Earth. I ask permission to ground to her so that I can be allowed to send any negative energy, thoughts, or feelings to her. If the negative energy can be converted to healing energy, I ask that she use it for herself or send it out to whomever or whatever needs it. Then, I activate by keeping my chakras open all the time. *(Kat Riegel)*

☼ I use oils. I automatically protect my aura. I like to have a candle. At the end of a reading, I like to use sage, incense and oils to clear the area. *(Marta Taylor)*

☼ I say prayers before I talk to a client. I have a mirror in the room so that energy can bounce off of it and not stay on me. I also wear certain colors which help the client's energy stay off of me. I tell people to eat before they come in so that they are grounded. After the session, I use the bathroom and I wash my hands. Then, I walk outside and say additional prayers. *(Rhonda Harford)*

☼ I try to wear something black or I hold a crystal in my hand. I was told that black protects people from negativity. *(Marianne Patyk)*

☼ I protect myself when doing a reading or any sort of energy work. I ask my Spirit Guides to assist when working with spiritual matters. Also, I have learned through energy work to use color to shield myself from unwanted energy. I learned a lot of helpful techniques by studying chakra energy. *(Jackie Chin)*

☼ My Guides always protect me from harm. However, it is a good idea to ask for additional protection during readings to retain my own energy. When I don't ask for extra protection, I find that readings can drain my energy. The extra protection works as an energy shield. *(Gigi Sample)*

☼ Sometimes bad energy is unleashed during a session. When people leave, the bad energy sticks to me. In that case, I will have to take a bath in Epson salt to separate it from me, or I will burn sage to clear the house. In addition, I wear a rosary around my neck. Sometimes when there is negative energy, the rosary breaks. The rosary has a St. Benedict cross which provides protection against evil. *(Richard Schickel)*

☼ When I am doing readings, I ask Mother Mary to protect me. I ask Spirit only to send people for readings who are on their spiritual path. I don't want people who are just looking for lottery numbers or boyfriends. If they want spiritual guidance, I am here for them. *(Laurie Hays)*

Prior to energy work

Energy workers have slightly different ways of protecting themselves while they are working on a client's body. Here are three examples:

☼ I ask Archangel Michael and his Angels of Protection to completely surround me with their wings and keep me safely protected. I ask that I be protected from any energy which is not mine, not of the Light, or a disease. After I do my healing work, I dump all of the energy and I fill myself with Light. *(Denise Singerline)*

☼ If I feel that the person I am working with has negative energy, I consciously protect myself. Most of the time, it's something I do automatically; I just don't allow that kind of energy in. When I need to protect myself, I visualize myself in a circle of white, healing, G-d light, and I am in my little bubble. *(Nancy)*

☼ I do a lot of work with the Angels and the Ascended Masters. I set up an energetic shield of light. Sometimes people ask me, "If we are all G-d and we are all interconnected, why do you need to protect yourself?" My answer is that G-d created fire too, but you are not going to see me walk into fire without the right protection. We all come from the same source, but not everyone is conscious of what they are doing. *(Raquel Spencer)*

After a reading

As mentioned above, PRISMS open their energetic systems to connect with clients and provide information. Because they are open, they sometimes absorb the client's negative energy or issues.

After a reading, or in-between readings, it is very important that the psychics shake off negative energy. If the negative energy is not removed, the psychics may experience headaches or other physical symptoms. In addition, this negative energy can affect subsequent readings. Similarly, clients should clean out their energy fields, close their chakras, and bring in fresh light after a reading.

Out in the world

Laurie Hays explained how she protects herself when she leaves her house. She is very "open." When she goes out, she asks Spirit to, "Protect me, guide me and not let anything which isn't love and light come to me." She prays that she only radiate love and light and she asks that anything sent to her that isn't love and light be returned as love and light – that the negative energy be transmuted into love and light.

What should a client do to prepare for a reading?

There are several things for a client to keep in mind when preparing for a reading. The following suggestions will help people get their best possible readings:

1) Clients should focus on what they want to know.

At the beginning of the session, the client should tell the psychic about any specific topics he or she wants to discuss. Psychics can talk about a wide variety of subjects, but they won't know to focus on a specific area, such as health, career or love, unless the client lets them know that is why the client has come to them.

In most cases, if someone comes to a reader and says, "Read me," it's too broad. For the psychic, it's like seeing a roadmap. The psychic needs to know which way to go or they might go down the wrong road. It's a perfectly fine road, and the information is solid, it's just not the road which takes the client where they want to go.

In addition, clients who have clear questions in mind, should ask about them specifically. When clients ask a question, it opens the energy and allows someone to give them an answer. One of the psychics pointed out that the Universe answers general questions in a general way. If the clients want to know something in detail, they should ask specific questions. They need to figure out exactly what they want to ask in order to receive a substantive answer.

On the other hand, some psychics prefer "open readings." They begin by providing all of the information coming from their Guides and the client's Guides. Once the client has heard all of the Guides' messages, the client can ask questions. Clients should ask psychics in advance how they prefer to work.

People who are trying to make progress in a particular area of their life and go to a reader who provides helpful oils or botanicals, should be very clear about the outcome which they seek. In addition to defining the problem, they should have an idea of what they want to accomplish so that the reader knows which oils or botanicals might work for them. It is often easier to say what is wrong than it is to pin down what people really want. Clients have to know what their answer *feels* like. This action forces people to jump on board with the *Law of Attraction* and to create the solution they seek.

2) Clients should prepare a list of questions.

Clients are encouraged to write down their questions before consulting a reader. They might not receive answers to all of their questions, but if they put them in priority order, they should get the answers which are most important to them.

3) Clients can ask the Higher Realms and/or people who have crossed over to assist with the reading.

Before the reading, people can ask the Higher Realms to send answers to specific questions. They can also ask for specific people who have already passed to come through during a sitting. There are no guarantees as to who will show up, but it doesn't hurt to talk to a loved one before a session and ask them to try to come through. However, clients should listen to, and enjoy, whoever actually does come through. People should not be so focused on hearing one specific message that they miss the rest of the reading.

4) Clients must come "clean."

Clients need to have a clear mind. They should not drink alcohol or take drugs before a session. People should not have a reading when they are very depressed or suicidal because this can complicate the reading.

The person who had the most stringent requirements for a session was an energy worker. She needs to be able to read her client's energy cleanly. She tells people not to have alcohol or drugs for a minimum of 72 hours prior to a session. Alcohol, drugs and even over-the-counter drugs can distort a person's energetic field. In addition, she requires clients to state that they are ready to step into their own mastery, strength and power.

5) Clients would be wise to bring a voice recorder or a pad of paper and a pen.

People should bring a voice recorder or a pad of paper and a pen so that they can remember what the reader has told them. Because of the energy in the room, voice recorders don't always work, so it's smart to bring along the paper and pen even if a recorder is available.

6) Clients should come with an open heart and an open mind.

A client should come to a reading with an open heart and an open mind. Being open helps expand the possibilities. When someone is closed down, it makes it difficult for the reader to connect with that person's energy. It's okay to have a healthy skepticism, as long as the person is open to the discussion. When a person works with a reader, they should try to make the reading easy for the psychic.

When discussing the need for keeping an open mind, Leah Taylor noted that there is more that we don't know about human consciousness than we do know. There are possibilities out there and even if it isn't the norm to have miracles and healings, they do happen. She added that people who come for readings should try to be open to exploring the limits of human potential and consciousness.

7) Clients should prepare to be "active listeners."

A client should think about being an active listener. This means listening without interrupting the reader. Interruptions may disengage the energy with which the psychic works. Check with the reader before the sitting and ask if they prefer to have questions during the session or at the end of the session.

8) Clients should come alone.

Clients should meet privately with readers. They shouldn't bring friends to the reading because the friend's energy might influence the session. In addition, the client may need privacy to discuss the issues which arise during the reading.

9) Clients should schedule time for solitude after the session.

People should leave time afterwards for solitude. They should try to minimize distractions after the session so they can think about what they have heard and allow time for the energy to heal deeply at their core.

So, now that we know how to find a reader and we know about preparation and protection, let's discuss the tools of the psychic trade.

Chapter 12 - Tools of the Psychic Trade

Some PRISMS use Tarot cards, crystal balls, astrology charts, numerology, candles, crystals, muscle-testing, or other tools when they work with clients. Other readers don't use any tools and can just look at someone, hold hands or look at their palms, and read their energy. Readers who use tools say that the tools either help them access the client's energy and bring in fresh ideas and information, or that they don't really need the tools, but they like having them around. Crystals and candles enhance the setting. Tarot cards provide pretty pictures for everyone to examine. In addition, cards provide a bit of a barrier between the readers and the clients so that the readers can maintain their personal space. The cards also provide a nice distraction from the intensity of the reading.

Tools, such as Tarot cards, often help the client feel more comfortable. Some clients don't like to think that a psychic is reading their mind. When Tarot cards are used, it seems as if the information comes from the cards and is just being interpreted by the psychic; not like the psychic is directly accessing the client's energy or information.

One reader explained that he can do readings just using Tarot cards. Or, he can do readings just using psychic ability. However, when he uses both the cards and his abilities, the readings are better. His Guides are able to influence the cards so that they reinforce the messages he receives.

Why do readers use cards, candles or other tools when they do readings?

I asked each of the psychics about the tools which they use. Here are some of their answers:

<u>I use tools to improve my ability to access information</u>

☼ I use crystals because of their strong, clear vibration. Depending on the person I am reading for, or where I am going to get data from, a certain crystal might align with their energy and I will know to bring that crystal with me. I also uses flower essences because they shift my energy into a state where I can more-easily hear, or receive, guidance. *(Beth Hays)*

☼ I use astrology charts to go back to the past and come forward to the future. Before I meet with someone, I have them fill out a form which asks for their birth date and time, and the birth dates and times of the people who are related to them. The astrology charts provide the technical answers. I try to look at the technical charts then paint a picture. This is my gift. I can read the charts and I often receive additional, intuitive, information. *(Rhonda Harford)*

☼ I like to use Tarot cards. I like the visual images. I like the stories. I am very visual. When I do a Tarot card reading, I do a general reading which includes work, life, relationships, and the house they came from. Then the client and I discuss their priorities, problems and goals; slowly we move towards those goals. *(Shirli Millmond)*

☼ I like the cards because I have a trust issue. I like having the cards between me and the other person. I am a very emotional person and I cry. I like having the cards in between us so that I can stay out of it. I just say what comes to me. In addition, the cards open up things. I see the cards, get ideas from the cards, and then things open up. I tell people what I see. I also get a feeling about it, an atmosphere. I am picking up the energy surrounding things. I will sometimes get flashes of something which mean nothing to me, but might mean something to someone else. *(Marta Taylor)*

☼ I use numerology because it is a tool to get me to a certain point. First, middle and last names all have a strong impact on the individual. That's why we have those names. We choose our own names. *(Patricia Kirkman)*

☼ I work with the *One Brain* system. This system uses muscle testing to understand what a person is experiencing. Muscle testing provides bio-feedback and information from the body. I don't know what someone's truth is, or their story, but their body knows it. Muscle testing is the body's validation of the person's truth. I just touch their arm and I ask "yes" and "no" questions. I talk really fast so that their brain doesn't get in the way. I do a light touch and it is almost like a pendulum test. I ask the body how it signifies "yes" and "no" then I ask questions and allow the body to answer them. *(Trish Silay)*

☼ I like candles because they draw spirits in and out. I think they help our thoughts go out into the Universe. I think they help me focus. I also like rocks and stones. Quartz crystals seem to channel energy. *(Marta Taylor)*

☼ I typically read cards for people. They are called Shustah Divination and Meditation cards and they are similar to Tarot cards. Shustah Cards have the same philosophy as Tarot cards, but they are a different deck with different pictures and numbers. In order to read the cards, I have the person shuffle the deck so that their energy is in the cards. I work with energy. If they have a specific question, I ask them to focus on that question. If they want a more-general reading, I ask them to focus on their breath and relax so that they don't get nervous. Once they give the cards back to me, I spread several of them out in a crescent moon shape. Then I read the cards. The cards trigger something in me and they give the client something to look at. I also like having cards to look at. If I did a five-card spread, the client would be the center card, with half of their cards in the past, and half in the future. Then, it triggers a story or an event and I just have to tell the client whatever comes to me. *(Gina Stanfill)*

☼ I use Mah Jongg cards. I have done Tarot card readings and I have a collection of card decks. Decades ago, I started with the Tarot cards and found that they had many layers of meaning and symbolism. When I started collecting cards, I found the Mah Jongg cards. I changed my focus to the Mah Jongg cards because they provide more-immediate information and that is what most people want. They reflect the here and now without going into a lot of esoteric information. I have also worked with the Akashic Records. *(Marta Taylor)*

<u>I use tools to help the client</u>

☼ I like to make the setting look nice for the clients. I really like stones. I had a teacher who told me that stones were atomic medicine; they worked with the energy of the atoms of the body. *(Leah Taylor)*

☼ I use Tarot cards for the person I am reading, not for me. People feel more comfortable if there is something they can look at. Or I can just open the calendar, lay it down, and read the calendar. However, when I just sit down and read people, it freaks people out because they don't have to say anything in order for me to read them. They can bring me somebody's name on a folded pieced of paper, or a photograph, and I can tell them about the person and about the things that have happened in that person's life without ever seeing the person, without having the person near me. People don't have a frame of reference for what I do. That's why I use the Tarot cards. People think that the cards are saying something, but they have no idea how much extra I am getting.

One of the difficult things when I do a reading is telling the difference between "spirit time" and "people time." There is no time over there and there is time here. In spirit time, "soon" could be anything from tomorrow until three months from now. With the Tarot cards, I can be very precise about time. The cards makes it easier for the person being read. *(Cherie Fraine)*

☼ Most people are frightened when you don't have a tool in front of you. That's why I always play with the numbers. It keeps them grounded and from thinking that I am reading their minds. I don't read minds, but I do pick up the vibrations of what is taking place. *(Patricia Kirkman)*

☼ Before I go out to do a reading, I ask the crystals what I should bring today, then I pick what I like. I think it makes the client feel better. I don't use cards or numerology. I'm just out there on my own and if I have stones around me maybe clients think I am a little bit more legitimate. *(Cynthia Rae)*

☼ I place a quilted table runner on the table because it is soft on people. I like something soft on the table. It is as if I have set a place for the reading. I also put out a sacred holy card, with the drawing of a hand, which has a protective energy. I also put out a holy card of Mary and a holy card of Mary, Joseph, and baby Jesus. These cards bring in the highest and best energy.

I also have Tarot cards, but I only pull them out when people ask for them or when Spirit tells me to use them. Some people need the cards for a distraction or as something to focus on. When I have read for someone several times, I don't want them to think that I am just remembering the things I told them at a previous reading, so I pull out the cards. The cards are impartial. I do my spread of the cards, I turn the tape recorder on, and I begin readings. *(Laurie Hays)*

☼ I use sage. Native American sage and sweet grass are used for purification of the environment and the person. Sometimes, I use a drum or feathers. *(Delphina Nova)*

☼ I use Tarot cards because the public likes cards. I can also work with stones which people have carried with them or held. I shuffle the cards until Spirit tells me to stop shuffling, then I interpret the cards the way Spirit wants me to interpret them – I just listen. The cards help organize the reading and the thoughts. I can also read shells and use a crystal ball. When I use the crystal ball, I see things in it. I get messages through the crystal ball. I can also do sand readings. I place my hand on the sand to get vibrations and then I sprinkle colored sand on top and do readings. *(Jan Class)*

☼ Sometimes when I do a reading I use Tarot cards. I can use the cards but, because I am clairvoyant, I don't need to use them. The cards are a tool, but I don't know what half the cards mean! Even when I use the cards, I ask Spirit to help me to step aside so they can work through me. I ask my Spirit Guides and angels to talk to the client's Guides and angels so that I can help them for their highest good for whatever reason they came to see me. I hold their hands for a moment and feel their energy, then I look at the cards and (in my head) I ask Spirit what they want to tell me. I step out of the way, then I hear the message and I tell the client. After that, I move on to the next card. Sometimes it's about the future and sometimes it's about the past or the present. Sometimes I will receive a message from a loved one. Often, I receive self-help tools to give to the client. I am activating people and helping them with their life's purpose.

I also have a beautiful crystal wand with gemstones in it. I use it in my healing work. I hold it in my left hand because the left hand receives energy. I use it to cut things out of a client's aura. I do psychic surgery and it is my psychic scalpel. It amplifies the energy. Energy comes in through the left and the crystal amplifies the energy. *(Denise Singerline)*

☼ When I shuffle Tarot cards and lay them out, I am not really using the cards. The cards are an excuse for me to tell people something. People are less prone to be offended when I use the cards and tell them the truth, than when I just tell them what I know. *(Erik Assman)*

<u>I don't need tools, but they make me feel good</u>

☼ I have a beautiful prayer box. I am drawn to holy objects. I picked up this prayer box and it felt right. I didn't even know what it was used for. I came home that night, laid in bed and asked for information on the box. I saw an image of a monk sitting in a lotus position with this box hanging around his neck; it was like his altar. It has been a traveling altar and it has great energy. I think there is still a monk attached to it who is one of my Guides. Sometimes when I am going to a psychic fair or to do Reiki work, it says, "Bring me." *(Denise Singerline)*

☼ Occasionally I put something on my table, but not as a tool. Sometimes I just want something on the table so I will ask, "Who would like to come with me?" and I will take something. I take a little castle or a candle with an essential oil; it just depends. I need the room on the table to do card readings so I don't take too much. *(Gina Stanfill)*

☼ I started out with a couple of crystals and people have brought new pieces to me. Other times, I have found interesting stones and added them. I don't really know stones, but when I find something that feels good, I use it. Crystals have energy. I have a labradorite piece that always seems to end up at the front of the crystals. *(Patricia Kirkman)*

<u>I don't usually use tools</u>

☼ I don't generally put anything on my table when I read. Sometimes, I use Gypsy cards. They are similar to Tarot cards, but you read them forward. I can also read sea shells. I only use the cards if someone asks me if I read Tarot cards. I tell them that I have Gypsy cards and I can use them if they are interested. I shuffle them, then I ask them to pick cards for a 10-card spread. I just read off the card and sometimes it shows me what the client needs to know. *(Marianne Patyk)*

☼ I have a Doctor's bag! My bag is always by my side when I do readings. I don't always open it up, but it is nearby. My bag contains Florida water (part of the hoo-doo tradition) which is used to cleanse and clear. I am able to call on several entities who work with me to open up energies. I also have my Mother Peace book which I received at the Harmonic convergence; my Mother Peace Tarot cards; my Medicine cards; my *Animals Speak* book; and a pendulum which I was directed to make.

The imagery on the cards can sometimes trigger information and bypass the rational mind. It's a tool. I rarely use the tools anymore, but they are always here just in case I need them. Once in a while, I use the reference materials. *(To-Ree'-Nee' Wolf)*

☼ I have a desk and on the top of the desk there is a handmade spirit house which contains a stone statue of Kwan Yin. On her house I hang my jade mala beads and a jade bracelet with Kwan Yin on it. There are two stones, one is jet and the other is quartz. Those represent balance in all things. I have a small statue of a Buddha who faces Kwan Yin. I do not use a Tarot card deck unless I need more information that I, for whatever reason, can't see for the reading. The cards do not make me more psychic. However, they give a second opinion on what I have already said or they offer more insight. Do I need these things to be a better reader? No, but to me they represent balance and that is what my clients seek. *(Jackie Chin)*

So, psychics use tools for many reasons. However, it seems that the tool is not nearly as important as the psychic's ability to connect to invisible information sources. Whichever tool they use, they still need a clear connection to transmit messages to clients.

All of this fascinating information is leading up to the big event, the reading. At this point, we understand how PRISMS and clients prepare for readings. We see how psychics work in a world of energy connections and we understand why tools are used. Now, we are ready for the moment of magic. The next chapter is "All About Readings."

Chapter 13 - All About Readings

Each PRISM has a unique working style. This chapter explains how they perform their work, how people can get the most from a reading, and what to do with the new information. Read on to make the most of this exciting experience.

The Actual Reading

What happens at a reading?

Most professional psychics have a preferred place for doing their readings. They either work out of a public office, an office in their home, or a specially-prepared place in their home, such as a dining room table. A client can expect to be met in a professional manner and to be escorted to the area where the reading will take place. Depending on the psychic, there may be candles, cards or crystals on the table and there may be incense burning. For a reading, the client will usually sit at a table across from the psychic. For a past-life regression, the client may lay down on a couch. For energy work, the client often lays on a massage table.

To start the reading, the psychic may say a prayer, ask to hold hands or ask to read a person's palms. Some readers use Tarot cards, crystal balls, muscle-testing, or other tools to open the energy. One way or another they will attempt to access the client's energy so it's important for the client to relax and keep an open mind.

A reading is an intimate event. People must be willing to be open to the Universe and be willing to share their deepest thoughts and issues. When the energy is open, the magic begins.

Once the reader has accessed the client's energy, information will come and the psychic will share the messages. People can ask questions and ask for clarification. Some psychics encourage questions during the reading and some prefer to get all of the information out first, then answer questions. The psychics often ask people what they want to know so that the psychics know where to look for information and can focus on the answers. Be prepared for some information to be clearer than other information. During the reading, it may seem that the psychic has had several "hits" and several "misses." This is normal. The information coming to the psychic may not be completely clear, or the psychic may need to interpret pictures and images which the client might not recognize immediately. Some of the information might not make sense right away but, a couple of days later, the client may understand what the reader was saying or the references the reader was using.

A reading can be an emotional experience. Some people have tears because they are connecting to their angels, Spirit Guides and Higher Self. Other people may have tears because they are discussing their private hopes, dreams and personal issues. In either case, it is smart to bring a tissue.

Here are the psychics' simplified answers to the question: "What happens at a reading?"

☼ I ask the client to put their hands on top of mine so that our hand chakras connect. I connect with the person's energy and I can get what they are thinking. I see their energy and what is in their mind and their heart. When we are talking about delicate issues, I can see the truth even if they are lying to themselves. I can see if they are not following their true course. I know about their past and future. I provide a lot of past-life connections. In addition, I can see who is around them, for example, their family. I also see auras and hear voices. *(Richard Schickel)*

☼ When a client comes to me, I take a moment and ask the Higher Realms to bring me the information which this client is seeking. I also ask for a bit of information which validates who I am. I communicate with Spirit Guides, angels and G-d. Sometimes I see a vision, sometimes I have an emotional feeling, sometimes I get a physical feeling. There's an internal conversation and then, when the conversation ends, I ask for something else and I might get a vision. *(Cynthia Rae)*

☼ It's almost like a part of my brain steps aside and I let this other part come through. It comes through very quickly, as fast as thought. I say it to the clients almost at the speed I get it so my working brain doesn't have time to interfere and say, "Don't go there. That would be rude." For me, I give it just the way I get it and it tends to pick up speed very quickly. I say what Spirit tells me and sometimes I can't believe the things which come out of my mouth. I have asked to be "Divine loving truth."

I see, hear and feel information. It comes in on all five of my senses. I don't rely on any one sense; I leave them all open. If someone from the other side wants to talk to the client, I will tell the client verbatim what the entity is saying. I also have Tarot cards, but I only pull them out when people ask for them or when Spirit tells me to use them. *(Laurie Hays)*

☼ I typically read cards for people. For me, I like it best when people are direct and tell me that they have a particular question. I try to pinpoint the question because the Universe answers general questions in a general way. If you want to know something in detail, ask a specific question. If you don't take the time to figure out what you want to ask, how can you get the answer? People usually ask simple, general questions. People will ask if someone is going to ask them out. The deeper question is whether the person wants to be asked out and what that means to them. If we don't follow the question far enough, we don't get to the answers which clients want.

In order to read the cards, I have the person shuffle the cards so that their energy is in the cards. I work with energy. If they have asked a specific question, I ask them to focus on that question. If they want a more-general reading, I ask them to focus on their breath and relax so they don't get nervous. Once they give the cards back to me, I spread several of them out in a crescent moon shape. Then I read the cards. *(Gina Stanfill)*

☼ We usually sit at a table. I give them a general reading so that their angels, masters [Spirit Guides] and loved ones have a chance to say something to them. After that, they can ask specific questions. I use Tarot cards because the public likes cards. I can also work with stones which people have carried with them or held. I shuffle the cards until Spirit tells me to stop shuffling, then I interpret the cards the way Spirit wants me to interpret them – I just listen. The cards help organize the reading and the thoughts. *(Jan Class)*

☼ I am clairvoyant and I am clairaudient (which means I see and hear what is coming). In addition, my Spirit Guides tell me what is coming; I hear them. I use Tarot cards for the person I am reading, not for me. People feel more comfortable if there is something they can look at. In addition, I can sit down and just read people. They don't have to say anything in order for me to read them. *(Cherie Fraine)*

☼ I just talk. I read cards, get ideas from the cards, and then things open up. I tell people what I see. I also get a feeling about it, an atmosphere. I am sensitive to energy. I am picking up the energy surrounding things. I will sometimes get flashes, or pictures, of something which mean nothing to me, but might mean something to someone else. I like having the cards between me and the other person because I am a very emotional person and I cry. I like having the cards in between us so that I can stay out of it. I just say what comes to me. *(Marta Taylor)*

☼ When I read for someone, I look at the person's palm and actually go into the person's energy stream. People have many streams of energy. Some are focused on home or jobs or life purpose. I generally ask the person I am reading to ask me a question. The question gives me a direction as to which energy stream to follow. This opens up other streams and doors and gets into that one energy that people are asking about. The energies are made up of feelings. It is my job, I feel, to disconnect my feelings from the person's feelings and just tell them what is there. I have had people call me when they are in crisis mode and I'm picking up on their energy. If I just shot back a quick answer, it would be wrong because it is connected to their fear. I have to pull myself away from their energy then, aha, I can see what is happening. The person in crisis mode is so involved in what is happening from their perspective that they can't see the whole picture. I try to give them the whole picture. I can do this by going into their energy stream. Nine times out of ten, when someone is looking for a psychic reading it is because they have a question which they cannot figure out themself. They want more clarity. When I talk to someone and they are panicking, they need to calm down so things can be discussed. People don't see the patterns in their life and what throws them into panic mode.

During readings, I receive information through my Guides, the client's energy field, and the spirits for whom the client has questions. My gifts are multi-faceted. I can see, hear and feel any beings who are around at the time of the reading. The information comes through clearly and the readings are never rushed. *(Cecilia Nemmers)*

☼ I tell people what I see. I don't need to hold hands. I can do readings over the phone. Sometimes, I will ask people for their name or the names of the loved ones with whom they want to connect. I will ask people what they want to know so that I focus on the right things. I see future possibilities and pasts. We have free will so there are lots of different possibilities for the future. I see people's lives, their childhoods, their thoughts, their hearts. I see what is going on in their relationships, I see their living and dead relatives. A lot of times deceased people come in during the readings. I see animals when they want me to communicate with them or if clients want me to find them on the other side. I am also a medical intuitive and I do healings. I work with Guides and I can have my Guides heal people.

What I see and hear I don't see and hear with my physical eyes and ears. I see it and hear it in my mind. It is like a voice in my mind. I can talk with deceased people, with Spirit Guides, and with people's Higher Selves.

Sometimes, I will look up and I can feel with my hands what is going on with somebody's body. It's almost like a whole image comes up that I can feel with my hands.

In addition, I can see and hear client's relatives. Even though I am looking at the wall, or I am looking at you, I am also seeing the other people and things. It really is the third eye and the other senses. *(Leah Taylor)*

☼ I can see the future and I can help people make the best of it. I can help people to be the best that they can be and to do the best that they can do. When I do a Tarot card reading, I do a general reading which includes work, life, relationships, and the house they came from. Then the client and I discuss their priorities, problems and goals; slowly we move towards those goals. At a reading, people will receive tools and abilities to deal with their problems. They will get more clarity about their life and the things that they want to achieve. It's an "Aha" moment for them. It's also a relief for them to know that they are not alone. They understand that someone knows them. *(Shirli Millmond)*

☼ My psychic ability is "connection." When I connect with someone, I am just gone. I am not totally there. I hear things. I look at the person I am reading and I zone out. I get a feeling about what the person is feeling and I get an idea of what they want to hear and what they need to hear. *(Erik Assman)*

☼ I am connected with the Spirit Guide and Angelic Realms. I have my own Spirit Guides and angels. In addition, each person I work with also has their own Guides. I create a very sacred space before making a phone call to a client. In that sacred space, and on the phone, I create an energetic environment where, as the Guides speak to me, I hear and see things. Ultimately, I have a feeling of totally knowing. *(Beth Hays)*

☼ Before a reading, I meditate and gather information on the client. I have a sheet of paper and I do a kind of automatic writing. I also have intuition during the session. I hear a very strong voice. I thought that everybody had that voice until I was about 19 years old. The sound of the voice depends on the level of the intuition. If it sounds similar to my voice, it provides practical information. If it is a bit different, like a conversation, it is applicable to relationships and health. When I connect to the Holy Spirit, it is extremely loud and not my voice. This level of energy provides answers regarding life path and other big decisions. *(Jeff Sonnenburg)*

☼ When a person comes to see me, I have them sit down and we talk. I listen. I find out why the person has come to me. Do they have an issue which is spiritual, emotional, mental or physical? I ask them what they need. Sometimes they know what they need and sometimes they don't know. Sometimes, they just saw my brochure and wanted to come see me. As we talk, I listen, and the person reveals to me what is needed.

Sometimes, all a person needs is to talk with someone. They want someone to listen. They leave and they feel so much better! I don't know what happened, but I will call it "love." I have been a vessel through which this person has been helped.

Other times, we will talk and the person will have a release and start crying. Then, I will have them lay on a massage table for an energy healing. I purify the body and soul with sage. I am directed by Spirit to send energy to the places where it is most needed. I don't always know where the energy is most needed, but the energy is directed where ever it needs to go. For example, someone might complain of a pain in the neck, but the problem is really the leg, or the problem is a relationship which is not working. Often, the symptom does not indicate the location of the actual problem. People will ask me about a pain in their neck, but it is really just the symptom of another problem. *(Delphina Nova)*

☼ All readings are different because each person wants to know different things; however, I have done readings when the only thing required was to see the present day. There are clients who want to know future information as well, primarily how they should do a particular thing, and that requires me being able to see past the present day. Sometimes a deceased person will enter into the picture, but those occasions are rare, and not really primary to most of my clients. It is not like dialing "1-800-the-dead" because I don't have a direct line to the other side.

I have the client think about specific questions which are immediately affecting his or her life. Usually those concerns have a lot of energy behind them. It is as if they have a high energy or spark to them; like a lit match. Once the initial question is asked, I tend to go backwards in time to where the initial spark of energy came from. Everything has a beginning and an end. It is easier for me to go backwards in time for a few reasons. They know their past and their situation. They also know that I do not know anything about them. Once I get the information for them about what initially happened, they relax and I am able to move more easily into their current energy and get the answers that they are seeking. If someone is relaxed, it's easier to work with them than if they are tense. Even skeptics relax when I tell them where they have been. It's a real ice breaker.

I don't actually hear voices. I get a knowing. I know that something will happen. This knowing is separate from seeing images because when I get a knowing message I don't see an image attached to it. Images do come when I am working with a client. I do see people that they are asking about, places where they have been or places where they are going to go. Sometimes they flash very quickly like an image that is passing by at a very fast speed. Usually those images are short lived, 20-60 seconds at best. However, there are some images which I receive that linger for hours and, sometimes, for days. I can go back and examine those images. Those are like mental snap shots. They are closer to a memory than a quick image. *(Jackie Chin)*

☼ I hear things. The validation is usually a feeling. I get a huge body rush. I get goose bumps (Guide bumps!). The Guides know that I recognize goose bumps as a validation. I have known for years that when I get a huge body rush, we are on the right track. *(Gigi Sample)*

☼ I sense, I intuit, changes before they happen. Intuition is different than sensing, feeling or understanding; it's a knowing. I am not speculating, <u>I know</u>. *(Delphina Nova)*

☼ I honestly don't know how this works. When I sit down with someone, I ask for their birth name and date and I get a thought. The answers come out and I don't always feel like it's me. It's there for me to use to help this person to do better. I never know which area I am going to be channeled into to help this person. Sometimes it will have an astrological bent; sometimes it's intuitive; sometimes it's numerological; sometimes it's a blending of all; or I can just sit down and start talking to someone and read them and they are standing there with their jaw dropping. Most people are frightened when you don't have a tool in front of you. That's why I always play with the numbers. It keeps them grounded and from thinking that I am reading their minds. I don't read minds, but I do pick up the vibrations of what is taking place. *(Patricia Kirkman)*

☼ I see symbols. For example, I can see a cross or a dog. Sometimes a whole paragraph comes into my head and I know what to say. Or a certain word comes in. I know thoughts. *(Richard Schickel)*

☼ The Medium: A person sits down and I ask them what they want to know or if they have someone specific that they want to talk to who has crossed over. If there is someone who they want to talk to, I ask for that person's name. I take a quiet moment to see if I can contact that person. Sometimes people want to know about finances or about love. I can also answer those questions, but I don't like being called a Psychic. I am very intuitive. I am empathic, intuitive, clairvoyant, and clairaudient. I hear things, smell aromas and can do pet readings. I am a channel and I do automatic writing.

It's hard to say exactly how I make a connection. Sometimes I can pick up on their energy; it depends on whether or not they are open. If they are not open, I won't be able to read them. That happens very rarely. I ask people if they want to know everything; if they want to know the truth. I just pick up on their vibes, on their energy. It's hard to explain. I don't know how I do it!

I can tell you what the person I am connecting with looks like, but I can't see them physically. I hear voices. *(Marianne Patyk)*

☼ The Astrologer: Before I meet with someone, I have them fill out a form which asks about their birth date and time, and the birth dates and times of the people who are related to them. We set up an appointment. I record the sessions on CDs. I ask the client if they want me to tell them everything. I run their chart and I set up a file. I ask if there is anything which they want to talk about. People ask me about their life's purpose. Most people want to know about their career and their health. I have a gift for helping people understand their health. I am supposed to help people heal.

I have the client's chart ready when they come in so I don't need to refer to the computer while they are here. I say a prayer and I bring in my Spiritual Guides. I bring in Djwal Khul. I ask for High Protection to bring in all of the good and all of the information which they are truly seeking so that I might be allowed to give that information to them.

In addition, if I receive intuitive information, I sometimes see people from the other side. I have had people appear to me. People can come back in any form, in any outfit which they loved wearing. Sometimes, I hear them tell me things. *(Rhonda Harford)*

☼ The Animal Communicator: I ask people to bring photographs of their animals. Before they arrive, I protect, ground and activate myself, and I ask the Universe to let the animal know that I might be talking to it later. When I get ready to do the reading, I look at the photograph, ask where the animal lives, the animal's name, and if the animal is alive or dead. Then, I put out a call to the animal. I introduce myself and let the animal know that I am sitting here with the client and that we want to ask a few questions.

I contact the animal directly. I have asked my Spirit Guides to help. Sometimes I ask my living cats to help. If the animal is alive, it is easy to establish the connection. If the animal has passed on, I go directly to their energy. The energy of a person or animal who has passed on is very different. I feel "swirly" as if I have been spinning in circles and then I am trying to stand still. It is like I have a bit of vertigo. I can tell that I have connected with someone who has passed on when I get that feeling.

There's an intuitive area near the solar plexus where a lot of emotions come through. I get a sensation, almost like my stomach is flipping, when I know I have made the connection with an animal. In addition, when I get "yes" answers I feel that flip. For "no" answers, or if I am on the wrong track, there's no feeling at all there. I also get pictures in my mind. Sometimes I hear sentences. It is like when you read a book and you hear different characters in your mind; you hear the different character voices. It is like I have a play going on in my mind with dialogue with different characters, different voices, different pitches. Emotions come through. If I am on a topic an animal likes, I will feel warm and good. If we are talking about their human, sometimes they express that they really love their human. When that happens, I feel like I am enveloped in a hug. *(Kat Riegel)*

In addition to the idea of "tapping into" information, psychics also have to "screen out" unrelated information. They have to be able to isolate the information which the client is seeking.

Are we all connected?

During readings, some psychics connect to intermediaries such as Spirit Guides, while other psychics connect directly to their client's energy. This direct connection allows the psychic to perceive the client's situation and access their information. The sense of separation between the psychic and the client dissolves. The idea of connectedness came up many times during this Project.

Although I didn't do a full interview with her, I asked April Cunningham, a psychic Medium in California, how she was able to read people. April emphasized that there was no separation between people's energies. She said:

> "Why do I know you? Because I have nothing in between. I don't have a judgement of you. I don't have a thought or an opinion. I look at you and I love you, and I love the ones who are with you and all of the sudden, the relationships are complete. The information is there because it is about love, the higher good, and healing."

In addition to the people who I interviewed for this Project, I have also read about other psychics. Elizabeth Lloyd Mayer, Ph. D., wrote a fascinating book about science and unexplainable, yet real, phenomena. She interviewed several psychics for her book, *Extraordinary Knowing* (Bantam Books, NY, 2007), and they provided insights into how they were able to access information. They explained that they moved between states of rational knowing and intuitive knowing. They also mentioned this idea of connectedness. Many of their observations were similar to the ideas I had heard from other psychics, but they were able to further refine this information.

One of the people interviewed for *Extraordinary Knowing* was John Huddleston. On page 52, he talked about his ability to do readings and emphasized that it was effortless. If he tried too hard, it didn't work. He couldn't "try," he could only "allow." He pointed out that a reading was as effortless as opening a garden gate and stepping into a new landscape. He didn't need to create the garden, he simply needed to observe the garden. The information about the other person was available simply because people were connected.

Helen Palmer was also interviewed for *Extraordinary Knowing*. On page 53, she explained that her key to giving readings was getting her mind empty enough to watch different inputs. In this state of emptiness, she was no longer aware of the room or her body. However, a separate type of awareness became available to her. At that point, she could begin to focus on an imagined object and wait. She could doubt herself and stay there anyway. Through this process of focusing and waiting, she could become whatever that focus was and know it from the inside out. She could read another person accurately because she *was* them; they stopped being separate.

Many PRISMS report that even though people think they are separate from each other, on a deeper level, they are somehow connected. Trees provide an example of connectedness. Trees in a forest appear to be separate from each other, but they are connected by an underground, intertwined root system. Similarly, all unconscious minds might somehow be connected.

Another way of looking at this is to think about personal energy systems. Psychics connect with the energy of the person whom they are reading. Their energies intertwine. When this happens, the psychic knows what the client knows because they are in the same energy field. How is it possible for psychics to access another person's energy and understand his or her unconscious world? Psychics make these connections every day, but there are no definitive scientific answers as to how this works. These are the kinds of energy questions currently being investigated by quantum physicists.

Can psychics see the future?

Psychics often see the direction a client's energy is flowing. They see if the energy will take the client where they want to go. They also see bits and pieces of the client's future. Because information comes in paragraphs, phrases, images and symbols, these pieces have to be assembled correctly to produce a clear view of the future. The pieces are part of an assemblage, a collage, a mosaic, a painting. Psychics are artists. The pieces are real, but because they require assembly, it can be difficult to see the future precisely. In addition, pieces and impressions are just part of the story. What people actually do matters.

As I understand things, each person agrees to an outline for his or her life before being born. Once a person is here, the person doesn't remember what was agreed upon or which lessons he or she is here to learn. However, the blueprint still exists and psychics can often access the blueprint and help clients see the overview of their life. This blueprint helps the psychic understand the person's future. For example, they can see if a person is destined for marriage, children or travel.

While the outline provides the broad brush strokes for lives, people use free will to fill in the details. Most things are not predestined. People have choices. So the psychics can see the most-probable future, unless the person uses free will to change this future. This ability to change course is one of the positive things which can come from a psychic reading. If a psychic sees someone's future, and the person doesn't want that future, they can use free will to make the changes which bring a different future. For example, if a psychic sees illness on the horizon, the person can choose a healthier lifestyle to ward off disease. This change works unless the upcoming illness is part of the larger blueprint; part of the required life lesson.

In her book *Gifts of the Soul* (Llewellyn Worldwide, Woodbury, MN, 2008, p. 35), Constance Rodriguez, Ph. D., provided a metaphor for seeing a client's past, present and future. She explained that doing a reading can be like traveling by airplane, looking down, and seeing a vehicle on a one-lane road. She can see where the driver has been and where he is going. She can see bends in the road which represent difficulties in life and she can see upcoming intersections where he must choose which road to take. It is as if she can see the person's past, present and potential future at the same time. She can see the road with the most energy with respect to the person's future.

When it comes to world issues, psychics' most-complete predictions come in prophetic dreams and visions, or as clear communications from non-physical entities. These experiences have a unique energy which indicates that they are prophetic. However, time frames may not be clear. The psychics have to wait and see if the events come to pass. And again, if the psychics see a world future which they don't like, they can enlist people to try to change that future.

In addition to glimpses of the future, psychics also see other kinds of information. They see the emotions surrounding issues, the decisions with which people struggle, health issues, strengths, weaknesses, personality traits, life challenges, and relationships with parents and children. They might also see relatives who have crossed or provide inspirational messages about how wise and wonderful people are and how people can gracefully overcome challenges. Potential futures are just one aspect of psychic readings.

What do people ask about? Are there common themes and topics?

According to the psychics, most people ask about:

Love; relationships; finding a soul mate
Finances
Jobs
Health (their own)
Health of a relative
Children

Loved ones who have died
Spiritual paths
Life purpose

People want to know:

Are they doing the right thing?
Should they apply for a certain job?
Should they get married?
Is their partner cheating on them?
Will they be moving?
Will they win the lottery?
How can they remove blockages when they feel stuck in their life?
Are their loved ones who have crossed over okay?
Will they see their deceased animals again?

Why do people ask these questions? What kinds of answers are they seeking? How do the psychics respond to the questions?

Clients are usually looking for insights on personal issues and/or insights on "big picture" issues.

Personal Issues

Some people are struggling with life events. They want a psychic to help them understand why things are happening the way that they are happening. Is a particular situation a life lesson or a detour? They want to understand why they are experiencing challenges so that they can make decisions which get them back on track or take them to a happier place in life. These people want to see their options and they ask the psychics to contact their Spirit Guides for advice. People want hope that things will improve.

Other people are very happy with their life situation and are just curious about the future. They want to know what is going to happen. Will they get a certain job? Will their relationship work out? What will their children grow up to be?

Many people want time frames for specific events, such as weddings and job promotions.

Some people seek validation for the decisions they have already made. Other people want corroboration of the psychic insights which they have already had. They want someone to confirm that their intuition was correct. In some instances, people talk to psychics because they feel confused about something they experienced and want to be certain that they were not just imagining things.

Sometimes, people want answers about their animals. They want to know what the animals are thinking and feeling. Other times, people ask if they, and their relatives, are healthy. Is there anything they need to know?

Many people recognize that they are on a spiritual path and that they have lessons to learn. They ask the PRISMS about their life purpose and their lessons. If they understand reincarnation, they ask about the large trajectory of their spiritual path. How far have they come and where are they now? How is this lifetime related to previous lifetimes? Is this lifetime resolving Karmic issues from previous lifetimes? Can this lifetime bring breakthroughs and great strides along their spiritual path?

Big Picture Issues

Some people talk to psychics because they want evidence that there is more to life than life on Earth. People want to know that PRISMS contact something real. They want confirmation of an invisible energetic universe.

The ability of a psychic reader to bring forward information about a client which the psychic should have no way of knowing confirms that something unique is happening. People want to hear specific information, such as names or details about current circumstances, so that they have confidence that psychic abilities are real. When a psychic produces this kind of detail, the client can accept that there is either an unseen information source, or that the psychic is able to read their mind. If the psychic transmits information which the client is not aware of, and the client can return home and confirm that information, there is evidence that something more than mind-reading occurs. For example, if a reader provides information about a grandparent and the client can go home and talk to their parent to validate this information, it means that the psychic is tapping into information which the client does not know. The psychic is not reading the client's mind. The psychic is accessing a larger stream of energy and information.

Another "big picture" issue is life after death. Some people talk to psychics because they want to know that consciousness survives death. They want to hear from loved ones who have crossed over so that they are completely certain that there is an afterlife. These people listen for specific names, phrases or references which assure them that their loved ones still exist and are doing well.

Other people want evidence of a connection to their Spirit Guides and angels. They ask for the names of their Spirit Guides and want to know how they can understand the messages which their Guides are sending to them.

Some people seek assurance that there are unseen forces helping the Earth. This has become a more-prominent concern as 2012 approaches. In addition, they want to know if their location is safe and if there are actions they can take to ensure that life survives on Earth beyond 2012.

People who are looking for evidence want measurable answers. They listen for specific names and pieces of information, and they ask detailed questions about future events so that they can wait and see if the events occur as predicted.

Answering the Questions: The Psychic Perspective

Here are a few insights from the psychics about the questions people ask:

☼ People ask if they are doing the right thing. Should they apply for a certain job? If they apply for the job, will they get it? If they have not applied for the job yet, I can't tell them much because they have not done anything to get the job. If they haven't applied, they haven't made the "cause" which can lead to the "effect" of getting the job. Should they apply for the job? Of course! Especially, if it's something they want to do. They have to open the door. Within certain parameters, I can tell them things fairly clearly, but if they haven't done anything, everything is still up in the air. People ask about jobs, about boyfriends and girlfriends, and whether they should or shouldn't get married. I tell them that if they don't know what to do, they shouldn't do anything. When they absolutely have to do something, they will know exactly what to do. *(Cherie Fraine)*

☼ Young and old people ask the same things, however, older people focus more on financial security and health. Younger people are more interested in jobs and love. They ask, "Will he marry me?" "Is he cheating on me?" "Should I stay with him?" If they are asking, the answer is "No." They already know the answer. Ninety-five percent of the time, they know the answer, all I do is confirm it. I do that by giving it to them in a way that helps them to understand their own feelings. *(Gina Stanfill)*

☼ People ask, "When will I meet my mate?" They think that meeting their mate is going to be the thing that solves their problems; it's not. [Ouch] *(Richard Schickel)*

☼ People ask me where the healing comes from. They want to know how I access this energy and if it is also accessible to them. They ask, "How can I protect my energy? How can I be more vital? How can I have more love in my life? More joy? How can I get out of this toxic situation?" They want their life to be better. They are not happy the way things are so they are coming to me for assistance. By coming to me and asking for help, they are opening up to the Divine. They are admitting that they can't do the healing all by themselves. That is the beginning of the healing process. *(Delphina Nova)*

Why can't we know the lottery numbers?

Several psychics remarked that people want to know lottery numbers, or want to know why the psychic hasn't yet won the lottery. The answer is that everyone is on their own life path. If it is in their best interest to win the lottery, they will. If it is not in their highest and best interest, they won't. Not even the psychics.

Do clients already know the answers?

Some psychics explained that they did not give answers to their clients, they just confirmed what the clients already knew. While this is the psychic's perspective, I'm not sure that the client realizes that he or she already knows the answers. On the other hand, some people talk with a psychic hoping to hear things they already know so that they can confirm the information.

How can a client get the most from a reading?

Here are a few tips to remember during the reading:

1) Listen with open mind.

A client should listen to the reading with an open mind. There may be surprises and insights which shake the listener. They should keep listening. If a deceased relative unexpectedly pops in, they should keep listening. Whatever happens, keep listening.

2) Stay calm and focus on what the reader is saying.

A client should not latch onto the first idea they hear and cement it in their mind. They should try not to let one thing capture their imagination so fully that they don't hear the rest of the information. They should continue to listen as the reader refines the ideas and discusses alternative possibilities. It is important to listen instead of reacting emotionally.

Similarly, the client should try not to focus on the one thing that they want to hear. They may miss chunks of information while waiting for a specific message or key word.

3) Be an active listener. Let the psychic speak.

A client should be an active listener. If the psychic is relaying messages, it is important not to interrupt as this can break the flow of information. If the psychic asks a question, the client should try to answer quickly and succinctly. They should not keep talking and explaining. It is okay to answer the psychic's questions and confirm information without providing too much additional information. If the psychic needs a quiet moment to recognize and relay the answers which are coming, the client should wait patiently. Some clients talk instead of listening because they are nervous or they think they need to fill the quiet spaces. It's okay to have a quiet, thoughtful, moment.

4) Control over-reactions.

If the client doesn't think the information is correct or doesn't recognize the references in the reading, they should try not to over-react. The psychic can find the client's body language distracting. There will be time to ask questions and refine information after the reader stops speaking.

5) Record the information.

The client should record the session so that they can review the details later. In the comfort of their own home, the information may make more sense. They will get the most out of the reading if they take the time to sit down and listen to the voice recording, or review the notes, without distraction.

6) Ask questions.

If a client hears something they don't want to hear, they should ask the psychic how to deal with the situation. Readers see energy potentials when they work with clients. The energy may be going in a certain direction, but people have free will and can make choices which turn the energy in a different direction. There are always multiple possibilities for the future and people can use their free will to influence what will happen. Very few things are set in stone. If clients hear something they don't want to hear, they may be able to take action to prevent the event from occurring, or to minimize the impacts of the event. If they hear something which scares them, they can ask for details or look for ways to improve the situation. Readers are here to help people figure things out.

7) Stay grounded.

During a reading, both the psychic and the client should try to remain grounded so that energy can flow freely. For the client, this means sitting in a chair with their feet flat on the ground. They should not cross their arms or legs because this can affect the energy flow.

How do psychics make their clients feel comfortable even when they have to deliver bad news?

Most of the psychics try to be gentle and encouraging when they give readings. They are here to assist and empower people. When they see something negative, they don't just blurt it out, but they may ask the client about the issue. For example, if they see disease on the horizon, they may ask the client when the last time was that the client saw a doctor and may gently suggest that it is time to go again.

Several readers revealed that sharing bad news is one of the hardest parts of their job. It can give them a sick feeling in the pit of the stomach. At the beginning of a reading, some PRISMS ask their clients if they want to know everything, including the bad news. Clients are given the option of hearing the difficult information. In many cases, clients tell the readers that they don't want to hear any negative news.

Richard Schickel noted that he has only had to tell people that they were going to die three times during his career and only because it was important. In one instance, the client was a cancer survivor who was afraid that the cancer would come back. He told her that it would come back if she kept holding on to that stress and fear. He had to remind her that everyone else was going to die too. He told her when her projected death would be and asked what she was going to do until then? He suggested that she shouldn't stop living just because she was afraid the cancer would return. He added that most of the time, there was no point in telling someone that they were going to die. His work was to tell them how they could live more-healthfully so that they would not die prematurely.

Laurie Hays explained that she has asked to be "Divine loving truth." She will not tell someone that they are overweight and are going to die. Instead, she will tell them that they need to watch their intake and be healthier. It's still the truth, but she wants to provide a gentle, loving truth. Her purpose is to help people, not hurt them.

A third Intuitive, Cynthia Rae, had this story:

> "One time I had a client who asked how long she and her husband were going to live. I said that that was up to them and up to G-d and that every time I gave her an answer, it was her opportunity to change it. People have a destiny, but they also have free will. If a person wanted to change the length of their life, they could change the way they lived that life. After she left, I received a message that she was not really asking for herself, but she wanted to know if she was going to have to be alone after her husband died (which was not going to be too far in the future). If I had told her about her husband, she would have lived every single day in fear of waking up and finding him dead. That's not my goal. My goal is to empower people so that they are courageous in their living, not fearful in their living."

She added that she had rarely been given information until after a client had left that something horrifying was going to happen to them.

When I asked a fourth psychic, Delphina Nova, how she managed to tell people what they needed to know, this is what she said:

> "I can sense in their energy field if a person's life force is diminishing. They also know when this is the case. I try to prepare the person by helping them complete unfinished business with loved ones, finances, personal obligations, connections to Spirit, etc. I help prepare them by letting them know that there is more to life than this life; there is more than flesh and bone. They are eternal and their souls live forever. I won't tell anyone that they are going to die. I would just suggest that people take care of themselves. If they tell

> me that the doctor has already told them that they are going to die, I will ask them what they think they need to do in order to leave here feeling completed.
>
> "I don't give bad news to people. No one has the right to tell anyone else that they are about to die. No one knows for sure and these are very powerful words to say. People are sometimes told that they have only a year to live, then they live for 30 years. No one knows for sure."

Another psychic, Jackie Chin, also talked about sharing difficult information:

> "When information regarding a matter is not favorable to the client, I begin by explaining that simply because they want an event to happen does not mean that it is right for them, or that the other person who is involved also wants the event to occur. I try to be firm yet compassionate because although I do not have any personal interest in their situation I know what it feels like to be disappointed, and even devastated. Bringing to the table my understanding of personal life events allows me to be a better reader and advisor. I have not had many traumatic readings although, when I receive information which is difficult to pass forward, I make damn sure I am right. No one wants to hear something horrible and then find out it was not true. If I am working with someone who has a missing loved one, I will go the extra mile to work with them until they are able to move forward on their own."

Several of the psychics reminded me that we are all here to learn life lessons. For the client, this means that unpleasant news and circumstances also provide opportunities for soul growth. The psychics may try to present this information with a positive spin so that people can understand what might be coming their way and can come up with strategies for dealing with the challenging circumstances. For the readers, their life lesson may be learning to present the information with clarity, honesty and compassion. Over time they find the words to convey the messages in a delicate way which helps the clients understand how they can improve their lives or deal with the future.

Some readers commented that it took experience to learn how to deliver difficult news. At first, the readers may have received clear information, but found it very difficult to deal with the client's emotions. One of the psychics said that she had given a reading for someone and the client had started crying. This psychic realized that it was too much for her; she was not ready to take care of the client. Giving information is a lot of responsibility, especially when the PRISMS want to empower people, not frighten them. Sometimes it is just too hard and they stop reading for the public.

On the other end of the spectrum, some psychic readers are brusque, very truthful, and may offend clients. Some clients need a rude awakening and this is the type of psychic which works for them. There is something to be said for psychic style. Just as people in some parts of the country speak more forcefully than people from other parts of the country, some psychics speak more forcefully than others. A couple of the psychics commented that sometimes they would not read for a client because they could tell that the client needed a more-forceful reader to tell them the truth. They recommended a different psychic reader who they thought had the right words and the right style to get the message through to that particular client.

Do readings affect how the psychics feel? their emotions?

Readings can have a big emotional impact on clients. Surprisingly, they can also have a big emotional impact on readers, especially when the readers are empathic.

Psychics work hard to retrieve information as clearly as possible. Most of them need to concentrate in order to hear, see, or understand messages. This work is easiest when clients are open and comfortable; but that is not always the case. Some people are so worried about what they might hear, that have trouble hearing the information which actually comes through. Other people come for a reading, but are skeptical of the psychic's ability so they limit access to their energy. These situations can make it difficult for the psychic to convey information.

Leah Taylor explained:

> "When someone comes for a reading who is skeptical and closed, and I am trying to connect to my soul, it is a hard feeling because I feel them being closed off." She added, "I open myself up to share this gift with people. For clients, it's just their time, but for me, my heart is out there. I can feel everything they are feeling during the reading. When they feel closed down, while I am so open, it can be difficult."

In addition, some people continually interrupt the reader and this can be distracting. And some people just won't stop talking. Instead of listening to the reader, they are busy providing background information, hoping that the psychic will give them the answer they want to hear. PRISMS find this behavior frustrating.

Many clients come to psychic readers because they have emotional traumas which they want to discuss or because they have recently lost a loved one. They are hurting and are seeking answers to life's big questions. It can be emotionally and physically draining to deal with the client's aching issues. In addition, empathic readers don't just listen to these traumatic events, they absorb the client's emotions. Readings can be exhausting!

On the other hand, Denise Singerline (a chakra-balancing specialist) mentioned:

> "Sometimes I feel very connected to the people I work on. One day I was working on a woman I knew and, in my mind's eye, I saw a ray of gold light come down over her and illuminate her whole body and all of her chakras. Then, the light spread and encompassed me. Wow. That was amazing."

Some psychics enjoy giving readings because it keeps the energy flowing through them. It's important to keep the energy flowing freely. And most psychics feel very fortunate to have a gift which helps people. It feels great when people want a reading or a consultation. Marta Taylor remarked:

> "I feel like every message I give, I am also getting something. Just like when you teach, you learn. It's a great gift."

Jackie Chin added:

> "When I am able to give information to people who are hurting and seeking answers, it makes me feel terrific. While I know that I am not the source of the answers, it gives me peace to be of assistance."

How do psychics feel when they know things about other people?

During readings, PRISMS often receive information about the lives (present and future) of their clients. How do psychics feel when they know things about their friends and clients which the friends and clients don't know?

All of the psychics remarked that they were very pleased to be able to help people understand what was going on in their lives. Helping people was why they provided readings. However, it was often disconcerting to know other people's stories; to know more about them than the psychic would like to know.

One psychic commented that it can be confusing to know things about other people. When she knew something about a client, she had to figure out what to do with the information. Should she share the information with the client? What if it scared them? What if it altered their life lessons? She always had to ask Spirit about the next step.

Denise Singerline provided additional detail on this kind of situation. She wondered why she was told certain things. She felt that if she was given information, she had to do something with it, but she was not always certain what to do with the information. When people came for a reading, she had to be appropriate and it was not always appropriate to tell the client everything she saw. She couldn't just tell people when she saw illness, death or divorce coming. It would scare them. One time she saw that her friend's husband was having an affair, but she couldn't tell the friend. The woman wasn't ready to accept the information and the situation was part of both partners' life lessons. Denise remained quiet.

Patricia Kirkman remarked that she had to work hard to make sure other people were okay; to give them what they were going to need, even if they didn't know that they needed it. For example, if a person told her that they were not feeling well, she might meditate on it and discover that the condition was much worse than they had thought. Then, she had to decide how much information to share. Alternatively, someone might tell her that their life was wonderful, but she might see a block. She commented, "You try to protect, guard and take care of people so that they are strong enough to do what they need to do."

She added:

> "I don't enjoy it when I can't make things better for someone, but I also know that these are their life lessons. It's like when you hold a child's hand when they are learning to walk because you don't want them to fall. But there is a point in time when you have to release the hand and let them try to stand on their own."

Cherie Fraine put it this way:

> "It's a double-edged sword. Sometimes it is really cool and sometimes it is a pain in the butt because you see someone going through hard times and you can't just tell them what is going on because it freaks them out. It can be painful when you know something and you can't do anything to help, but it's wonderful when you know something and you <u>can</u> do something to help."

What does it mean when a psychic says that they can't read for someone?

People have told me that a psychic refused to read for them and that they were frightened that it meant that the psychic didn't want to tell them that something terrible was about to happen. What does it mean when a psychic says that they can't read for a client? Not much. It just means that, at that particular moment, there wasn't a connection. Or, it can mean that there is a different psychic who would be better able to convey the message which needs to be heard. Sometimes a different psychic has just the right words or the perfect connection. They can present ideas in a way that allows the person to truly understand what they need to hear. In this situation, one psychic may send a client to a different psychic. Each person who is supposed to get a reading will get one. People shouldn't worry if a psychic can't do a reading at a particular time. They can find someone else.

Gina Stanfill explained further:

> "It doesn't mean anything if a reader can't read someone. It just means that, at that moment, the psychic can't read them. There might have been a connection from another lifetime. Or the client's energy stunned the reader and threw them off-guard. A reader needs to be in their zone and if they are stunned sometimes they just can't get into their zone. It is nothing more than that. It has nothing to do with the person. That particular reader is just not the person to read them that day."

Of course, there are people who come for sessions just to test the psychic. If they close their energy to prove that they can't be read, they will be right – they can't be read. They win . . . and they lose . . .

Can most psychics read most people?

Yes, professional psychics are able to read most clients. However, psychics pointed out that they only read for people who ask to be read. It would be an invasion of privacy to read people without their permission. They don't just walk down the street picking up detailed information on strangers.

Here are some insights from the PRISMS about "read-ability":

<u>Some psychics can read everyone</u>

> ☼ There isn't anybody I cannot read . . . I was doing a class and there was one guy who no one could read. I tried reading him and I read him just fine. I knew where he lived as

a child, I knew addresses, and I knew what the house looked like. I opened my eyes and looked at the guy and beads of sweat were rolling off of him. He looked at me and said, "Wow." I said, "See, it doesn't hurt." He sat back and suddenly three other people could read him. He had been so blocked that no one could read him. *(Cherie Fraine)*

<u>Sometimes it is difficult to read people</u>

☼ I can read some people more easily than others, but I haven't come across anyone who I have not been able to read. However, I might not get as much information from some people because they are afraid and it might take me a little longer. After a half hour or so they relax and I can get additional information. *(Denise Singerline)*

☼ I have always been able to read people who have hired me to do a full reading. Occasionally, I have drawn a blank with someone at the psychic fair. They will sit down, we will chit chat, and I will be sitting there with nothing. Either I will tell them to see another reader, or I will take a breath, look at the cards, and go back to basic readings from the book. As soon as I do that, it begins to flow. It is something in me. Either something about that person is a challenge to me, or there is something I am going to say to that person that I also need to hear. I need to get past my own block. If I start with the basics, it always starts to flow. *(Gina Stanfill)*

☼ Any time someone has asked me for a reading, I have been able to read them. The only people who I have not been able to read have asked on the spur-of-the-moment at public venues. Typically, if I can't give a reading it is either because I am very distracted by something which is going on, or because that person is very distracted by something which is going on. If the two of us can't hold our intention of coming together for the purpose of new information coming through, then we don't have the connection to bring it through. *(Beth Hays)*

<u>Sometimes people can't be read. This is why it happens</u>:

☼ Some people jam your radar. There are people who are very intense, and they don't want to tell you anything about themselves. They close off their energy so you can't read them. If you want a reading, you need to keep the energy open. I tell them, "You're really uptight. Why don't you walk around and try to loosen up a bit then come back." Then they say, "Well, I thought you were psychic," and I say, "I am, but your energy is closed off." *(Cecilia Nemmers)*

☼ To me, it means that I am not the one to deliver the message. Someone else has the correct vocabulary or the heart connection to be able to give them the information which they need. I tell them that today is just not the day for us to connect. Some people think it's because they are too skeptical, but that doesn't have anything to do with it. Often, I give information to people who are skeptical and later they tell me that the information was correct. *(Cynthia Rae)*

☼ This happens when the person is afraid, or doesn't believe I can read them. It is like they are in their own little castle and they won't lower the drawbridge so that I can get in. I don't know why they come for a reading. Maybe so they can de-bunk the idea that they can be read? They want it, but they don't want it. Their logical mind is saying, "No, it can't happen." *(Richard Schickel)*

☼ Sometimes I have a bad day and my energy is not there, or sometimes we are just not connected. The main reason that I may not connect with a client is that the client has come to test me and really isn't interested in getting a reading. In that case, it does not work. *(Shirli Millmond)*

☼ There are times when I can not read someone. If the person has decided to play "stump the psychic," use illicit drugs, or alcohol, or intentionally try to deceive, it is difficult to read for them. What does it mean? It means that Spirit will not allow me to mingle my energy with the person who is asking questions. *(Jackie Chin)*

☼ When I do bodywork, I ask the body for permission to do this work. If the body says we can't do it, we can't do it. If their energy is blocked, they need to shift their energy. If their body is telling me it's not for their highest good because the timing is wrong or the person isn't ready for the information, we can't work. I have to trust that the body knows best. *(Trish Silay)*

☼ When I sense that the person wants their healing to come from me versus the healing coming from the Universe, I will tell them that they need to trust more in the healing energy. If I feel like a person is blocking their own healing energy, I will ask them why they have come for healing. I can read people pretty easily if they allow themselves to surrender to the process of healing. If someone doesn't want healing, they won't allow themselves to be healed. For example, they can eat all the right foods, but they won't allow themselves to be healed. Some people would rather just be sick. They go to healer after healer, psychic after psychic. They want the attention, but they don't want the healing. That person is not going to get better. I tell them that they need to find another healer or another psychic. *(Delphina Nova)*

<u>Sometimes the psychic can read the person, but doesn't want to read them</u>

☼ I don't know if I <u>can't</u> read them, or if I <u>don't want to</u> read them. Sometimes it just doesn't feel right. It's not an energy with which I would want to be involved. *(Marta Taylor)*

☼ I don't remember having a time when I couldn't read somebody, but I have had people sit down who were agitated and I could feel they were waiting for me to do something so they could say "Aha! You're wrong" or "Why are you saying it like that?" We have had people at the Psychic Fair and I have said that I didn't think I was the right reader for them, then I recommended that they talk to someone else. Intuitively, I knew that I was not going to connect with this individual even though the individual felt they were going to connect with me. The reader gets that feeling. I haven't told people that I couldn't read for them, but I find that some people are there to be a challenge; it's a test for them. We have had people go to two or three readers, sit with their arms crossed, and say, "Tell me what you know." This isn't show and tell. I didn't come to them, they came to me. I can't help people who don't want to be helped. *(Patricia Kirkman)*

☼ One time I was doing readings in a public place and a gentleman sat down with me. I was going to read him when Spirit rolled a shade down with a skull and cross bones on it. I looked at him and told him that I wouldn't read him. Spirit must have known something about that person's energy and given me a signal not to read him. I protect myself. When they told me not to read him, I didn't read him. *(Laurie Hays)*

What about reading animals? Kat Riegel, the Animal Communicator, explained that there were times when she could not read an animal. This was usually because the animal felt accused of bad behavior and was defensive. It could also be due to the human's poor attitude. The animal might be afraid that if it did not give the correct answer, it would be given away. Animals don't want to be given away, they want to fix what is wrong. Animals can shut down out of fear of what might happen.

More information on Animal Communication can be found in Chapter 16.

After the Reading

First of all, after a reading, clients must remember to pay the psychic! They have bills to pay too. Clients with money issues should try to have a positive attitude when paying for a reading. Money carries energy and money which is paid out reluctantly creates an invisible energetic resistance which can affect the psychic's ability to read for the client in the future.

Second, both the psychic and the client should disconnect their energy, clear out any negative energy, and fill themselves with white light.

Third, the client should take some time to think about their reading.

What should a client do with the information they hear at a reading?

It is always fun to listen to the recording after a psychic reading. There is so much more to be heard the second (and third) time through. Clients should listen for ideas which may have been missed in the moment.

After reviewing the recording or the notes, people should use whatever information is helpful. Some of the information will confirm what they already knew. Some of the advice will help them figure out how to deal with family members, friends and/or co-workers. Some of the details might not seem relevant right now, but will provide something to think about.

Keep in mind that psychics provide guidance and respond to questions at the time they are asked. The responses may not be "forever" answers. As situations change, responses can change. If someone asked the same question five years ago then asked it today, the answer might be different. Think of the answers as current responses and remember that answers can change as people evolve.

Although a reading will be full of information and insights, it should not be taken <u>too</u> seriously. It is a tool which provides wisdom to be used in the client's decision-making process. The future depends on the client's choices. If clients hear something they don't want to hear, they need to think about the steps which can be taken to change the outcome. They should think slowly. There is no need for drastic, reflexive, changes based on the information from a reading. They should marinate in the information and think about the changes which can be made.

Clients might enjoy talking to a good friend or spouse about the reading. The messages can provide an interesting starting point for discussion. Reviewing the information with a friend may help solidify it in the client's mind.

If someone is fortunate enough to find a reader who provides a glimpse of the future, they can wait and see how things play out. See if the events come true. Check them off when they do!

However, it's important to remember that not all messages are fact-based. Sometimes people receive wonderful, inspirational messages from psychics, or messages from deceased relatives. In these cases, clients can just bask in the miracle of extraordinary inter-realm communication. They can feel that they are making good choices and that their future is bright.

When clients leave a reading, they should either feel good about themselves or feel like they have learned something which might have been difficult to hear, but can be used to improve their life. If they leave the reading feeling despondent, they should seek a different psychic for future readings.

Do psychics remember what they tell clients?

Most psychics report that they are like radios or conduits. They receive information and pass it along to the client, but they don't remember what they tell each specific client. Sometimes this can be awkward if they run into the person a few weeks later and the person wants to tell the psychic about what happened after the reading. The psychic has to listen carefully and try to remember the messages. However, one psychic told me that she immediately taps into the other person's energy when she sees them again. She doesn't have to remember what she told them in the past because the information is always right there and she taps into it as soon as she sees the client.

What else might be involved in a reading?

After the reading, some psychics do short energy-healing sessions for their clients. They may have the client lay on a massage table for this energy work. The reader will float their hands above the client's body and clear blocks so that there is an improved energy flow. Even over the phone, many psychics are able to work energetically on their clients.

Additional information on Energy Work can be found in Chapter 15.

Chapter 14 - Accuracy

Can you depend on the information which a psychic provides? If you understand how psychics work with energy and how they see bits and pieces of lives and futures, can you use their information to plan your life? Remember, bringing in information and using it to paint a picture of someone's life is an art. This chapter provides insights on psychic accuracy and explains why what was accurate in the moment may, or may not, happen.

How accurate are the psychics?

Psychic accuracy is difficult to quantify. I never tried to test or score the psychics' abilities. Instead, I asked them, ***"On a scale of 1-10, 1 being "not much" and 10 being "incredible," how psychic do you think you are?"***

Only 15 readers provided a numeric answer. The average score of these professional readers was 8.93. Some of the psychics based their scores on testing which they had undergone to be certified by various groups.

One of the readers reported that she was a certified ESP psychometrist. She had been certified in 1978 and part of her certification included training to use her abilities accurately. Cherie Fraine explained:

> "In order to be certified, you have to run at least 80% correct all the time. You have to have an 80% score-able 'correctness' percentile. I run between 95% and 100%. This

> testing is done through the Southern California Society for Psychical Research which is a branch of the American Society which is an offshoot of the English Society."

Jeff Sonnenburg told me that the first 3-5 years he was doing this work he asked people to fill out an evaluation form. His accuracy rate was 92.5%.

Jackie Chin explained that she was a ten, according to her husband. He had tracked her predictions and they were 75-85% accurate. She was very conservative in her work, and tried to make absolutely certain that what she told a client was to the best of her ability.

Other readers explained why they did not provide a numeric score:

<u>There isn't any way to score accuracy</u>

Psychic ability isn't a measurable talent. If someone is good at math, or sports, results can be measured. Psychic ability is more like being good at art. Science has not yet figured out how to score psychic ability. Readers added:

> ☼ There isn't any way to scale that. I don't know that I'm psychic at all. I think I'm pretty intuitive and I think that I have a very bright, clever mind so when the information comes I can glean it and provide it for my client. I can't compare myself to anyone else. *(Cynthia Rae)*

> ☼ I am as psychic as anybody who I have met in my life. At the same time, I don't know what the possibilities are. *(Leah Taylor)*

<u>Accuracy depends on the listener's ability to understand the information</u>

There's no way to know, in the moment, if the listener can identify the references in a reading. Days after the reading, things may become clearer to the client.

In addition, some people might be in denial about the messages. Laurie Hays explained:

> "You could be accurate and a client might not recognize it. That's when you think you are wrong, but it could be that they are just not ready to acknowledge the situation. I was told that my first marriage would end in divorce. I never thought it would happen [so I thought the information was wrong], but it happened."

Here's a slightly different perspective on accuracy from Beth Hays:

> "My accuracy changes based on circumstances. By 'circumstances' I mean that the person I am interacting with has an influence on me. It has to do with that person's level of 'asking,' and their levels of openness, intensity and expectation. This controls how well I perform, from their perspective. All I have is their perspective to gauge the accuracy of what I am telling them. I can get something from the Universe that I know is absolutely true, but if I can't present it to them in a way that they know it's absolutely true, then that same information still moves me down the scale of being psychic because there is a way of presenting data and truth that should get through no matter what. If I can't present it correctly, then I think it lowers me on the scale.
>
> "To me, 'psychic' is a two-way street. If I have the answers, but they can't hear them, then I have given them nothing. 'Psychic' has to be that round trip where the client aligns with the information."

Accuracy may change from day to day

In some cases, personal accuracy changes from day to day; sometimes people have it and sometimes they don't. Here are some thoughts from the readers:

☼ I think that accuracy changes day-to-day for me. When I need it, it is always there, but if I get too emotional or scatter-brained from all the things which are happening in my life, I lose touch with that part of myself. I become more concerned with day-to-day things. *(Erik Assman)*

☼ Some of it depends on how prepared I am for readings. If I am not concentrating on things, information sometimes comes more easily and I would be higher on the scale. Other days, I want to give information so badly that I think I shut it down somehow. *(Kat Riegel)*

☼ I want to do everything perfectly and sometimes I need to relax and take care of myself. The more tired I am, the more I let go, and the more I lose control of the situation, the more information comes to me. Sometimes when you let go, great things happen. *(Shirli Millmond)*

Modesty and practicality

Because there is always more to learn, or because they are focusing on other things in their lives, some very good readers are reluctant to give themselves a 10. They commented:

☼ I am an "8." When I can get names, addresses, and phone numbers, then I'll think I'm a 10! [lol] *(Laurie Hays)*

☼ I am an "8" mostly because I am very practical. I don't want to let myself go too far. There is a bridge between the spiritual and practical aspects of our lives. I want to find the balance. Maybe someday I will be a 10, but right now I want to live a more-grounded life here. If you let it, and you are ready, the spiritual part can become a bigger and bigger part of your life. I am not ready for it. *(Shirli Millmond)*

What was accurate in the moment, doesn't always happen

Because people can change their choices at any time, predictions for the future may not come true. For example, a psychic may see a particular future if the person stays on the path they are on. If the person changes their path (for example, changes their major in school or their chosen profession), the prediction might not come true. It was accurate at the time of the reading, but not accurate in retrospect.

To-Ree'-Nee' Wolf provided this example:

"Several years ago, I had a reading with a woman and I saw very clearly that she would be living in Turkey or Istanbul. I very clearly saw her doing archaeological and anthropological work. I heard that that had not happened in her life and I remembered wondering why it had not happened when I had seen it so clearly. Years later, I ran into her and I asked what she was doing. She told me that she had shifted her major from anthropology to cooking. The time line I had seen had totally evaporated.

"The future is made up of all the minute choices we make in the moment. There might be four appointments in your lifetime which are predestined, but if you choose not to show up, they don't happen. I think that the future is very flexible and very fluid. It changes. The future which is set in concrete changes as soon as you get out of your car and decide to go a different way. A whole new time line opens up."

Without formal testing, how do the psychics know if they are any good?

Several readers mentioned that when they do readings, they are confident that the information is accurate. There is no question in their mind that they received and relayed the information well. The only question is what people did with the information once they were aware of it. Most of the psychics did not follow-up with their clients; however, they received phone calls, letters and e-mails from satisfied customers. In addition, they had high rates of return clients and many referrals. They noted:

> ☼ I have never needed to follow up. My clients are very good about getting back to me and the Universe is very abundant with its validations for me. People often call me and rave about the results. I try not to get emotionally involved in whether the [flower] essences work, but people call me all of the time. Repeat business is 70-80%. In addition, about 75% of my clients call or e-mail me to tell me how well things worked. *(Beth Hays)*

> ☼ I get affirmation after affirmation that what I saw really happened. People tell me that I am correct. I get letters regarding how accurate I was. I receive lots of confirmations. People come back and bring their friends and relatives. *(Jan Class)*

Why don't most psychics follow up with clients after readings?

Psychic readers generally do not follow up with clients to find out how accurate the readings were, or what the clients did with the information which they heard. Cynthia Rae explained that the whole point of this process was trust. She said:

> "As a reader, you have to trust that the information you are giving is the right information. Whatever they do with the information is up to them. I just have to know that I have done the best I could do. It doesn't help me to know if I was right or wrong, because it might have been how they perceived and used the information."

Gina Stanfill echoed this idea saying:

> "Sometimes after a reading, people ask if I want them to come back and tell me how things worked out. I politely tell them that I don't need to know. I have to trust that what I gave them was what they needed to hear and that they will take that information forward. I have no control over how the information is used. I just give them the information so

> they can make choices. I don't dictate that someone must do, or not do, something. I can just tell people about their choices and the consequences of those choices. For me, personally, following up is ego-oriented, and I have to stay away from it."

And To-Ree'-Nee' Wolf commented:

> "The other reason I don't follow-up with people is that I don't have an attachment to the reading. This is their reading. The information is for them."

Scientific Measurement

If you are interested in scientific experiments which are being done to gauge the accuracy of psychic information, there are colleges and groups which are working in this area. One of the most-prominent researchers in this field is Gary E. Schwartz in Tucson, Arizona. Another good information source is the ***Institute of Noetic Sciences***. Searching the Internet will provide information on current research.

Chapter 15 - Energy and Healing Work

Many PRISMS perform energy work and assist with healing. It's difficult to draw a distinction between energy work and healing as they are intimately intertwined. Both promote good health. In some cases, energy work can help prevent disease. Healing work is often done after a medical issue has been identified.

Some PRISMS provide psychic readings followed by energy work, some only provide energy work, and some provide energy work followed by psychic readings. For energy work, the client usually lays on a massage table while the reader floats their hands above the client's body and clears blocks in his or her energy system. Even over the phone, many psychics are able to provide energy work for their clients.

Why do people benefit from energy work?

Our bodies are energetic systems and the energy needs to flow freely. According to psychics, there is a subtle energy field around, and through, the human body. This personal energy field has several layers. People who see auras are seeing this personal, subtle energy field around the body. In addition to our personal energy field, we live in a multi-dimensional, universal energy field. People can use their personal energy fields to interact with the larger universal energy field. The personal and universal energy systems interact through each person's chakra system. Chakras are the energy portals between the physical body, the personal energy system and the universal energy system. Clearing the energy around and through the body allows people to feel well and to perceive information from the universal energy field. Information brought in by psychics is often accessed from this universal energy field.

Where are the chakras located?

Chakras are the energy centers along the spinal cord which extend out of the physical body as energy portals and intersect with the personal energy field around the body. To simplify, picture the personal energy field around the body with the chakras going through the body and intersecting each layer of the body's personal energy field. Think of the chakras as perpendicular to the body's energy field. Chakras rotate at different speeds and can become blocked or unbalanced. Energy workers can often see the rotating chakras and clear imbalances.

There are seven major chakras in the human body: the Crown chakra, the Third Eye chakra, the Throat chakra, the Heart chakra, the Solar Plexus chakra, the Sacral chakra and the Root chakra. In addition, there are many smaller chakras throughout the body, including the hands and feet. Each of the seven major chakras correspond with an endocrine gland, a color and a musical tone. The chakras bring in energy and stimulate consciousness. Because the chakras correspond to colors, people often wear colored gemstone jewelry to keep their chakras balanced.

Here's another way of looking at chakras. In her book *The Lightworkers Way* (Hay House, Carlsbad, CA, 1997, p. 190), Doreen Virtue, Ph. D., explains that we can clean and balance our chakras. She suggests that we visualize the chakras as round, transparent, stacked balls of energy in our body. When our chakras are balanced, they are all the same size and rotate at the same rate.

When I interviewed the psychics, they talked about their personal work with energy systems, but they didn't talk much about the actual energy fields in which we live. People who are interested, can find information on chakras and human energy systems in books and on the Internet.

What is energy work?

People can develop blocks and imbalances in their personal energy systems. Energy work can clear these areas. Energy workers see and feel energy moving through the body and around the body. Sometimes they feel disease, or pre-cursors to disease, and may make suggestions which help clients prevent illness.

Acupuncture is one well-known type of energy work. Acupuncture assumes that there is a "chi," or vital life force, flowing through the body. This energy flows along twelve invisible meridians and can become blocked. An imbalance in the flow of chi through a meridian allows disease to arise. Acupuncturists insert very thin needles into specified points along the meridian lines to restore balance to the flow of chi.

There are many other kinds of energy work including cranial-sacral therapy, Shiatsu, Therapeutic Touch, Polarity Therapy, Emotional Freedom Techniques, color therapy and sound therapy.

One type of energy work which is often employed by psychic practitioners is called "Reiki."

What is Reiki?

According to The International Center for Reiki Training (www.Reiki.org, 2011):

> "Reiki is a Japanese technique for stress reduction and relaxation that also promotes healing. It is administered by 'laying on hands' and is based on the idea that an unseen 'life force energy' flows through us and is what causes us to be alive. If one's 'life force energy' is low, then we are more likely to get sick or feel stress, and if it is high, we are more capable of being happy and healthy."

The Center's website goes on to explain:

> "A treatment feels like a wonderful glowing radiance that flows through and around you. Reiki treats the whole person including body, emotions, mind and spirit creating many beneficial effects that include relaxation and feelings of peace, security and well being. Many have reported miraculous results.
>
> "Reiki is a simple, natural and safe method of spiritual healing and self-improvement that everyone can use. It has been effective in helping virtually every known illness and malady and always creates a beneficial effect. It also works in conjunction with all other medical or therapeutic techniques to relieve side effects and promote recovery."

What happens at a Reiki session?

Reiki sessions are very relaxed events. Four energy workers described their Reiki experiences:

Reiki Practitioner #1: Energy work is done on a fully-clothed person who lays on their back on a massage table. People should wear comfortable clothing. Most of the work I do touches the body, but there is nothing invasive and I always ask in advance if they are comfortable being touched. I like to use soft music and I might light candles. I want the client to be as comfortable as possible. When I am working with a client, my intuition tends to draw me to the areas I need to work on in the client's body. I have learned to trust that if I am drawn to someone's left knee, I need to work on it even if they came in for something else.

During an energy session, information may just pop into my head; it's a knowing. I know to work on a place in the client's body, or I feel a presence in the room. I don't always see something. I am more likely to feel it. Later, it will be confirmed by the client. When I feel something very strongly, I honor it and recognize it and when the session is over, I tell the client about it. The client often knows what it is that I have felt. On one occasion, I was working on a client and felt a presence. The client later confirmed that it was her mother who had passed away from an accident in a hospital operating room.

I don't hear anyone talking to me, the words just come into my head and trip off my tongue. I wonder where the words are coming from! Sometimes someone will ask me a question and the answer is just there and I will give them a long answer without knowing where it came from.

When I work on someone, my hands turn red and feel hot. That has always happened. I have taken a lot of massage classes and whenever I worked on people, they would tell me that my hands were hot. This was a clue to me that I would be able to do the energy work. *(Nancy)*

Reiki Practitioner #2: First, I explain what I am going to do. Then, the client lays on a massage table and I explain that I am not going to do a massage. I am going to place my hands on top of their chakras and do energy work. I may use chakra stone bags, place stones on top of their body, use tuning forks or use crystal bowls. I put on nice music so that they can relax. I put a lavender eye pillow over their eyes and I use essential oils on their feet and on their third eye. The oil goes into their blood stream and prepares them for the chakra work. Some people have been coming to me every month for several years and now, when I use the essential oils, they have begun seeing visions, astral traveling, and connecting with their Spirit Guides.

When I start doing healing work, I ask Spirit to help me to step aside so that they can work through me and attach themselves to the backs of my hands. I ask them to show me what needs to be done; to guide me and lead me. I step out of the way and I start channeling energy through my body. All of the sudden I will see a little movie inside my head. For example, I will see a cruise ship and I will figure out that the client is going on a cruise. Or a book will pop up and I will suggest that the client read the book. Or I'll see a symbol like the Star of David and know that the client is Jewish. If I don't understand the symbol, I'll ask what they are trying to tell me and I will hear additional information. Sometimes I hear that there is an issue with one of the client's organs so I'll clean it out [etherically]. *(Denise Singerline)*

Reiki Practitioner #3: People should expect to be comfortable. They usually lie on a table and I touch them lightly or float my hands over their body. There may be incense or relaxing music. I talk during the session. It's important for people to know when and where they are going to be touched so that it doesn't surprise them. Talking out loud keeps the client informed so that they can relax. I also tell people what I see in their bodies. I see the whole body as an energy matrix and I try to align it. I look for places where things aren't right. I try to put energy in to re-align the matrix. Sometimes I see the beginnings of disease manifesting in the body. Sometimes I can see actual disease in the body. *(Erik Assman)*

Reiki Practitioner #4: In the end, all healing arts are the same thing: I have to be beyond myself; I have to allow the person to heal themself. That is where all healing comes from, from our selves. People take the first step in healing themselves by wanting to come to a healer. They are open to doing something. Then, I just guide the energy into their bodies and help it move around to where it needs to flow. It is a hands-on "touchy" thing. People like the hands-on work. Truly, I could sit here, write your name down and do the exact same thing as I do having you sit there for an hour while I touch you. There is no difference, but people like the intimacy of being with someone and being touched. I can touch someone and focus energy into a spot or I can do that without touching them. It is about my intent to send the energy to them, not about touching them. The energy flows through me. I call it in and I am a conduit for it. But it is their healing. I can call it through, but they have to accept it. Otherwise it goes through them and back out. They have to be willing to accept it into their body for their highest good. *(Gina Stanfill)*

After Reiki treatments, some people experience a huge emotional outpouring.

Do readers do other kinds of energy work?

In addition to Reiki, there are many other kinds of energy work. This is a summary of work done by the people who are part of this Project:

One of the practitioners, Raquel Spencer, works with the Higher Realms. When she looks at someone, she sees things in an energetic format. She sees grids and laser light shows. For her work, she sees what needs to take place to help the person clear out and upgrade the body. Her vision is in pure energy. Sometimes she gets pictures of a client's issues, but mainly she works on an energetic level.

When someone comes to her in person, they usually lay on a table. When she works remotely, it doesn't matter what the person is doing because she is looking at them on an energetic level. If they are at home, they are usually in their meditation spot, in a chair or on a bed. People often fall asleep while she is working on them.

Raquel explained:

> "I help people with their own ability to tap into their Highest Self. I help people to be better at their spiritual work. I help them to figure out their life's work and then to do it well. When I do the energy work, I access their energetic information and bring in the person's Divine Blueprint. If people are ready, I can give them direction and help them to work with the Ascended Masters, angels and Guides who have information for them. I can help them to improve their meditation by raising their personal vibrational frequency so that they start to get information. People can begin to receive clear information about their life's work. I am a guide who can give someone an energetic push so that they can pull in their own information and guidance."

She went on to say:

> "I connect with the Higher Realms. I connect into the higher frequencies and that is where I do my work. I go into a certain 'space' where I connect with clients energetically in the Higher Realms on the higher frequencies (energy vibrating at a faster pace). I connect to the client's Higher Self. My Higher Self works with their Higher Self then it comes down into physical reality. Most people who are sensitive or intuitive can feel me working on them. I end up showing up in people's dreams or in the room while they

are meditating. They can feel the changes in their body; they can see bits and pieces of what is happening."

Another energy worker, Trish Silay, uses the *One Brain* system. This system helps people understand their personal belief systems and how their beliefs may block them from being fully who they are. Muscle testing is used understand what a person has experienced and why they might have blockages. Muscle testing provides bio-feedback and information from the body. While this intuitive energy worker might not know someone's story, their body knows it. Muscle testing is the body's validation of the person's truth.

I asked how muscle-testing worked and Trish explained:

"I just touch their arm and I ask 'yes' and 'no' questions. I talk really fast so that their brain doesn't get in the way. I do a light touch and it is almost like a pendulum test. I ask the body how it signifies 'yes' and 'no' then I ask questions and allow the body to answer them. The person's forearm provides biofeedback."

This work allows Trish to access the time when the person began to feel a certain way about an event and it changed his or her life. She can clear blockages and diffuse the emotional energy around the blockages. Using the *One Brain* system, she has seen many lives improve.

During the interviews, at least three people said that they see energetic gridlines on people. When they look at someone, they can see "in" and it often looks like a hologram with grids.

Did the psychics provide examples of healing work?

Energy work and healing work go hand in hand. However, healing work is often done after a medical issue has been identified. Healing may include prayer, herbs, and the "laying on of hands." It is often used in conjunction with western medicine.

Cynthia Rae is one of the Intuitives who does healing work. I asked Cynthia what happened when she touched clients and she answered, "When I touch someone's body, information begins to come through . . . It's just a natural talent." She went on to say that she can feel pulses between each section of the body. Each section has its own rhythm and the rhythms need to be in sync. For example, if there's a pain in a muscle, she can put her fingers on the patient in a particular way and feel the inconsistent pulses. She holds her fingers until there is a consistent pulse. When she takes her fingers away, the pain is gone.

Richard Schickel explained that according to some Native American traditions, he is called a "hand-trembler." He can put his hand over someone's body and do a scan. If his hand trembles, he is feeling trapped energy. He can see and feel issues. He has to be careful about what he says to clients and must refer them to doctors when necessary. He is a medical intuitive and a healer. Once he has identified an issue, he has to determine how to heal the person. Sometimes he takes people back to a past life and helps them finish off issues from that life. According to Richard, when people release their anger and fear, healing can occur. Anger and fear are the basis of disease.

Leah Taylor has many psychic gifts, including medical intuition and healing ability. She revealed that when she does readings, she is often be able to look up and feel with her hands what is going on in someone's body. It's as if a whole image comes up in front of her which she can feel with her hands. She uses this ability to check her client's health.

Leah provided a couple of examples of her healing abilities:

> "I diagnosed my Mom's cancer. She had a terminal cancer. She was having pain in her side. I felt like it was coming from one of her spinal vertebrae and that the pain was radiating from the side. It turned out that she had a tumor in the spine which was causing the pain. Before the doctors had looked at her seriously, I took her into the emergency room. They told me that they had taken an x-ray and said that she had normal degenerative spine problems due to aging.
>
> "One day she was screaming in pain, and she is a tough woman. I talked to EMTs who told me that she had probably just pulled her back out. Finally I took her to the hospital because she was shaking, crying and vomiting. They kept her there for several hours just because of the pain and finally they saw her and admitted that she had spine tumors and multiple myeloma. They kept her in the hospital for a few months. The doctors said she had a 5% chance of living more than 6 months; she had end-stage multiple myeloma, a terminal cancer. Her friends were worried and I told them she was not dead yet. I did not have her write her will and I told her friends that she was going to be fine. I also told them that if she died, I did not want her to die scared.

> "I took her home. She ended up going off of a lot of her medicines. In addition to chemotherapy, we did herbs, Reiki, and healings, and she is still alive. They told her she would never walk without a brace, but she moves, gardens and does everything. She is in remission. Her doctors didn't recognize her when she went back in. That was in 2003. She was so ill she couldn't even hold down water. I started her on herbs, then we went to get Reiki. After Reiki she never vomited from the cancer again. She had chemotherapy, but never got sick with it, never lost her hair. Now she is on a drug which allows her to be in remission. We used a combination of western medicine and other healing techniques. I am so happy that she lived through it. I think it was her own desire to live; she never thought about dying."

In another case, Leah was able to help a woman prepare for pregnancy. She recalled:

> "I had a client who came to me and was talking about adopting a child. I mentioned that she didn't want to adopt a child; she wanted to have her own child. She was crying because it was true. Then her father came through [in spirit] and said, 'You can do this!' She came for energy healings every week because I felt that there was a lot of congestion in her uterus. I felt that there was a thickening, a swelling, of the uterus. I worked on clearing the congestion out and she went to see her doctor. She wanted to try IVF [in vitro fertilization], but her doctor told her that she had a lot of fibroids in her uterus and would need surgery if she wanted to try to get pregnant. She had never had any symptoms from the fibroids. He told her that some of the fibroids were really deep in the lining of the uterus and in the muscle, so he didn't know how well surgery would go. She came to me and I worked with her to try to get the fibroids to come to the surface, to come out of the muscle. She told me, "I just want the doctor to say to me: 'They popped right out. It was easier than I had thought it would be.'" After she had her surgery, she said that the doctor had told her that the fibroids had come right out. He used her exact wording. Everything had been better than he had thought it could be."

Other PRISMS emphasized that people are responsible for their own healing. Energy workers can't force a healing to occur; however they can guide healing energy into a body and hold positive expectations. Patients must be willing to work with the healing energy.

Laurie Hays is a volunteer Chaplain at a local hospital. When I asked how she helped patients, she answered:

> "I tell them to connect with their G-d energy. I remind them that they are G-d, they are that spark, they need to turn up that pilot light. All healing is internal healing. Doctors may cut and stitch us, but people do the internal healing. If it is a broken bone, see the health, claim it, own it. It is yours! I pray for everyone I have ever seen or met. One lady was suicidal and was killing herself by not eating. I always ask what people want to pray for; I don't assume. She said, 'I want to die.' It was the only time when I circumvented what she wanted. I prayed that she may know how precious her vessel was and what a wonderful opportunity it was to live in this vessel. I recognized that only she could represent G-d as her expression and I told her that she was not here by mistake. G-d had not forgotten her.
>
> "I went to see her about four days later and she looked like a different person! She looked like life had been pumped into her. A few days after that, she was doing even better. It felt good to be a small part of her healing."

Delphina Nova echoed the idea that all healing must come from the patient. She sees herself as someone who gives people a jump-start. When someone comes to her for healing, she reminds them that the healing is within them and that she is there only to assist them on their healing journey. She added:

> "When people come for a healing, it doesn't mean that they are going to get physically better immediately. They want a magical cure. A healing means that we are going to get to the core of the issue and the effects of healing may come up after the session. Toxins may be released. It may also be that six months later they find out that they are dying. Coming to a spiritual healer doesn't always means that people are going to get better physically; that's also true for medical doctors. We think that 'getting better' means staying on this Earth because we are attached to this Earth plane. Getting better can mean that someone has finally learned their lessons and that they are done here and have graduated. They can move on. No one really knows when it is their time to go home. Spiritual healers can help someone in their process, but what if that person isn't supposed to be here anymore?"

Ah.

Chapter 16 - Animal Communication

In my life I have had many pets who I have loved, loved, loved. I have had two dogs keeping me company as I write. In my own way, I communicate with my dogs and they communicate with me. If the truth were known, you would see that my dogs have trained me well. They clearly communicate when they think it is snack time by standing in front of the pantry. I get the message and I oblige – treats all around! But what if I needed more information than what kind of snacks they liked? What if I needed to know if they felt well or if they were happy? Is there a way to communicate with animals?

Can psychics communicate with animals?

Of the twenty-six people interviewed for this Project, nineteen communicated with animals, four did not communicate with animals, and three did not discuss animal communication. Several of the psychics said that they communicated with their own animals, but had not tried communicating with other people's animals.

The PRISMS who communicate with animals can understand what the animal is thinking and can send messages to the animal. They say that animal spirits sometimes show up during readings and that the psychics can convey messages from the animals to the clients. This skill is being fine-tuned by one psychic who specializes in animal communication.

How does animal communication work?

Animals communicate telepathically in images. One psychic uses her third eye to send images to an animal and she can tell by the way that the animal responds that the animal has received the image.

Erik Assman mentioned that communicating with animals is soft and gentle. They don't have lives in their heads. They are "cleaner." They can be easier to read than humans because people sometimes have static in their heads. Erik has an empathic connection and feels what the animals feel. He finds that mammals and birds are very interesting. He especially enjoys communicating with grey squirrels and racoons. At one point, he made friends with racoons and they would sit outside and gossip.

Richard Schickel also said that he communicates with animals. Sometimes he talks to animals when they are under stress. For example, he has spoken with pets whose owners are sick. When the animals know the owners are sick, they worry about who is going to take care of them. It is self-based: "What about me? Who is going to feed me? Where am I going to live?" He explained that animals understand when he tells them the plan for their future. However, many people don't realize that they are sick so there is no plan. The animals can sniff out cancer so they may know about illness before the humans know. Animals don't like change. Richard added that animals may be a lower life form, but they are still able to love and to have fear.

Some clients ask PRISMS about specific problems which they are having with a pet. For example, the animal pees in the house or barks too much. Beth Hays explained that she can try to help an animal change its behavior, but if that animal refuses to work on the issue, that is where it ends. She can't force the animal to do something it doesn't want to do. She communicates with animals on an etheric level. She feels that animals are much better at living authentic lives than people. They easily adjust to her asking to communicate with them; however, they have their own personalities and if they don't want to interact, she can't make them interact.

Several psychics mentioned that cats protect them. In most cases, these are living cats, but one person told me that when she does readings, she has unseen lions by her side protecting her. Another psychic astral travels with her cats. Some psychics pray with their animals and other psychics do Reiki and energy clearings on animals.

One Intuitive commented that he had helped a friend's pet transition when the pet had to be euthanized. He heard from the pet that it was okay and that the pet understood what the person was trying to do. This person saw the spirit leave the pet.

Another psychic who has never had pets told me that she talks to everything. One time she was with her husband who was dove hunting and she heard the doves crying and telling each other to watch out. She couldn't go hunting again.

What about animal communication as a specialty?

There are many good Animal Communicators. I spoke with one, Kat Riegel, and she explained her method of animal communication. Of course, other Animal Communicators may have different working styles. Some of the information from Kat has been presented in pieces in previous chapters. Here, it is pulled together as a single psychic's story.

Kat Riegel helps people and their animals have better communication. Many people come to her because they are having a problem with their pet and they are not sure what is happening. By looking at a photograph of the animal, Kat can ask the animal what is going on and relay that information to the person. She thinks of herself as an interpreter for the animal.

For the most part, Kat contacts the animal directly. If the animal is alive, it is easy to establish the connection. This is the best energy connection. If an animal has passed on, she goes directly to their energy. The energy of a person or animal who has passed on is very different and it makes her feel dizzy. It feels like having vertigo.

Kat noted that there is an intuitive area near her solar plexus where emotions come through. She gets a sensation, almost like her stomach is flipping, when she makes the connection with an animal. In addition, when she gets "yes" answers she feels that flip. For "no" answers, or if she is on the wrong track, there's no feeling at all. She also receives pictures in her mind. For example, if she asks a dog if he likes his food, the dog will show his food. If there is a placemat under the bowl, she will see the placemat and the bowl as well as the color and the shape of the food. Then, she will ask if they like the food or if they want something else. Sometimes they say that the food is fine and sometimes they show her something else which they would prefer to eat which they have eaten in the past.

Occasionally, Kat hears sentences. This experience is like reading a book and hearing different characters in her mind; she hears the different character voices. Or, it is as if there is a play going on in her mind with dialogue from different characters. Emotions come through. If she is on a topic an animal likes, Kat feels warm and good. If they are talking about their human, sometimes they express that they really love their human. When this happens, she feels like she is enveloped in a hug.

Mostly, she reads what is happening right now with an animal. She can also see what has happened in the past. Occasionally she receives hints about the future. An animal may tell her what they think might happen. Animals who have passed on might tell her that they think they are going to come back; that they want to come back.

Kat explained that some people have told her that they did not want a reading because they were afraid of what their animal would tell them, or tell on them. She has never had an animal tell her something about their human that the human would find embarrassing. An animal has never shared anything about their humans which the humans wouldn't share with their friends. Animals respect those boundaries.

I asked Kat if there were times when she was not able to communicate with pets and she said:

> "There are times when I can't read an animal. Sometimes an animal feels accused. For example, an animal may have had an accident in the house. This is upsetting to the humans and it is also upsetting to the animal, but the humans may not understand that. It could be that the animal asked to go out, but the human ignored the requests, or the human isn't doing something the animal needs so the animal is seeking attention.
>
> "When I can't read an animal it can be because the human has such a bad attitude towards the animal that the animal is ashamed and afraid that something will happen or that it will be given away. Animals don't want to be given away, they want to fix what is wrong. If I can't read an animal, it can be because the animal has shut down out of fear of what might happen. I try to be neutral and not accuse the animal of anything. I don't want to put them on the defensive."

I asked her how "normal" people could better communicate with their pets and she responded that people needed to really think about what they wanted to communicate. Then, they should talk aloud to the animal. When the human says it out loud and thinks the picture in their mind, the animal understands. People tell her that their dogs have totally changed behavior using this technique.

Kat provided an example illustrating the uniqueness of animal personalities:

> "One dog who I work with is a thinker. When I talk to that dog, it takes the dog 24 hours before it will change its behavior. It is as if the information has to be processed and the animal has to decide if there is going to be a compromise. The animal will wait to make sure that the human is holding up their end of the bargain. As long as the human does their part of the compromise, the animal will compromise too. Sometimes people think that they are not getting a response from their animal, but really the animal is just watching to see what happens."

Can psychics communicate with animals in their natural environment?

Several PRISMS communicate with animals in the animal's natural habitat. They communicate with hawks, doves, owls, racoons, wolves, dolphins and whales.

Gina Stanfill explained her belief in the Shamanic world where spirits live in all things. She communicates telepathically with plants, trees, and animals. She feels that her Spirit Guide in life would more likely be an animal than a human, although she has also had human and plant Spirit Guides. She understands that her house and garden keep her safe and that she has spirit beings living in her yard. Her garden has been a huge teacher.

Some psychics sit in their gardens and communicate with nature spirits and animals prior to readings. Being in nature enhances their connection.

One particular reader has spent time swimming with dolphins and whales. When swimming with them, she knows which oceans they have been in. Delphina Nova explained:

> "My energy is connected to the whale or dolphin. That dolphin is not separate from me; it is part of me. I don't see myself as separate from the animal. I am one with the dolphin. It is part of the molecular structure, the atomic energy, which the entire universe is made of. This is not something I have read about; I have known this since birth. This dolphin and I are one so I don't need to access anything to get to the dolphin. For a long time, I didn't even know this was a gift because it was so natural. Deep down, we all know that

> we are connected. The reason that we have pain in the world, we cry, we are in despair, we give money, is because we know that we are connected. It's that bond that we have with everything. How do I know that? Probably because I have done this for thousands of lifetimes. I have always known about this connection."

Delphina communicates with animals instantaneously and telepathically. Animals also come to her in dreams. After the devastating oil releases in the Gulf of Mexico in the summer of 2010, Delphina had this experience:

> "Last week [June 2010] on the new moon, at 3 a.m., I awoke to the sounds of humpback whales. I was asked to 'Listen!' In the sounding, the whales said that they were emissaries, messengers on Earth, and that they cleaned up the imbalances on Earth through *Sound.* I listened to the sound of the whales and I cried! They were crying! They were overwhelmed. They spoke for all sea life: dolphins, turtles, birds and sea creatures. I asked the whale who was speaking to me what we could do to help. The answer was, 'We need Sound. We need humans to send Healing Sound to us, to the Gulf of Mexico and to the oceans of the world.' So, I promptly organized a Sound Healing for sundown on the Summer Solstice, June 21, for all of us to send out Love and Sound from our hearts to all the whales, dolphins and sea life."

She added:

> "Dolphins tell me about changes on the planet. The dolphins which I swam with were able to tell me what was going on within myself, with my friends and family, and with the environment. They have a very ancient memory. They are close to humans and I am connected with the dolphins. As I spent more time with the dolphins, I returned to my childlike state. We were on the same wavelength, which was play. The dolphins imparted a lot of joy."

Kat, the Animal Communicator, finds it easy talk to dogs and horses. She has also spoken with iguanas, chickens, cows, parrots, owls, fish, cats and a ferret. When I asked if she had spoken with zoo animals, she remarked, "I haven't gone to any zoos because I don't know how to help an animal if I find out that the animal is not happy."

Then, I asked her about communicating with animals in the wild and she replied:

> "In a lot of ways I am in touch with them. Whales are considered the record-keepers, or librarians, of the world. Whales can tell us things from the past, present and future. They are credited with vast amounts of knowledge. Most animals are aware of other animals. They know what is going on in other places. They understand that humans are encroaching and that humans have better tools than they do: guns vs. claws. Humans don't want to understand that they have shoved animals to their limits as they have expanded and pushed them out of their homes. I would like to see better use of all of the world's resources. I think that animals are part of the world's resources. Ecological systems are important. I think we see problems in plants and animals before we see them in humans. I have tried talking with animals in the wild. For the most part, they have accepted that they are getting shoved around."

She added:

> "If I had one wish for humanity, I would wish that people could be more open-minded about things. It doesn't mean that people need to change what they do or how they act, but I would like them to be able to accept other people's ideas and think about them."

Chapter 22 has additional information on the spiritual life of animals including the PRISMS' understanding of what happens to animals after they die.

• • •

This Section of the book has explained how psychics work with invisible information sources and has shown us that there is an unseen world which operates at a higher frequency than our physical world. We understand how intuition accesses information for our personal readings. Beyond the personal information, PRISMS can also bring us broader insights about life, death, and spiritual evolution. The next Section expands our understanding of how the Universe works.

Section IV

The Wheel of Incarnation

or

Life Continues (for us and our Pets) and it Circles Back Around

Chapter 17 - Death and Dying

As humans, we struggle with ideas concerning life and death. We hope that we are making the most of our lives. We want to find out if consciousness survives death. We want to know why things happen the way that they happen and if it is possible to live happier lives. All of these issues are discussed by people working in the spiritual field. If you speak with a psychic reader, you can ask about your personal life, your place in the universe, or how the universe works. Your choice. Each psychic reader has a specialty. If you find one who speaks about the universal truths which interest you, pursue that reader. Learn and grow.

This Section contains the psychics' information and opinions regarding life and death. These insights form a mosaic: no one particular piece is crucial, but when you assemble them, you get a picture of the possibilities. In addition, very-detailed information from a channeling event by one of the psychics is included. This channeled communication came from non-physical entities who entered the psychic's body and used her voice to impart wisdom. The channeled material greatly enriches the discussion. Even if you struggle with the concept of "channeling," you may find that this event presents highly-useful insights.

What happens at the moment of death?

The psychics all agree that at the moment of death, a person's soul vacates their body. Their life force leaves their "vessel." The soul hovers above the body, connected by a silver cord, to observe what is going on prior to their transition. Sometimes there is a light or a tunnel to which the soul is drawn. Then, the silver cord is released. If the person crossed over in a peaceful way, and they were ready to cross over, they go to the Light. After that, they transform and review their life. The body is a transient thing so that the spirit can learn, experience, and grow in knowledge and understanding. The soul survives.

Several people who lived through near-death experiences (NDEs) reported that there is an immediate life evaluation, and it is determined whether or not it is the person's time to leave. If it's their time, they go to the other side. If not, they come back to Earth. Sometimes, before coming back, people are advised that they need to improve the way they live their lives.

At the time of death, many people don't immediately understand that they are dead. People are confused and rely on spirits from the other side who explain what has happened to them. Most people see deceased relatives or Spirit Guides who take their hand and help them either go over a bridge, or into the Light. People who are afraid of the Light can go over the bridge. Children, and people with Alzheimer's disease, go over the bridge. On the other side, there are family members and friends waiting to greet the deceased. The transition is easier for an elderly person who has fulfilled their desires than it is for a young person who has an unexpected death.

One psychic reported that he had witnessed someone at the moment of death and that he could see a tunnel at the end of her bed. An angel hovered at the bedside, along with the woman's deceased parents. G-d was at the other end of the tunnel. However, the woman was afraid to die. This psychic noted that people are given the time to let go. However, after a certain period of time they are advised that it is time to go. Once this woman let go, she went through the tunnel.

In our culture, the Angel of Death has been regarded as something to fear. It might actually be that this angel is specially trained to assist the person who is dying; to greet and comfort this soul.

Several psychics mentioned that our souls are tethered to our bodies by a silver cord. At the time of death, we float out of our bodies. The silver cord is severed and our souls are released from our bodies. There are a few different ideas regarding this silver cord.

Delphina Nova saw things this way:

> "There is a silver cord which connects us to this earth plane and at the moment of death, the silver cord is snapped. It's released through the fontanel in the head. That is why there is a soft spot on a baby's head. That is where the soul leaves. The silver cord snaps

> and the soul leaves through the top of the head. Many people have seen this in hospital rooms. The soul is eager to leave and happily returns home."

Jan Class further explained:

> "Our soul, or spirit, is connected to our body with a silver cord. Death occurs when the silver cord is severed. It is severed because it is that person's time according to the agreement which that person made with G-d. The spirit lifts out of the body, goes to the other side, and is greeted by loved ones and counselors who help with the transition. Some people may go through a tumultuous death and wonder what happened, so counselors are there to help them with the transition. The transition period and the recovery period take place in a beautiful garden."

Cecilia Nemmers has a different understanding of the silver cord. She thinks that the cord runs from the solar plexus to the other side. When we are ready to go, it opens up and our soul is free and able to go. Releasing the cord creates the white light. People who are waiting for us on the other side know we are coming because the soul blinks when we are ready to go.

One of the psychics interviewed for this Project channels information from a group of Spiritual Guides. Leah Taylor allows this group to enter her body and speak through her. One prominent Guide who speaks through her is named Anneo. When Anneo speaks through Leah, the wording sometimes sounds a little stilted because Anneo doesn't normally speak English. During a channeled-information session, this message about the moment of death came through:

> "Most people, when they are making their transition out of their body, will say, 'Why was I so scared of this? My whole life, why was I so terrified?' Their whole life may have been leading up to that moment of death and they were scared. Maybe they were making decisions throughout their life to help them avoid death and run away from death, but when it happened, they were not afraid. They asked, 'This is it?' This is usually the experience people have. Then, they remember. They start remembering who they were before they came to Earth and they start connecting with their relatives on the other side. More than that, they start connecting with loved ones on the other side who may not have been involved this lifetime.
>
> "From the other side, we observe that if you cross over with a clarity that you are re-taking your place inside the vast Universal Truth, that is the easiest way to pass. The

biggest struggle people tend to have when they die is to release control and to trust. It is that struggle of not wanting to leave the body when it's their time that causes a lot of the conflict and fear around the death process. This is especially true when somebody is watching someone they love going through the death process. What they are seeing is that person's struggle to surrender and to release and to join the Universal Truth. When they do, it's always, always, a sigh of relief."

Raquel Spencer provided this consistent additional perspective:

> "We are all multi-dimensional beings and we exist on many levels of existence at one time. This physical reality is just one dimension. When a person dies, it is just a small portion of them which dies. It is like a drop of water in a glass."

What do the psychics' near-death experiences tell us? What did they actually experience?

Seven of the twenty-six people I interviewed have had at least one near-death experience (NDE). Another person described an NDE, but called it "astral planing." This person told me that she had gone to Heaven during a seizure and was told to go back; it wasn't her time. Some psychics had NDEs complete with the tunnel, the Light and the choice to stay or to go. Other people were clinically dead and were revived, with no memory of the event. Although some of these stories have already been included in other chapters, they are worth repeating to fully answer this question. These are some of the things which happened during near-death experiences:

☼ When I was giving birth, my blood pressure dropped and I was in the blackness. Most people talk about seeing a light. I was in the tunnel and it was black. I was conscious. That was when I was about 21 years old. After that, [intuitive] things really started happening. *(Cynthia Rae)*

☼ When I was a teenager, I had a near-fatal asthma attack and I saw my grandfather, several angels and a group of people. I was out of my body and I could see the doctors and nurses, as well as my parents. They were frantic. I was dying and it was nice to be out of my body and to feel no pain. I was very light-weight. I was looking at all of these people and wondering why it was taking so long to die; I was ready to go. I heard them say, "We just want to make sure you really want to do this." Then I heard my mother bawling and I looked down at her and I said I couldn't go. I was only 16. I told them that I had to stay and immediately, as soon as I said it, I was back in my body. It was extremely painful! No wonder babies cry when they are being born. If their souls are coming in while they are being born, it hurts! *(Jan Class)*

☼ I had a car accident and when I walked through the Light, I had a life/death experience. Walking through the Light was like trying to stare into the sun. When I walked through that Light I met a woman who said, "Come walk with me." I remember the beginning of the experience and I remember the end, I don't remember anything in between. In the beginning of the experience, she told me I was okay, I was fine. There was a beautiful, peaceful brook. At the end, I remember there were a lot of people I knew and it looked like we were in ancient Greece, although I knew we weren't actually in Greece. There were pillars for the house, but no ceiling. There were animals everywhere, including dogs and horses. I have a gift with cats and I know that they are my protectors. I know that I have lion cats who sometimes sit around me, but are not always here. I knew people on the other side, but I couldn't tell you who they were. At the end of the experience, she told me it was not my time and that I had to make a choice. I could either stay or go back. She told me that I had not yet done my greatest work. I asked about the guy I had been with in the accident and about his children who had also been in the accident. As soon as I thought about them, whoosh!, I was out of there and I was waking up. *(Rhonda Harford)*

☼ I don't have any recollection of what happened. I did not have an NDE or go into the Light. My parents told me that on several occasions I sat straight up in the bed and spoke to them in "non-language." It was a language not of this world. Some people might call it "speaking in tongues." It scared my parents. I was pronounced dead three times and I came back three times. *(Raquel Spencer)*

Marta Taylor has had four NDEs. She observed:

"I remember waking up after one event and thinking, 'Huh? I was on the Ponderosa Ranch from Bonanza.' That was weird. I never saw any white lights or remember anything from being so close to death. My psychic daughter said that I appeared to her and I apologized for not being able to get back into my body. She saw me psychically. She told me to do what I had to do, but that she was not yet ready to let me go. She encouraged me to get back in my body. I could have been dead and I wouldn't have known it. Nothing happened to me. I didn't see anybody. But every time I came out of an anesthetic or an intubation, I was immediately conscious. I wasn't in a dream state, I was immediately aware of what was going on. I was also aware that I had no memory of what went on while I was out of it, or that nothing had happened. That was a real change for me. I believed in the white light, but I never saw it. I don't have a clue what happens. I have no fear of dying. I've been there and it didn't hurt.

"In some ways I think that people get what they expect when they die. For example, seeing G-d, or ending up on the Ponderosa Ranch!"

Richard Schickel has had three NDEs and described two of them this way:

"The first time was when I was five years old and had an out-of-body experience. I was in a children's ward at the Cook County Contagious Disease Hospital. Because I was contagious, I was in a ward where the children had been taken away from their parents. I could see myself laying in my bed while I was floating up by the ceiling. A silver cord was attached to the base of my spine. A lot of children were dying and I could see myself just laying there. I remember a large white presence off to my right and then I was told that I could float around for a while, but that I had to go back to the body on the bed.

"When I was 12 or 13 years old, I nearly drowned on a rafting trip. I was caught in a hole under a rock under the water. That was the first time I saw my life flashing before me; like a wide-screen movie. It was scary. Then I felt them grab my ass and push me up. There have been three or four times when I could have died, but I just didn't die. People have 'exit points' throughout their lives when they can die, but they don't die because it is just not their time.

"After the three near-death experiences I have had, I realize it is just a natural thing. Nothing to be afraid of. You are just afraid for the people who are left and you worry about how they will react. It's a win-win situation for the dead person."

Delphina Nova has had six NDEs. I asked her why she thought she had experienced so many of these events and she replied, "Each time . . . it's almost like I'm asking, 'Am I done here yet?' I am no longer afraid of death at all."

She added:

"After having these NDEs, I am ready to share these experiences to help people remember that they are not their bodies. So many of us are attached to our material things, our jobs, who we think we are. For me, I've gone through certain situations in my life to be able to help others.

"So now I have said 'Yes' to my life. I had been reluctant to say 'Yes.' Have you heard the story about the reluctant messiah? It's like asking, 'Can't you find someone else?' I wonder if I have had these experiences so that they can keep asking, 'Are you going to say 'Yes' now?' When I was little, I knew why I was here. Then I was experiencing my life and thinking that I wasn't old enough yet to say, 'Yes.' I thought, 'No one is going to believe me; I don't have the credentials.' Now, I am coming from a place of love. Three of my dear friends passed away in the last two years. We had always thought that we would be here together. It keeps reminding me that I need to get this work done. I need to do this interview. I need to publish my book. Earthly time is limited. There is no such thing as time, but we have gone through many, many experiences in our lifetimes which need to be shared with people."

In addition to her six NDEs, Delphina has also had a Shamanic Death Experience. What is a Shamanic Death Experience? Delphina explained:

"It is an experience where you are in the body and who you think you are, dies. Your ego personality fragments. You see yourself completely shattered. You disappear as if you don't exist at all; there is an elimination of the ego. When you come back, you need to bring the personality back in so you can function on Earth, but you have a new understanding that you are pure soul and that this is a temporary body. I know, 100%, who I am. I am not my body. It all had to disappear so that I could come back and help people with healing and Shamanic work. I needed to remember that I am more than my body. In order for me to help people who are in life and death situations, I had to be able to go to the other side and come back. It is part of my training."

Does dying hurt?

I often heard from people who had been through near-death experiences that dying didn't hurt, it was coming back into their body which hurt. When they died, they felt light-weight and extremely peaceful. Coming back into their dense bodies, which had been ill or in accidents, was very painful.

Many of the psychics commented that while they were comfortable with the idea of being dead, the process of dying could be harrowing. No one wanted to have a difficult death. They were concerned that the circumstances of their death might be painful or frightening. No one wanted to be in a car accident, a fire, or any other unpleasant situation. However, a few psychics mentioned that in the case of a traumatic or violent death, the soul would be whisked from the body, greeted by Spirit Guides who acted as counselors, and escorted to a beautiful place where healing could begin. There would be no suffering.

Do we have a choice when to leave?

Several psychics mentioned that we have some choice in how and when we die. There are a few "exit points" during out lives when we can choose either to leave or to stay. One psychic mentioned that people are not supposed to be trapped in a collapsing body. People are supposed to have a hand in when they leave and be able to leave consciously. NDEs are often exit points.

Can psychics help people who are dying?

In some cases, psychics can see a person's life force diminishing. They can see that death is imminent. They often suggest that people make amends, if necessary, and get their affairs in order.

Cecilia Nemmers works as a home health care provider. Her job is to take care of the elderly. She works especially hard to ensure that people who are near death are prepared. This is her story:

> "When I work with people who are depressed or very ill, I may ask them, 'Do you want to live, or do you want to die?' I only ask the people who think that I know what the doctor has already told them. I let them know that they don't have to die from this if that's not what they want. I ask people who are young enough to have a life after they recover.
>
> "Some people say, 'Yes, I want to get well,' and some people say, 'I think I'm making my peace.' Whichever answer I get, I help them do whatever they want to do. There was a 50 year old who had a stroke and I thought that hypnotherapy could help her. It took a week for her to decide that she wanted to try hypnotherapy, but once we tried it, she got better. She had to make the choice. Until they make the choice, I can't help them; my hands are tied, because it's their free will.
>
> "I give them basic physical care while they are deciding, then I help them with psychic healing. We talk. I find out what their belief system is; some people believe in G-d and some people don't. Some people believe that they are going to turn into cosmic dust.

Depending on their belief system, one of two things can be done if they want to get well. First, I help them take responsibility for their sickness and I help them clean any energetic blockages which they have. I sit with them and in my mind I repeat the Ho'oponopons: 'I love you, I forgive you, I'm sorry, thank you.' I say that over and over, and it changes the energy. I clear my energy system and because my energy is connected to their energy, it clears their system too. It fills people with Divine love. Second, I can go to them and clean out their aura.

"If people tell me that they are ready to go, we talk. I listen to what they think they are going to be up against over there. Sometimes they say, 'I just don't know.' So I say, 'Well I've heard . . . . ' and I tell them what I know about the other side."

Another psychic uses Reiki to help people gently cross to the other side.

Two "normal" people with whom I spoke said that while they were not psychic, they could tell when a person was going to die soon. One person said that she could tell if someone was going to die within the next three days, whether they were ill or not. Sometimes, she was able to suggest that they take certain steps in the next day or two, without letting them know what she suspected. The other person mentioned that he had looked at someone and was puzzled that he could not see an aura. The aura-less person died the following day.

How can people deal with loved ones who are dying?

The answer to this question could be a whole book! However, I have just a few thoughts to share. This is part of the wise message which was channeled through Leah Taylor/Anneo:

"If any of you has had somebody who is standing on the brink between life and death and you love them and you don't know what to do, you don't know how to bless this situation to make the passage easier for them because it so painful for you, the best thing you can do is to surround them with Light. Have your tears for a day or two. Let yourself feel that sadness, feel that grief that they are leaving, but try to give them the space to do what they need to do.

"When we are sad and we are around somebody who is between the worlds, our sadness gives them a situation where they are going to need to come back and comfort the people they love. It is important to let people go. We know that. We all know that. I am sure you hear that in the spiritual world, in the metaphysical community, that you release people when they are ready to go and when they need to go. But a lot of times we can't practice that because the sadness comes in and, when our faith is tested at that point, we forget some of the metaphysical principles that we learned before: that it is okay to go. It is okay on the other side. It's okay to pass. It's human for that to seem to be one of the biggest fears that people have. You spend your lives trying to find a way to be okay with dying, but when it is close to you, you get scared and you tend to forget what you have learned. It's a situation where instead of going into the fear, instead of letting yourself go into the sadness, try to remember the principles that you have learned, the love that you have learned. Then, you can extend that love instead of extending the sadness and the grief.

"A lot of times, as someone is leaving their body and going to the other side, they will feel that they need to come back to tell everybody that it is okay on the other side. They will try to get back in their bodies. They think, 'I'm just going to tell them it's okay and then I am really going to go,' and then they end up being in the flesh again and going through more of the disease process; or the death process takes longer. We need to be able to say, 'It's okay. It is okay there. We know. You can go…' That's part of the reason why, as humans, it's so wonderful to be able to have glimpses of the other side so you can see that it is okay. These glimpses give you faith because you know from personal experience, because you remember, because you have touched that in Spirit or in meditation. Instead of forgetting all of these wonderful principles that you have learned along the way, you can go back to that moment of faith. It is important to streamline yourself and your belief system, and to release the fears that you hold onto."

Are psychics comfortable with death?

Twenty-one psychics remarked that they were comfortable with death. Only one psychic stated that she was afraid of death. She was just not ready to leave! However, several psychics mentioned that they did not look forward to the process of dying. Dying could be difficult, but once they were gone, they knew they would be fine. Beyond these shared views, there were variations in how the psychics felt about their own death and the deaths of their loved ones.

Here are a few of the PRISMS' thoughts:

☼ I am not afraid of it; I am comfortable with it. I work with a lot of people with AIDS because I am very comfortable with death. Death is just another part of the process. There is nothing to be afraid of. The only thing which dies is the physical body. The spirit, your true essence, keeps going. The spiritual part of us is in a body to have a physical experience. *(Cherie Fraine)*

☼ I am very comfortable with death. I am not afraid of death. I don't mourn when others go. I have lost friends and pets. It was sad to think I wouldn't hug them again, but I didn't feel that they were gone forever. I felt that I could have a connection again if I wanted it; I could feel their love for me. I don't grieve anyone's death. I am not scared of my own death, although I am scared of the scenario of my own death. I am not afraid of the passing or what happens afterward, I just don't want it to be scary, for example, driving my car off a cliff and into water and drowning. *(Beth Hays)*

☼ I'm not afraid of it. Sometimes, I'm quite anxious to go. Not that I want to shorten my time here, but it's like going home. I don't think I belong here. *(Cecilia Nemmers)*

☼ I am very comfortable with death; I am more afraid of life. If my philosophy holds true, I really need to be cognitive of what I am doing. If I am messing up, there will be consequences. Living life is about being human. Being human is often about self-judgment and judging others. In my deepest spiritual understanding, I know I shouldn't be doing that. *(Cynthia Rae)*

☼ I'm not afraid of death. I know that a person who dies is okay, but I would miss being able to see them in this physical world. I am an emotional person so I like to be with the people I am attached to all the time. Even though they could be with us, it's not the same as having them here. I would miss them. I'm not afraid, but I'm not ready for anyone to go. I know that people will see each other again. *(Gigi Sample)*

☼ I look forward to death; I don't look forward to dying. I know I can have enough awareness to let go when I am dying. *(Laurie Hays)*

☼ On a human level, it is always difficult to deal with the death of someone close to you, especially if it is sudden. It tugs at your emotions. The realm of them being "gone" doesn't bother me. *(Gigi Sample)*

☼ I am comfortable with it. We all have to pass away eventually. I know there is something bigger out there than we have seen before. I had a glimpse of it when I was younger so I know what to expect. It is peaceful. *(Marianne Patyk)*

☼ I don't think about it one way or the other. It is part of birth. We start dying the moment we take our first breath. It is what we do with the space in-between that counts. *(Patricia Kirkman)*

So, what comes next?

Chapter 18 - Between Lives

If we are spiritual beings in physical bodies, our souls must continue their journey after the death of the body. What do the PRISMS believe happens after death?

After dying, where do we go?

Many psychics believe that once people cross to the other side, they review how they lived their life on Earth and make plans for their next incarnation. People go through a unique flashback of all they have done. They see things that they didn't realize about their parents and the reasons why they acted like they did. They see their own errors, but they also see their positive impacts. If the person is fairly enlightened, the life review doesn't take long. If they are more dense, it may take longer.

After the life review, people are able to visit with friends, relatives and pets. They can learn with teachers or explore things on the other side. They are often in a peaceful place with beautiful gardens. Colors are pure, vibrant and intense, and there are tables and cathedrals made of light.

On the other side, souls experience love and forgiveness. The only time when souls may feel sad or distressed is during the transition period after their death. There can be remorse over how they lived on Earth, especially if they injured others. People who were alcoholic, mean-spirited, or abusive may suddenly comprehend their impacts on friends and family. People who died tragically, or unexpectedly, may need a moment to regroup. In addition, souls can realize how they wasted time on Earth. When they remember what they were supposed to have accomplished, and see that they did not learn their lessons or achieve their life purpose, they may become depressed. Specially-trained Spirit Guides help these souls come to terms with their life choices. The key is to learn from their mistakes, then forgive themselves.

Many PRISMS mentioned that what we believe about death while we are alive, influences our experience of the afterlife. For example, if we believe we are going somewhere beautiful, we will go somewhere beautiful. If we believe that the afterlife is a dark void, it will be a dark void. We are able to create our reality on the other side, just as we create our reality on this side.

Erik Assman believes that there are different levels and realms in reality. There are infinite possibilities as to where souls can go. After death, some people choose to remain in the "dead zone" and reflect on what happened to them in a previous life. Some people go to nicer, fluffier realms. Some people go to scary ones. Where people go is based on several criteria, including where they hope to go, their level of experience and the lessons which they have learned. If they expect to go somewhere wonderful, they will go there. However, if the soul doesn't have the Karma or capacity to live in a place that is truly love, it can't go there even if that is what is expected. These souls may stay in the "dead zone" and reincarnate in a place like Earth where there is a mixed bag of good and bad. When they return to Earth, they can learn new lessons, re-try situations and burn off old Karma [burn the negative energy which is carried from one lifetime to the next lifetime].

In his book, *born Knowing* (Hay House, CA, 2003, p. 205), John Holland (a psychic Medium) explained that there are different levels in the spirit world. He wrote:

> "Every lesson and deed here determines what level you'll go to when you leave this physical world. You're incarnated into a physical body to assist you in your soul's growth, which is why it's so important to try to be the best you can be while you're here. You should continually strive to be compassionate and kind, and give assistance and love to others. This will always increase your rate of vibration. And when it's your time to pass, your spirit will gravitate to its rightful level."

Souls gravitate towards the afterlife level corresponding to their level of spiritual understanding.

Gina Stanfill, explained that at the time of death, people transfer out to the Universe and choose wherever it is they want to go to rehash what they have experienced and decide what they want to do to further their development. They can choose to stay in the Universe or to be a Guide for someone else. They can choose to be reincarnated as anything – there is no limit. Death is a transition. In life, people progress from children to teenagers to adults to wives to widows. These changes are all deaths of one thing and births of another. Ultimately, human death transitions souls back to the realm of spiritual life. It is the beginning of something new.

Other psychics commented that people can go anywhere they want to go including different planets and different realms.

Here are three more answers to the question, "Where do you think the soul goes?"

> ☼ We are spiritual energy beings having a human experience and when our spiritual energy is no longer held within the body, there are a number of things which can occur. This energy can go directly into the 4th dimension where ethereal energy resides (the other side), it can stay bound to the 3rd dimension (stuck on the Earth plane due to trauma), or it can reincarnate. As with all things in life, we have a choice.
>
> In my 45 years, I have seen a lot of death, helped people cross over with Reiki, and counseled many clients about these issues. I know for a fact that there is life after death, but I believe that each person has their own idea of what death will be like for them.
>
> I had one client who grew up as an Orthodox Jew and believed that there was nothing after death. She did not come to me asking about a deceased loved one. Her worries regarded her business and other personal issues. However, towards the end of the reading, I told her about a man I kept seeing. He was dressed in traditional Orthodox clothing: dark suit, white shirt, dark shoes. His outfit looked like something he would wear to Temple. He told me personal things about his life, his likes and his dislikes. I told my client everything I could gather from him as it seemed very important to this man to let her know about him. One thing that bothered me was that I could see him plainly, but he was standing in complete darkness. For many years it bothered me that there was no color around him, no objects, nothing. This woman told me that she would ask her grandmother about the things I relayed to her. I did not hear back from her for at least three weeks. Finally, she wrote me and said that for the past three weeks she had been fighting with her religious beliefs. She had told her grandmother what I had seen and her grandmother was certain that this was her deceased husband. *(Jackie Chin)*

☼ Some people say that we go to the dark side of the moon for a transition period. I was shocked when NASA bombed the moon in October 2009. There is a lot of spiritual energy on the dark side of the moon. Our souls don't just shoot out to nowhere; our souls need a rest. The planets are all connected. It's almost like a transit station. From the moon we go to other places. There is a place called Arcturus which is supposed to be a station where souls go before they are born again. *(Delphina Nova)*

☼ People have soul groups: Gail 1 could be sitting here doing this interview and Gail 45 could be out tripping the light fantastic on the Crab Nebula, but you are all part of the same soul group. I believe that a person's existence continues after physical death. I have met too many people from the other side not to know that. People have come by to say good-bye. They absolutely continue on the other side. *(To-Ree'-Nee' Wolf)*

Cherie Fraine provides a time frame for certain experiences on the other side. She believes that people spend the first 49 days reviewing the Akashic Record, which is the record of their soul. They look at what they needed to learn in life and determine whether or not they learned it. Then, they look at what the soul still needs to learn. She added that we are not physical people trying to have a spiritual experience, we are spiritual entities having a physical experience. We need to find out what the spiritual entity still needs to experience on a physical level. This information dictates where and how the soul comes back. This cycle of living, learning, dying and coming back into a body is known as reincarnation. After 49 days, entities may choose to take time off, or they may choose to come back. Once the spirit has learned everything it needs to learn, it is re-absorbed back into *that which is.*

Leah Taylor/Anneo's psychic-channeling event provided a new depth of information on where people go and what they do:

"As humans, when you pass, where you go generally depends on what your idea is, what your theology is about the other world. You have people who pass into the arms of Shiva or pass into the cosmic Wheel of Creation. There are people who pass to the energy on the other side and connect to G-d, connect to the idea of Christ, connect with the energy that they have created as part of their theology on Earth. That often happens. You will see vast areas on the other side where people with similar consciousness gather together. Theology carries over into the next world which is interesting because all theology is trying to explain the same universal truth: that there is love. Life is love. The other side is love and when you pass over you feel this amazing feeling of love and freedom.

> "Sometimes, people who are sure they are going to Hell, are sure it is going to be fire and brimstone, will take that fear with them and it will cloud their vision of being able to see the Truth of the Love there. One the other side, you are minds. Whatever the mind is feeling with that energy, it is able to create around it. That's why people with similar theologies will group together on the other side. They are all creating the same "illusion" or picture of what that Universal Force Energy is. They will draw together so that they can experience that and create that together. It's all mind. You are only limited by what you allow yourself to perceive. The real truth is that it is the same here, it's just that you also have a body here and you have things you can touch. The illusion is so solid that you forget that changing the way you perceive reality also changes your experience of reality."

Where is "the other side"?

A few of the psychics tried to explain where "the other side" is physically located. Richard Schickel looked to his Guides for an answer:

> "They say, 'It's like we are right next to you, but at a higher level.' People are at a slow physical level because of their skin and bodies. Entities are at a higher, free-er level of just spirit."

Other psychics commented there was a "veil" between worlds and that the other side was right here. One person thought that the other side was all around us, at a higher vibration and about three feet off the ground.

Do Heaven and Hell exist?

When I asked this question a few times (but not to everyone), no one seemed to think that Heaven and Hell were actual, physical places. They thought that Heaven and Hell were religious constructs, but that people could believe in them so strongly that they could actually create these illusions. This is similar to what came through during the channeling event when we were told that, "Whatever the mind is feeling with that energy, it is able to create around it."

Cecilia Nemmers commented:

> "I think people can get stuck in their belief systems. I think that Hell was created by various religions as a means to control people through fear. People are creators and people created it. But I don't believe there are devils or people trying to take your soul."

Richard Schickel surmised:

> "Heaven is like a thousand-story building. Everyone gets in unless they have killed themself, but they might be in the sub-basement, depending on how many levels they have experienced in their own life. The more lives that a person has had where he or she has done hard lessons, the higher up they would be in the building. Heaven is really whatever people want it to be; it's spiritual enlightenment; it's being one with G-d. Heaven might be a dinner table with loved ones. However, after a while, souls feel drawn to more learning. It's boring to be in perfection all the time.
>
> "At that time, souls can choose to reincarnate. If they stay on the other side, it's harder to move up the ladder because it's harder to learn lessons. It's much easier to learn lessons on Earth. The lessons are harder here, but it is easier to learn them. When a person says a prayer here, it goes out to the universal consciousness and is multiplied billions of times, so one prayer can help billions of people. On the other side, they are not able to pray in the same way. On the other side, everyone loves everyone else. It is easy to pray for people you like. On Earth, it's hard to love people you don't like. If you can pray for the people you don't like, you are doing well."

What happens to "bad" people?

There are three kinds of answers to this question:

1) People who have behaved badly go through their life review and see the areas which need improvement. Then, they design new incarnations which provide the lessons they need to learn and the opportunities they need to re-balance their Karma. These new lives may include having to experience some of the things which they did to other people so that they learn not to do them again.

2) People who are truly evil, immediately reincarnate so that have a new chance to work through their issues. They do not have the opportunity to rest on the other side.

3) Life on Earth is an illusion and every person plays a role. We need people in the "bad" roles, so that other people have the experience of reacting to these people and to the situations which they create. How could souls advance if they were not trying to overcome challenging situations?

"Bad people" have volunteered to play their evil roles in order to provide the opportunity for other souls to learn their lessons. In this case, bad people go to the other side and decide which roles they want to play in subsequent lifetimes.

What happens to people who commit suicide?

This is a very sensitive topic. Only three psychics commented on suicide so this is a limited explanation which may be colored by religious upbringing. I am including this information because it may help some people think about the implications of suicide. These are the psychics' comments, based on their personal experiences:

☼ The soul survives. In the case of suicide, a person might not be up there yet. The soul must wait until the right time to go up. If a person takes their life, it is not natural and there is a lesson to be learned between worlds. *(Shirli Millmond)*

☼ If you kill a child, molest a child, or commit suicide, you are coming right back as a brand-new baby. You might be deformed or have something wrong with you. If you commit suicide because you want to leave this Earth plane, you are coming right back. Then, you can work your way through it; you can heal yourself. *(Rhonda Harford)*

☼ Sometimes people who are suicidal come for readings. I explain to them that it is wrong to commit suicide. G-d put them here and G-d will take them back when it is their time.

On the other hand, people sometimes ask to connect to someone who has died and I can't connect to that person. If that person killed himself, I can't connect to him. I just feel a dark shadow next to the client. The person remains here. They will still be in every situation they would have been in if they were alive, but they won't be able to affect the situation for good or bad. If they see their child is going to step in front of a truck, they won't be able to stop it. Normally, people are surrounded by loved ones who have passed who may be able to give them advice like, "Don't go to 4th Avenue today," and people can feel the warning. People who have killed themselves can't do that for others. People who have committed suicide have to stay here, feel helpless, and learn from their mistakes so that they won't kill themself again in another life. People remain here on Earth until the time they would have died if they had lived the normal life span G-d had intended. Then, they go to Heaven. *(Richard Schickel)*

Because so few psychics commented on suicide, and this is an important topic, I am including thoughts on suicide from two books written by psychic Mediums.

In 2008, Concetta Bertoldi wrote a book entitled, *Do Dead People Watch you Shower?* (Harper Collins, NY, p. 49). In this book, she provided her understanding of what happens to people who have committed suicide. She believes that the other side is filled with justice, forgiveness and healing. Spirit Guides help the individual who has committed suicide to forgive and heal himself. It is the spirit who killed himself who must be able to forgive himself. However, this isn't easy because the spirit is aware that it has done something wrong. The person has lost the opportunity to balance that life's Karma and has created additional Karma which will need to be re-balanced in another lifetime. She felt that people who committed suicide would be forgiven by G-d, but would have to struggle to forgive themselves.

In his book, *born Knowing* (Hay House, CA, 2003, p. 208), John Holland explains that there is no running from problems. Since there's no real death, there's no escape from dilemmas and issues. He has a very different kind of feeling when communicating with people who have committed suicide. They are usually full of regret because they can see how those left behind were affected. On the other side, they begin to understand the differences they could have made in their own lives, as well as the lives of others. When these spirits communicate with John, they rarely want to talk about how they passed and they don't communicate with him for long. He believes that these spirits are going through a process of healing and need all of their energy to work on themselves. He suggests that people pray for those who have taken their own lives so that they can be assisted in the healing process.

What do people do between lives?

When a person dies, their soul leaves their body, yet the soul lives on. One of the psychics commented that life after death can be very similar to life on Earth, but that it is heightened. Whatever we have here, they have there. There is beautiful scenery with intense color.

Most of the psychics remarked that we don't have physical bodies on the other side, we have ethereal bodies. We are energy. We can do things with our minds and our energy. It's a thought world where people communicate telepathically. There is no time, and space is different. People don't take up as much space as they do on Earth.

Jan Class provided this description of the other side:

> "Everyone has a job. There is no eating or sleeping, unless you want to, but you figure out that you don't need to eat or sleep. People are busy doing pretty much what they were doing here. The other side is just like Earth. The landscape is very similar and you can learn how to play the piano or sing, or you can attend lectures. People do research and begin planning their next life. You can even go to a party. You can be a teacher or a librarian. You can take care of animals or help people who are transitioning."

In addition, people who were in tough situations here, may still have to work through those problems on the other side.

Right now is a busy time for both sides because we are all working toward the same goal: having the people on Earth ascend to new dimensions. Many souls want to go to the other side because they feel that they can help from that side. Other souls are clamoring to be born so that they can have an up-front seat for the coming changes on Earth.

Do the psychics remember what they did between lives?

Several of the psychics remember the meetings which had on the other side where they planned this life and developed contracts for this incarnation. (Additional information on contracts can be found in the chapters on "Reincarnation" and "Life on Earth.")

Cecilia Nemmers had this more-personal memory:

> "I have memories from before I was born. I was waiting to jump. It was a cloud embankment of some kind and I was talking to my sister. We were really good friends on the other side. I said, 'See you in a little bit,' and she said, 'Okay.' I was only 15 months old when she was born, and it felt really good to see her again. We were close until my Mom died; we haven't been as close since then. We will be close again on the other side."

Do our personalities change on the other side?

According to the psychics, people's basic personalities don't change much on the other side. People are still people and they retain their personalities and quirks. If someone had a good sense of humor here, they will probably have a good sense of humor there. If they were quiet here, they may be quiet there. Personalities come through during psychic readings and that is one of the ways to recognize the spirit who is speaking. When communicating with the deceased, some Mediums take on the attributes of the person with whom they are speaking. They may begin to talk with their hands, or giggle, if those were the person's characteristics. However, our earthly personalities can be influenced by our human circumstances. People who didn't get along on this side, can love each other on the other side.

Keep in mind that people who die don't automatically turn into enlightened beings. They may see an expanded perspective, but they are still working on their lessons and may have remnants of their ego. These souls are still going through the educational process of reincarnation and integration.

Can we eat chocolate on the other side or should we just eat it now?

For all of us who have been denying ourselves chocolate to save the calories, and hoping that we can eat endless chocolate in Heaven (isn't that what Heaven *is*?), there is some bad news: none of the psychics think that we can eat chocolate when we don't have a physical body.

On the other side, we will have lighter, ethereal bodies. These etheric (energy) bodies become less and less dense the longer we are not incarnated and, if we are energy balls, food is not the same concept as it is here on Earth. One of the psychics noted that chocolate is a human type of "good."

Cherie Fraine explained:

> "I don't think there is chocolate over there. Chocolate is about a physical body having a physical experience and when you are over there, there is no physical body so who cares about the chocolate? Why would you need chocolate when you are in a place of such completeness and balance? Chocolate is about filling a need, wanting hugs and close personal contact. The body needs that, the spirit doesn't. The spirit is that."

Leah Taylor noted that when she contacts the other side, she often sees people smoking or cooking, but she thinks this is just a symbol of those things. These symbols help us to recognize who is speaking; they remind us of the person's characteristics so we can identify who is coming through.

On a brighter note, one of the psychics commented that we can do whatever we want to do on the other side. If we want to have a body, we can have a body. We can eat chocolate if we want to. It's not the physical thing; it's the sensation of eating chocolate.

Other psychics agreed that you can eat food on the other side, but it doesn't taste the same as it does on Earth. Some people really miss burgers and sandwiches, so other spirits try to please them by making food. Unfortunately, these cooks don't know how food is supposed to taste so the consumers are disappointed. That is why people come to the physical plane: to eat, have sex and enjoy sensory experiences.

Another psychic reminded me that most of us will reincarnate and the presence of chocolate depends on where we choose to go. He didn't think chocolate was available anywhere else but Earth. However, he theorized that there might be things in other realms which tasted even better.

The bottom line is "Why take chances?" Enjoy chocolate and all of the sensory pleasures while you can. Stock up now!

What is the difference between a ghost and a spirit?

A **ghost** is the essence of a person who has died, but has not yet gone through the Light and completely passed to the other side. A **spirit** is the essence which has crossed to the other side. On this side, we have "souls," on the other side, we are "spirits."

Why do ghosts stay on Earth?

Many psychics think it is possible for ghosts to remain on Earth. Some psychics think that ghosts do this by choice; they are not "stuck." Ghosts may have had strong attachments to people or places. They may be so attached to their home or business that they don't want to leave.

Or, they may not be dealing well with their actions on Earth. They may have unresolved issues which make them afraid of what might be waiting on the other side. They may be afraid of judgement or retaliation. Some ghosts may stay to try to undo the harm they caused during their lives.

In other cases, ghosts are just comfortable on the Earth plane. They don't want to go to the afterlife. Some energies are unaware that they are dead. There are angels and entities on the other side looking for these lost souls and they shine a white light, but the ghosts are so scared that they hide in the shadows and elude the light.

Another explanation for ghosts is that souls don't want to go to the other side because there is a person here who is longing for them to stay. This intense grief can hold someone back from crossing over. The ghosts don't know what will happen once they cross over and they think that they can be closer to the living person if they stay on Earth.

Cecilia Nemmers commented that ghosts are often very-religious people who don't know where they are supposed to go when they pass. They don't think they deserve to go to Hell, but they also don't think they deserve to go to Heaven. They think those are the only two choices, so they don't know what to do.

Gigi Sample was adamant that ghosts did not get lost like they did on TV shows. Energies hung around because they had messages to relay or they wanted to help their loved ones, but there was no in-between world where people got stuck. They went to another realm. She felt that much of the Hollywood folklore was not correct. Her impression was that "haunted" houses were due to spirits who had crossed over and returned. Either they liked the place where they were staying or they wanted to get someone's attention.

However, April Cunningham explained that some ghosts are earthbound due to trauma. Until someone on Earth witnesses their trauma and encourages them to move on, they are held hostage by the trauma. Some traumatized ghosts might not even be aware that they are dead. They need to be told about their situation and encouraged to cross to the other side.

And, some spirits who have crossed return to Earth because they miss it and they miss their loved ones. The grieving is on both sides. Even though they are in a positive atmosphere and they don't feel the pain of, "I don't know how I'm going to live without you," when they come back and re-connect with their loved ones, they realize how much they miss them and they want to hang around.

Do psychics see ghosts and spirits?

Many of the psychics see ghosts and spirits. In some cases, this was the first clue that they were psychic; that they were different from other people.

As a young woman, Cecilia Nemmers moved in with a family who lived in a mortuary. She recalled that there were bodies laid out in caskets in the living room. Spirits would walk up, look at the bodies, and walk away. It was her first experience with the deceased checking themselves out in the casket.

Marianne Patyk, a Medium, had this experience as a child:

> "My grandfather came to me after he had passed away. That was my first experience with the other side. I was about 8 years old when he came and sat on the corner of my bed. I still remember it. I had a conversation with him. This was about three days after he had passed away. He came and sat on the corner of my bed and I felt him sit down. I opened my eyes and it was my grandfather. In fact, all of my relatives have come to visit me after they have passed. It's like having a normal conversation with them."

Denise Singerline, who has seen ghosts since childhood, recollected:

> "When my ex-husband's brother Vinnie died, I woke up at about 5:30 a.m. and felt him standing next to my bed. He had died in a trailer fire that night, but I hadn't yet heard about it. I felt someone standing next to me all night. The phone rang around 7 a.m. and they told me that Vinnie had died. His ghost stayed in our house for about two weeks and I would see him standing around and walking down the hallway. At night, he would stand next to my bed and want me to astral travel with him. He talked to me. I started praying that he would go into the Light and after about two weeks, that is what he did."

Sometimes, spirits who have crossed over are able to help us through difficult times. Here is an example from Denise:

> "When I was going through my divorce, my ex-husband and I lived on opposite sides of our house for a year until the divorce went through. His whole family lived in town, and I didn't have any family in the area so I asked my grandfather who had passed away if he could come down and help me. Immediately, I felt him standing next to me. The next day, a videographer came over and told me that, in addition to photography, he did psychic readings. He asked if I wanted a reading. He told me that my grandfather was there and that he was protecting me with shields all around my body.
>
> "At times, I could feel my grandfather standing next to my bed. When I went to my car, he would come with me and sit down next to me. I could actually see the seat sink down.
>
> "After the divorce, when I was settled, I thanked my grandfather for helping me and I told him that my brother Tom had cancer and I asked that he go help my brother. After that I didn't feel him around any more. About a month later, I went to one of my

> spiritual teachers for a reading and I asked if she saw my grandfather. She didn't know if he was alive or dead but she responded, 'Oh yes. He's in Heaven. He was helping you for a while, through your divorce, but now he is helping your brother.'"

Another psychic, Jackie Chin, has welcomed ghosts into her family. She shared:

> "Wherever we have lived, my husband and I have had members of the spirit world follow us around. Mainly they are children who are lost, confused or just comfortable around us because we acknowledge them. One such child is named Rachel. She came into our lives about four years ago and appeared to our children and, occasionally, to my husband. Rachel had a pet cat who we called 'Ditto.' We called her cat Ditto because we have a black cat that looks exactly like Ditto. Ditto liked to show himself to me and, many times, I actually tripped over him. Ditto liked to run into walls. One evening our cat, Witche, saw Ditto and chased him smack into the wall. A few weeks ago, Rachel decided that it was her time to go to the other side and be with her loved ones. It is odd to miss someone who we never had Earthly contact with, but we miss her just the same.
>
> "Not all spirits who end up in our home are welcome. There have been times within this past year when my children have run screaming into my room crying about the scary ghosts on the wall or telling me about something which was presenting itself in a horrible manner. When this happens, I go into full warrior mode, grab the holy water, holy oil and sage, and blast the thing back to where it came from. Just like people on the Earth plane, there are spirits who are benevolent and there are those who are demonic. If you find that you are experiencing any sort of paranormal event, and you are not capable of dealing with it on your own, get an expert."

Other psychics see spirits in a different way. When I asked April Cunningham, a California Medium, what she saw, she explained:

> "There are layers. It's like layers of spirit. It is almost dimensional. Sometimes, there will be a little round thing which is a confirmation of someone around you. This little round thing will come up close and I can see within that dimension."

April also sees full-size spirits in their earthly attire. However, she doesn't think that is necessary. It is theatrical. She commented:

> "When people come in with the hair and the hat and the bow tie, that is all theatrics for whatever people are comfortable with. I see that [version] if I'm with people and that is what they are comfortable with. I see their grandpa or smell the tobacco. It's comfortable for them. But I would know who it is anyway. In order to make them feel comfortable, and for that confirmation, they will show me what he looked like at that time. But he could also come in as anything and it would still be that same energy. It could be several lifetimes back."

When she is alone, April often sees movement, flashes of light and beautiful colors.

Is it frightening to see a ghost?

Denise Singerline remarked that seeing ghosts can be scary because it is so unexpected. Most of the time there isn't anything to be afraid of, but it is surprising to wake up and find ghosts looking at her. Occasionally, there are scarey-looking ghosts, but most psychics are able to limit what they see and they choose not to see such frightening sights.

The psychic who, as a child, saw her grandfather wasn't frightened at all. She said it was just like seeing him in real life. However, she had a different kind of experience when, as an adult, she was unknowingly led to a room where a gruesome murder had taken place. She became physically ill and remained sick for several hours. It wasn't until the person who had brought her to the room explained that there had been a murder that things began to make sense. She is empathic and empathic psychics can find it very difficult to deal with crime scenes.

What happens when psychics visit hospitals?

A couple of the Mediums mentioned that they need to close down their psychic abilities in certain situations, such as visiting hospitals. There can be spirits in hospitals who are waiting for anyone who can get a message to their loved ones. One Medium mentioned that there are spirits all over the grocery store who want to communicate with her. She doesn't know them. She had to learn to close her third eye, to turn it off, in order to function in public.

Can psychics contact our loved ones who have crossed to the other side?

If our loved ones still exist on the other side, can we contact them? The psychics' answer is, "Yes." Psychic Mediums contact our loved ones directly (all Mediums are psychics, but not all psychics are Mediums).

Marianne Patyk explained how this worked for her:

> "I talk to loved ones. That is my specialty. When a person sits down, I ask them what they want to know or if they have someone specific that they want to talk to who has crossed over. If there is someone who they want to talk to, I ask for that person's name. Then, I take a quiet moment to see if I can contact that person."

Marianne added that she had always had psychic abilities, but in her 40s she had experienced a great trauma which had brought forward her abilities as a Medium. She started hearing things she had never heard before. She could smell aromas which reminded her of deceased relatives. She realized that she was communicating clearly with people who had crossed over.

Another Medium, Jan Class, explained:

> "I connect with the Holy Spirit and I can connect with people who have passed on. I call myself a 'Holy Spirit Communicator.' We talk to angels, masters [Spirit Guides], and people who have passed on, and they like to talk to us!"

In addition to Mediums, psychics with other specialties often receive messages from the deceased during readings. It's not that these psychics put out a call to any particular person, it's just that the spirits who know the client show up and become a part of the experience. These psychics pointed out that when they did readings, they tapped into a source of information which provided whatever advice or validation the client needed to hear. If the client needed to hear from someone who had passed on, that message would come through during the reading.

And, sometimes, random spirits show up because they see an opening to get their messages through to people on this side.

Kat Riegel commented that the energy of a deceased person or animal was very different from a live person or animal. This connection made her feel off-balance; like she had vertigo. She could tell that she had connected with someone who had passed on when she had that feeling.

As much as people enjoy reconnecting with their loved ones, they should remember that people who have crossed over may not be any wiser than the people who remain on Earth. Just because someone on the other side has an expanded perspective doesn't mean that clients should take their advice without thinking about it. These spirits are still working on their own enlightenment.

In addition, talking to a Medium is not a cure for bereavement. When someone passes, the people left behind must go through all the stages of grief and deal with their loss. They may need to attend a support group or see a therapist. Some Mediums think that people shouldn't try to make a psychic connection until they have dealt with their grief. After going through the bereavement process, Mediums can confirm that our loved ones live on and can assist with healing.

Even psychics can be awestruck by their ability to see spirits and to relay messages from deceased people. They are often surprised that these spirits continue to be so closely involved with their loved ones on Earth. Mainly, they are pleasantly surprised when they can clearly see and hear the deceased.

The ability to contact people who have crossed over has been the subject of much scientific study and debate. Evidence is mounting that consciousness survives death.

Chapter 19 - Reincarnation

According to the PRISMS, our souls survive physical death and we go to other side to integrate all that we have learned on Earth. Then what happens?

Is reincarnation generally accepted?

Everyone I interviewed believed in (and often remembers experiencing) reincarnation on Earth. They all agreed that consciousness survives death and that we can choose where and when to reincarnate. We come back into bodies to learn lessons and to further our soul's growth. Once we have learned all that we need to know, we are re-absorbed into the Universal Source of Energy.

One psychic commented that she had met too many people from the other side not to know that consciousness continues. She had also met many people on Earth who she recognized from previous lifetimes.

Here are some interesting, summarized, comments about reincarnation, from the simplest ideas to the most complex:

> ☼ I believe in reincarnation, although it may not look like what we think it will look like. We are all here learning; it's an experiential place. We came here to experience the qualities of life. When people die, they review their lives and try to decide if they received all of the information and all of the experiences which they came here to get. Then they

decide where they want to go next, where they can be of service and what they would like to experience. Consciousness is experiential. *(Raquel Spencer)*

☼ I am a firm believer in reincarnation. At the moment of death, the soul leaves the body. Who we are is what is inside, not what we look like. I am using this body right now, but I firmly believe I will come back and use a different body next time. I can't believe that the soul would be wasted, thrown out and not used again. *(Nancy)*

☼ We evolve during each lifetime. We are here to experience things and the sooner we experience them, the faster we can move to the next thing we get to experience. *(Gina Stanfill)*

☼ In this incarnation, I came to help. I have the belief that I have never died. I don't look at past lifetimes as past lifetimes; there is a continuum. The "I" in me has never died. For me, there is no sense of time. Of course there have been historical changes on the planet and evolutionary changes. However, I feel that if I have done healing work in the past, I still have that ability. That hasn't changed. I have done this for thousands of lifetimes. I don't see a separation between lifetimes. *(Delphina Nova)*

☼ This lifetime we are having a "past-life teacher reunion." Everyone who has been a healer, a teacher or a messenger in another lifetime is here this time. *(Gigi Sample)*

☼ I believe in reincarnation, but not the way that some people believe in it. I do not believe that Bob becomes Carol in another life. It's not a one-to-one correlation. You will die and your spirit will come up here and may have three reincarnations to work on your three issues, or you may have one life to work on the three issues. *(Jeff Sonnenburg)*

☼ I am starting to understand that there were people who lived a long time ago, and that I might feel that they were who I was in former lifetimes. For example, I may feel that I was a specific person such as Joan of Arc, or Jesus; I connect with that energy. But other people might also think they were Joan of Arc, or Jesus. This may be possible. I am coming to understand how time really does not exist. Time is the platform that we choose for living our lives so that we can separate one instance from another.

As time goes on, consciousness is forever expanding. That's why we keep coming forth: because we keep expanding. Whether it is through technology or the concept of metaphysics, we are constantly expanding in all ways, all the time. So maybe the energy that was Jesus two thousand years ago has split into 5000 different people who all feel like they were Jesus, because they were. Jesus' consciousness has expanded into a space which can embody 5000 different conciousnesses. A single consciousness can expand, break off, and form new conciousnesses. *(Beth Hays)*

☼ I told my husband that I would never have picked this life. Up until my husband, life was terrible. He took me on a past-life regression and I ended up between lives. It felt like some guy was pointing to a small girl and I saw her life unfold. I knew she wouldn't survive that life if she didn't have someone strong in her and I said, "Put me in." My essence went in to help that little girl survive what she was going to go through. I felt that I could be strong enough. Then, it made sense to me. I would be compassionate enough to do that for someone else, not stupid enough to have chosen that life for myself. Some other soul might have gone into that little girl, but she would not have survived. *(Laurie Hays)*

☼ People can choose how often they want to reincarnate and they can remain on the other side for a long time. In my last lifetime, I was a German SS guard in World War II and I also worked with the Underground. That was only 12 years before I was born. A lot of people who are more aware were here during that time because it was such a horrendous time. A lot of us wanted to be here because there were a lot of lessons to be learned. It was a booming market for learning lessons! *(Richard Schickel)*

☼ I absolutely believe in reincarnation. Do I think it is as straightforward and linear as we think? Not always. But I have met relatives from other existences. I have met family members from past lives. One of the most challenging situations was with my high school Algebra teacher. Whenever I stood near her, a place between my 4th and 5th ribs used to hurt. I was terrified of her even though I knew she was a wonderful woman. Her body had not changed in eons and I recognized exactly who she was. I tried not to be alone with her. However, one day we had an Algebra test and I was the last one to finish so I was stuck alone in the room with her. She said to me, "I know you, don't I?" I said, "Yes." She told me that whenever she stood near me, her ribs hurt. I apologized to her and we both knew that we had been together in Mesopotamia. We were able to discuss the situation.

This is what had happened in Mesopotamia: She had been a dancing girl, a courtesan. I had been a stupid thug-boy. She knew a merchant who had received a caché of jewels and I told her to knock him out and steal the jewels so we could run away together. So she stole the jewels and we ran away, but because I wasn't that bright, we pitched a tent right outside the city. The merchant figured out what had happened and that night the merchant's henchman came for us in our tent. My first response was to run so I took off into the night. Then, I remembered that she was still in the tent so I ran back, but she had been stabbed. I felt terrible. Apparently, there was such a big wound on my spirit that I had to bump into her as my Algebra teacher so that she could forgive me. *(To-Ree'-Nee' Wolf)*

☼ I have had many discussions with learned people regarding this subject. There are many instances of children remembering things which they did in previous lifetimes. An example of this actually occurred with one of my children. One day my 4 year old was talking to his father while he was coloring. He said, "Hey daddy, remember when we used to jump out of airplanes in the dark?" My son is named after a man who served in the Army with my husband in the 1970s, Nicodemus. My son has exhibited many of the traits that my husband's friend was well known for: he gets a particular little smile when he is going to do something he should not be doing and he has the ability to disappear quietly into the background when he doesn't want to be seen. A couple of times when he was watching military shows on TV, he asked his father about things that Nicodemus and my husband had done in the military. I know that these things happen. I am Buddhist and part of the Buddhist belief is that all things change and come back around again, but to see it in my own family was a shock. *(Jackie Chin)*

Why do people come back to Earth?

Life on Earth can be hard! People sometimes wonder why they would choose to come back to a place where their circumstances can be so difficult. Are there other, easier, places to reincarnate? The answer is that Earth provides a unique place in the universe and, if we are seeking to learn our lessons, Earth can supply all of the situations we need to keep moving forward.

The following information came through during Leah Taylor/Anneo's psychic-channeling event and speaks directly to this question:

> "Life is an adventure. Life is beautiful. Being a human being alive on this planet is one of the most beautiful things in the whole universe that any spirit could ever, ever, hope to do. It is precious and that is why you come back. These bodies are precious. You embrace each other physically. How beautiful is that? In the spirit, it doesn't work the same way. This planet is gorgeous and you can learn here.

"When there aren't challenges, when you know who you are every day, how do you really learn about yourself? When everything is easy, you don't learn about yourself. That is why you come in here to learn and grow. You get to find out who you really are and how evolved you are spiritually because you get to rise above pain, suffering, and fear. On the other side you don't necessarily get to do that. It's just whatever you create in your mind. You learn here. You learn here. And you teach here; and you share and you play and you create.

"Earth is similar to the Holideck on the TV show *Star Trek*. That is what this is.

"When you are on the Wheel of Incarnation in this reality, you go to the other side and you come right back because you learn so much. When you come back, you think you are going to do it right. It's going to be the lifetime that you always wanted. Then you get in here and you find you forget again and it's the same struggles, the same lessons and you go back to the other side and you say, 'This time I'm going to get it for sure. I'm coming back in and getting it right.' This is what they call the Wheel of Incarnation. You are just going around on the Wheel.

"Eventually, when you have graduated from here, when you have learned the lessons you need to learn, you will ascend to realms that are fantastic. Realms which are very, very different from this reality. That are nothing like this. So to think that the end all and the be all of your being is to be reincarnated here on Earth, that is not a truth. It is just a place where you are stuck right now because you feel like you need to keep coming back to get it right. A lot of amazing teachers have evolved off of that Wheel of Incarnation and have come back to help and assist people who are stuck here in that rut, to get out to the higher realities when they pass."

Another reason to come to Earth? Earth is where the action is. This is why we keep coming back. Enjoy the fun! Enjoy the food! Enjoy all of the sensual pleasures of Earth.

Chapter 20, "Life on Earth," has more-detailed information on how we learn our lessons.

Can we go to other places to reincarnate and learn our lessons?

According to the psychics, people can cross over and go to other places, other planets, other realms and other dimensions. There are many dimensions to reality and these realms are being discovered by quantum physics. Free will allows spirits to choose where they want to go. They can explore different galaxies, then decide if they would like to come back to physical form on Earth or elsewhere. If they choose to come back to Earth, spirits can learn new lessons or re-try old situations to see if they can evolve through them in a different way.

During Leah/Anneo's psychic-channeling event, the answer to this question was extremely enlightening:

> "All of you are very lucky because, being on your spiritual path, when you pass over you will have the choice to ascend to the Higher Realms and to experience realities which are very different from this one here. The way that you do that is by loving yourself, by not carrying guilt with you, by not carrying 'would have, should have, could have.' You need to release those kinds of judgements on yourself so that when you get to the other side, you are going in light and clarity and there are no unresolved issues to come back and work though (because they have been blessed). Then, when you come back it's because you choose to come in for whatever reason you want. And maybe there are other parts of the universe that you would rather explore.
>
> "The way to get off the Wheel of Incarnation is to love You. And that is You beyond the ego. The ego says that you are worthy based on things about you that could change: money, appearance, what you do, what you think. All of that stuff. The ego says that is who you are. In reality, you are something very different from that. You are Light, you are love and connecting back to that source, that higher spiritual source of You is going to make it very, very easy to pass over and to leave this reality behind. The fastest way to do it is to love yourself with no judgements. To not believe what other people tell you about you.
>
> "Other people look at you and, this is very common as humans, only see the role you are playing in their play. They are so stuck in the ego world of role playing and being a character that they only see who you are to them: the role you are playing. They see that and tell you things, and you might believe what they say about you. Then you start taking that role with you and playing it out in the world, in other places with other people and internalizing it and maybe thinking that it is who you are. That is not who you are. Who you are is incredibly wise. The souls and the beings that you came from have been around for thousands of years. They are very, very wise. They wouldn't be here without a good reason. To maximize your experience on this planet you have to release the illusion because it is easy to get lost in the illusion when you can't remember, when you don't have the memory of, your soul's history here with you on Earth."

Erik Assman provided a more-technical way of looking at where souls can travel. He explained that where we reincarnate can depend on our frequency. A person with a high vibration who thought about going to a terrible place, probably wouldn't go there. However, a person with a high vibration who wanted to come back to Earth, probably could come back to Earth. People would need even higher frequencies to go to other galaxies or realms.

To further complicate this picture, some psychics believe that souls live simultaneously in several dimensions. Souls can stay in those dimensions while experiencing human form on Earth. There is a Higher Self overseeing these voyages. PRISMS believe that people can access these experiences, they just don't know that they have that capability.

More ideas regarding simultaneous lifetimes can be found in Chapter 21, "Past Lives."

Do souls come back to Earth even after they have learned their lessons? Who are the "volunteers"?

Some souls have completed their lessons on Earth and are ready to relax on the other side or move on to other realms, but they are asked to return to Earth. They don't need to come back for their own growth, but they volunteer to return and help other people evolve to the frequency where they won't need to come back anymore.

These volunteers are also called upon to help humanity move through times of trouble. Several of the psychics told me that they were here for World War II either because the traumatic events allowed them to move quickly through their lessons or because they were asked to help humanity move forward through that difficult period.

Many souls have been asked to return during this lifetime so that they can help with the upcoming ascension. This is a particularly precious time on Earth as people strive to leave war and destruction behind and awaken to a new reality. Gigi Sample calls this the "past-life teacher reunion," suggesting that all of the teachers and healers who have been on Earth in previous incarnations are here now to help with humanity's ascension. Additional information on ascension can be found in Chapter 24, "Looking forward to 2012."

To-Ree'-Nee' Wolf explained her experience of volunteering for this lifetime:

> "I came back to be of service. I remember the conversation I had before I was born; I came back to be of service. I was not an altruistic soul. My last life was during the Holocaust and I did not survive the war. During the conversation before I was born, I stated that I did not want to do this job. At the table where everything was made of light, the Beings said, 'We need you to come back.' I refused to come back. I had a huge chunk of rest due and I said, 'Get someone else.' They replied, 'We need everybody.'
>
> "I have what's known as a 'coming back' clause. I have a series of things which will not happen to me in this lifetime. It is a list of agreements which were made before I agreed to come back and be of service.
>
> "I have updated the contract a few times during this lifetime. I was on a plane one time and we hit big turbulence. I knew that as a part of my contract the plane was not going to go down. I was able to re-assure the other passengers that everything would be fine."

What role does Karma play?

Karma is seen as a re-balancing of energy as souls learn lessons and act on what they have learned. Reincarnation on Earth provides the opportunity for souls to clear old Karma. In addition, people must continue to work on their life lessons and life purpose, so that they don't incur new, negative Karma. The psychics didn't see any conflict between Karma and traditional religion.

Here are the observations of three psychics:

> ☼ For me, Karma is experiencing things and learning lessons. If a person causes a terrible car accident and someone is really hurt and the person who caused the accident feels badly and wants to know what the other person felt, they will come back and have the accident happen to them. That is how they develop empathy and learn not to do it again. That is how I look at it. I don't look at it as building good or bad Karma, although some of that may play into it. *(Jan Class)*
>
> ☼ With Karma, people may get pissed off if they think someone is doing something to hurt them, but that second person may be balancing out what the first person did to them which the first person is not willing to acknowledge, or which occurred in a previous lifetime.

Or it could be that one person hurt a second person who hurt a third person and the third person is now hurting the first person. It all balances out, but it is not necessarily a one-to-one correlation. Spirit uses whatever it needs to balance Karma. *(Jeff Sonnenburg)*

☼ I don't see any conflict between religion and Karma balancing. Karma is used to burn off negative issues so that people can get closer to the G-d energy. A person can really only deal with one or two or three issues during each lifetime. That's why people need to have a lot of lifetimes. It's like we are rough diamonds. We need to polish one facet of our diamond, then we need to return to polish another facet of ourselves. *(Richard Schickel)*

Do we see our friends in subsequent lifetimes?

According to the psychics, we travel in groups and help each other grow. Each lifetime, the souls in our circle play different roles so that they can learn from their role while also helping the rest of their group. For example, a mother may have a daughter in one incarnation, but the next time around, the daughter is the mother and the mother is the daughter . . . or the husband . . . or the cousin . . . or the employer. This is why people often recognize souls from previous lifetimes.

Kat Riegel believes that people and animals can travel in the same group. She remarked:

"I think that energies travel in groups. There may be a dynamic where there are 10 very close people in your life. As the energies pass, they go into this holding area and wait for all 10 energies to get up there. Once all of the energies are there, they discuss their experiences and decide how they want to change things the next time. Then, the energies begin filtering back to Earth one at a time in their new roles. They work with each other again when they come back to Earth. The energies travel in 'packs.' While they are up there, they just sit and wait for the others to show up."

Denise Singerline took things a step further commenting that people can be part of the same "soul family," which means that they came from the same egg. They split off and came here together to help each other. She remembers her brother from a past life when she was his mother. She and her brother tend to go through the same spiritual experiences at the same time, but in different ways. For example, they find that similar things are going on in their personal relationships at the same time.

A few words about Autism

I asked many of the psychics about autism. I had started with a personal curiosity about whether psychics could assist people with autism to better-communicate with their families. What I discovered was a few theories linking autism and reincarnation. I always find it interesting when I hear similar answers multiple times. One of theories put forth by several of the psychics had to do with these children being new to Earth and not having as much Earth experience as older souls. One psychic thought that these were spirits who agreed to incarnate and then arrived here and felt like they really didn't want to be here. They still felt close to the other side. On the other side, everything was very positive and these people might be homesick. However, she added that there were a lot of things which could be done to ground them here on Earth.

Another psychic, Leah Taylor, echoed this idea stating, "I think that there is a rash of people with autism coming in with souls from a different soul group -- a little tear between the realms. They haven't had a lot of lifetimes on Earth and the way that they articulate their bodies and use their human brains is different."

A third psychic, Gina Stanfill, thought that these children were coming in highly exposed and that our Earth realm couldn't come close to matching their world. She thought that people with autism were in a human body yet had a highly-developed psychic mind. Their communication didn't work on the same level as the rest of us because they were more internal. They used mind waves for telecommunication. She noted that autistic kids were usually "within themselves" and speculated that they had a more-evolved mind stuck in a human body.

A fourth psychic thought that people with autism were a higher level of being which we just didn't understand.

A fifth psychic reminded me that it was important to foster all the senses of a child with autism. They should be taught to use all of their gifts and their strengths. She also thought that, in some ways, they were more psychically-gifted than the rest of us; they were wired differently.

A sixth psychic, Trish Silay, thought that autistic children had brains which were very open to everything. They were getting a lot of information. She felt that these children were very gifted and that people needed to figure out how to access their information. She sensed that it was important to look at these children and see their gifts instead of their disabilities because these children could teach us things.

One woman with a special needs child believed that people had choices about how they came to Earth. She thought that people were both students and teachers. She explained that no one wanted to see starving children, disease, crime, war or people with Alzheimer's disease, and that the only explanation which made sense to her was that there was more going on than we knew. She speculated that before coming to Earth, people chose the situations which would help them, and the people around them, learn lessons. Some souls might choose specific physical conditions in order to learn and to teach.

Now that we understand that souls can choose to return to Earth to further their growth, let's hear what the PRISMS said about how we learn our lessons.

Chapter 20 - Life on Earth

We live, we die, and we can choose to live again. We are circling around on the Wheel of Incarnation. With all of our choices, why do we keep returning to Earth? How does life on Earth help us learn our lessons? What lessons are we here to learn? The psychics shared tremendous insights on soul evolution and how living on Earth keeps us moving forward.

Why are we here on Earth?

Our souls are on a journey of experience and discovery. On the other side, we don't know everything. We know the joy of being on the other side and we understand that we must continue our soul's journey until we have learned all of our lessons. On both sides, we are striving for self improvement and mastery. However, it is faster, easier and more dramatic to learn lessons on this side so we keep coming back to accelerate our learning. Leah Taylor believes that most of our building is done on this side. People can learn lessons in the soul world, but to build a true spiritual legacy, develop a talent, or refine a deep character trait, that work is best done in the flesh. Eventually, we attain mastery, go back to the other side, and return to Divine Light.

Cynthia Rae's philosophy about being here on Earth is that we come to learn lessons for our personal growth and also to provide the opportunity for "The Source of Life" (G-d) to benefit from our experiences. It's a form of connectedness. She explained:

"The Source of Life has never lived every single moment on this planet; has not lived every single moment in a different refraction, a different life, a different emotion. If you look at each of us, there are millions of different opportunities. That's why everyone is so different. If you look at Source as in the middle, and know that everyone is connected to Source, you understand that every person is allowing Source to live vicariously through them. Source can feel the emotions, can see the things we see, and can understand because of our brains. We are here to learn for ourselves and for Source. We can call the Source 'G-d,' or any other name: the Creator, the one who has the pulse on everything that is going on in the whole of existence. G-d might be the name of what is only the CEO of this space and He might have a higher somebody-else to talk to. Who knows? I don't know. I'm just doing my part.

"We are all fulfilling the contract we made with our souls before we came down here. Whether or not I am happy and joyous every single moment of the day doesn't matter. It is the human essence of what I have chosen.

"Why are we here on this Earth? To experience and grow in ways that no other soul has the opportunity to do. I think that we are very honored to be here. No other souls that we know of, not even the angels, Guides, or masters, have the opportunity to taste. They can't spit, they can't make love, they don't touch. They don't have the senses we have.

"I think that we are the honored ones. There aren't very many people on this Earth who have joy every day of their lives, who get up and skip. If they are doing that, they are not experiencing, they are not learning. All of the knowledge already exists on the other side. Here, we are learning, we are taking knowledge in. Every leaf we look at is different from another leaf. Each of us is different. We are here to experience things. We each have the opportunity to affect other people's lives and whether we do it in a positive way, or a negative way, is up to them and up to us."

Do we have contracts for each lifetime?

Several of the psychics remember negotiating contracts for this lifetime. Denise Singerline explained:

"Before we come to Earth we meet with a Council to decide what we want to learn in each lifetime. We form a contract and then we come down here. We have free will, but all of the major things in the contract are already in place. For example, the contract may state when a person is going to marry or when they are going to die but, in between, the person has free will. We come down here and when we pass, we leave our 'vehicle' behind and our spiritual body is released. Our spirit leaves and goes back to the Divine.

"After we pass, we meet with a Council which shows us all of the things which we have done with our life, the good and the bad, and asks what we have learned. Then we have a choice as to when we want to come down again to learn more."

Jan Class added:

"When you come down, you have pretty much planned your life out. When we pass on, we are very busy on the other side planning our next life. That takes a lot of work. People stick to their outline pretty closely because they have a contract with G-d. They may get off the road for a while, but they get back on the road. They may get busy sightseeing, but they get back on the road. There's leeway, but people get back to what they agreed to accomplish."

The contracts state several experiences which we agree to live through. However, we are free to choose all of the other aspects of our lives. For example, we may have a contract to experience marriage and raising a family, but we can choose whom we want to marry.

In her book, *The Lightworker's Way* (Hay House, Carlsbad, CA, 1997, p. 72), Doreen Virtue, Ph. D., provided a lovely passage about contracts and life purpose which had come to her in a meditation. She wrote:

"Before your birth, you and a spiritual council of guides created a life plan tailored to meet your material, spiritual, and karmic needs. This Divine plan has three elements: a purpose, personal growth lessons, and relationships with other people to support the overall plan.

"Your purpose is a task you are to do through your career, volunteer work, or a special project that uses your natural talents and interests to benefit humanity. Your plan's second element entails well-timed life events that teach you about love and help you to shed self-defeating personality traits. The third element involves pre-birth arrangements you made with certain people who will serve as catalysts for your purpose and personal growth. These people may function as your family members, co-workers, friends, or acquaintances. Your interactions with these people simultaneously help them to fulfill their own plan.

> "You predestined your plan as a rough outline of what your life would look like, including your purpose, significant life lessons, and relationships with particular people. Because the plan is only a rough outline, you must choose the finer details of your plan as you go through life. You are free to ignore the plan completely, but the emotional and societal consequences of this choice can be devastating."

She continued:

> "In our previous incarnations, many of us didn't fulfill our purposes. During our post-death life reviews, we felt ashamed that fears and material desires thwarted our plan. This lifetime, we swear to ourselves before birth, we won't forget our purpose. The trouble is, we design the Divine plan in a 'true self' state of peaceful mindfulness. When we experience ego-based fear during our human lifetime, we can't remember why we came here. If we do remember, fears keep us from ever starting our plan."

According to Dr. Virtue, people who procrastinate or forget their plans, feel a deep, low-level anxiety. They unconsciously know that another painful life review awaits them if they let themselves down again. They feel depressed, as if they're forgetting to do something important. They are forgetting to fulfill their contract.

Earth was created with everything we need to create ourselves as unique human beings. We have a Divine plan and we have free will. We use the free will to live our lives. However, if we don't use our free will to follow our Divine plan, we create negative Karma which has to be resolved in future lifetimes.

Why do things happen in our lives the way that they do?

There are many answers to this question! Here are a few:

Our soul doesn't know everything and is trying to learn through experiences on Earth. We create our soul's blueprint before we come to Earth so that we can set up the conditions which allow us to live whatever experiences we need in order to learn our lessons. Until we understand our lessons, we are exposed to them over and over again.

We set up our childhood events, and select the families we are born into, so that we can create the challenges which allow us to learn our lessons. Not realizing that we pre-arranged these conditions, we think of them as "things which just happened to us." We may feel like victims as we spend our lives trying to overcome childhood issues. As adults, we set up new challenges. Did these things just happen to us or did we pre-arrange them to provide growth opportunities? When we change the way we think about these events, we can change our perspective about our lives. We begin to look at events and ask, "What can I learn from this? What is the lesson?"

Shirli Millmond remarked:

> "People keep getting the same lessons in G-d's universe in order to give them the opportunity to change. If they don't change, they keep getting the same lessons. They have to stop for a second and try to get the lesson. If they can't get it on their own, they should get help. A reader can provide a different perspective on the situation."

Gina Stanfill refined this idea:

> "We spend a lot of time going in circles. I talk to people who have been married four times. What is the common denominator in four divorces? That person. They may still be blaming their exes, and if they are, they will have a fifth ex. Until they decide that they didn't put what they needed to into those relationships, the situation is not going to change. The lesson for that person is going to be how to deal with relationships. We each have something we are trying to deal with and when we stop and think about it, we can see that we have common themes in our lives."

While we are working through these lessons, we are also presented with people and situations which are carried over from past lives so that we can re-balance our Karma. There is a "big picture" filled with lifetimes.

What lessons are we here to learn and how do we learn them?

The most complete, inspired, answer I heard was during Leah Taylor/Anneo's psychic-channeling event. Please remember that this passage came from a non-physical entity speaking English through Leah:

> "Your lessons are to love this life. Your lessons are to love You. Your lessons are to release the illusion, the game and the fear, and to become masters of your destiny, of your reality. You all come in with special gifts.

"Your lesson is to love yourself. To love yourself, not to judge yourself. To release the pain, the fear and the judgements on yourself because in your mind, you are hard on yourself. It is to feel some joy and happiness. If you do one lesson this whole lifetime, it is just to love yourself. And that is true for everybody, always. That is it, to love yourself. Because when you don't love yourself, you are hard on yourself and you punish yourself and you tell yourself that you don't deserve. 'Well, if I was different, I would deserve this,' or 'If I hadn't done that, then I would have deserved happiness.' No. Just love yourself, then you can have the things which bring you joy.

"Let's say you are going through your life, you are an actor in a play. You've got your script, you are learning lessons with other people. You might be playing the villain in somebody's life, the victim in another person's life, the hero in somebody else's life. These are all roles and illusions that you set up; they are different ego games that teach you. You grow from it. You came here to experience that, to grow. But the problem is that you start thinking that those lessons and those experiences are actually who you are, instead of ways to learn.

"What happens is that instead of evolving beyond that, we start thinking that that is who we are and then there is no way to get back to the spiritual truth which is that this is all an illusion and that you are spiritual beings and that we are ready for you to come home when you are ready to come home. There is no shame in that. There is no shame in going, there's no shame in life, there's no shame in whatever roles you are playing or lessons you want to learn. It's all experience."

During our lives, we grow from children to adults to parents to grandparents so that we get to see the issues we are working on from all sides. As a child, we see how it feels to be loved or not loved by a parent. As an adult we can see this issue from a more mature perspective, then as a parent we can see how it feels to love a child and be loved by a child. As a grandparent, we get to see another aspect of the issue. All of these perspectives help us to form a healthy mindset and to learn our life lessons. Somewhere along the way, we learn the lesson. If not as a child, then as an adult and if not as an adult, then as a parent or a grandparent. Or, we can spend another lifetime working on the same issue.

We create our own illusion. We write our own play. We can create drama and despair or love and support. We create the illusion of a loving and supportive Earth by hanging out with people who have the same positive beliefs and religious attitudes as we do. This is creating our reality on Earth just as we create our reality on the other side.

Why do we choose situations which we really don't like?

The channeling event provided a great depth of information for this answer:

"For humans there tend to be a couple of different situations. One of them is that you are on the other side and you are planning this lifetime and you are thinking, 'Wouldn't it be nice to experience this or that? to learn about this part of reality?' Then you come in and you start acting it out and you realize it really isn't what you want to be learning about and experiencing. Maybe you would like to learn your lessons with a little more happiness involved. Whether you want to shift the lessons you came in to learn, or the lessons you created in this lifetime, you do it the same way: you change your mind about how you want to live and what you want your play to be. You all set up for it with childhood, with pretend play. Like cowboys and Indians . . . or princesses, whatever you want to be like. You practiced that as a child naturally. As you grew up, instead of it being pretend, it became real life. You started thinking you are the role which you created.

"The reason that people will create uncomfortable circumstances in their lives is usually by default, because they are not actively creating something; or by confusion. Something might happen which shocks them; something which is scarey or shocking. Instead of stepping back and looking at that, and that feeling, they will continue perpetuating that over and over again. They identify with it so strongly because they weren't expecting it to happen. For example, somebody who is very prosperous loses their job. That can oftentimes set them on a whole course of being a victim or having a poverty consciousness. Maybe their friends turn against them, maybe they draw people in who will support them in the role of being fired, being poor, being rejected. If they want to change that, what they would start doing is: before the outside started changing, they would start changing the seeds of awareness so that they start seeing themselves pretending, playing with, and finding joy in thinking about what they want to have and how they want to be and putting out an intention that that was going to be their new role. For a while, every time you start harvesting those old seeds that say your are a victim, you are rejected, you are poor, you are fired, you say, 'Oh no, actually, that is not my new role.' Then you can set that aside and move into something else.

"I will tell you this. When we look at the world, we look all over the world and I will tell you that there are the poorest people in the world who don't know it. Some of them think that they are the richest. It's all relative to the game that they want to play. If you are in that mind of 'havingness,' being wealthy, being comfortable, that might be having five extra goats and you might be able to live that role, to have the same joy as someone here who has a beautiful home. You might live in suburbia and be working very, very hard to make your payments for your house and your car and be completely in a poverty space even though you have stuff around you. It's really the role and the game and the *feeling* that that role and that game give you; more than what you can see externally about somebody. It's going to tell you more about what is really going on in their life.

"If you start to see patterns in your life, you start to see that every day you are waking up and there is a little feeling of unsettledness, of disquietude, inside you and you are not sure what it is, but you kind of override it and you go about your life. Well, what that is telling you is that that disquietude inside you is your spirit trying to get you back on track. Trying to get you back into a space where you can have that joy. So it will come up and if you can connect with your inner self and connect with that little bit that is telling you that something doesn't feel right, even when life is going smoothly around you, a lot of times it will show you that you are too caught up in roles that are not serving you any more for where you want to go spiritually. If you can look at those parts of yourself, they might be relationships, or ideas that you have had, or ideas that other people have had about you which then you have had to act out so that you could prove them wrong, or move past it, then you can release and you can move into who you really are.

"Who you really are is infinite, is any game you want to play, it's anything you want to do here, anything you want to learn about, anything you want to feel. It is not going to look the same for everybody. Wealth consciousness isn't always going to be about being a millionaire for every person. Love isn't going to look the same for everybody. Just like no two relationships are going to be the same. But it's the feeling which goes behind it. It's what you want to experience, it's the experience of it, that is what life is all about. Get back to that force of knowing that you are not from here, that this is a game that you are playing. This is one of the hardest things about working with humans: you try to tell them that, 'This isn't really you.' This is just you today or you this lifetime, or you with this background and this body and these friends and this upbringing and this life; but it's not You. You are much, much bigger than that. When you can remember that, when you can connect with that even for just a few moments, it can change your life. It can give you the strength to change anything that you need to change in the way that you are living. That way you are never trapped. You realize there are infinite possibilities. It's not right or wrong, except by the context of the role your character is playing. If you don't like it, then you change it. And you bring new people in.

> "It is true, one thing to be conscious of because we see it . . . let's say you have been the victim your whole life, since your childhood. Let's say you were abused as a child, no one liked you in school, you didn't have any friends, everybody rejected you and you were victimized your whole life. The people who you bring into your life, you are playing that character for them. As soon as you stop being the victim and you start changing, and you say it's a game you are playing, it isn't the real you, and you release that and start changing the energy patterns of your life, you might find that they are angry. They are going to push you to go back to that role because that is what they want you to play in their life so that they can learn about power maybe by being abusive. Maybe they want you to be a victim so that they can learn about rescuing someone. Maybe they want you to play that role for any number of reasons and when you refuse, you might find that the whole cast of characters changes in your life. Sometimes changing who we are for the better can also mean losing people that we have been very close to and that we love. That's okay. That is part of the process. They will find somebody else to be that role in their life, and you will find somebody to play a role in your life that is about equality, respect, and kindness." *(Leah/Anneo)*

So wise. So deep. Blows me away every time I read that passage.

How can we change the roles we are playing, the lives we are living?

Back to Leah Taylor/Anneo's psychic-channeling event:

> "If you want to change it, if you come to a point where you are tired of the role you are playing or you are tired of the role other people are playing in your life, you just change your script. You change your story so that you live the life which brings you joy instead of unhappiness. It <u>can</u> happen. It sounds simple talking about it. We know people say that if it was that easy, they would all be doing it, but it <u>is</u> that easy. It's so simple. The fact is that it takes a little while from what you set into motion, from when you plant seeds, until the harvest. If you are planting the seeds for changing your life and you are expecting to have it happen instantaneously, or 30 seconds later, and it doesn't and then you lose faith, it's because what you are harvesting right now are the seeds that perhaps you planted six months ago. It is as easy as changing your mind about what games you

want to play in life and what stories you want to act out in the play; but remember that whenever you plant seeds, it takes a while to harvest. It is a natural part of being in this reality."

Summary

To summarize, we create a contract for our life before we are born. We set up our life situation with all of the challenges and opportunities which we will need. Then, we come to Earth with our outline and our free will. We use our free will to fill in the details of our life while fulfilling our contract. We have a life purpose to work on, personal lessons to learn, and Karma from previous lifetimes to re-balance. All the while, we are allowing G-d to learn vicariously from our experiences. Our life purpose is often a project, while our life lesson is to learn to love our self. We circle through incarnations with a group of friends and help each other achieve our goals. If, mid-way through our life, we realize that we are not enjoying our journey, or think we made a mistake when we set up our life, we can change the circumstances of our life and change the roles we are playing. We can sow new seeds. Yet, even as we change our circumstances, we continue to fulfill our contract, work on our project, learn our lessons, burn Karma and allow G-d to work through us.

Whew. It's a lot to comprehend. The more often I remind myself how this works, the better I understand the concepts.

Chapter 21 - Past Lives

It might be easier to accept all of this information about living and dying if we remembered our past lives and our trips to other side. But when we were born, most of us forgot our previous lifetimes. Does anyone remember clearly?

Do the psychics remember their past lives?

Many psychics are aware of their past lives and recognize people from previous lifetimes. Some psychics report that they feel like they are living one continuous existence spanning many lifetimes. A few psychics discussed how past lives influenced current lives.

Patricia Kirkman thought that past lives helped people know certain things they should not logically know. For example, the first time she and her husband were driving around Virginia, she told him that she wanted to see the church down the street. When they turned the corner, there was a little white church. He just looked at her. Sometimes people know and feel things, but they don't know why.

Erik Assman was born remembering many of his past lives and the people he knew in those lifetimes. His mother helped lock in those early memories by accepting the memories instead of questioning them. Erik can remember lives from several centuries ago. Interestingly, he often travels with the same woman and they recognize each other in different roles in each incarnation.

Jan Class said that she and her husband had lived several lifetimes together, but had not been able to marry until this lifetime. They kept missing each other for various reasons. They had met in Atlantis and had been engaged to be married in previous lifetimes. Finally, this lifetime, they agreed to marry and raise a daughter. When they met in this lifetime, there was a feeling that they knew each other. They had similar qualities and interests, and were instantly comfortable with each other.

To-Ree'-Nee' Wolf also remembers Atlantis. Her memory is very long. While she doesn't remember all of her incarnations, she remembers a few and they keep her humble. According to To-Ree'-Nee', she wasn't always the nicest, brightest person. Her recollection of a life event in Mesopotamia was included in Chapter 19.

To-Ree'-Nee' also recalls her most recent lifetime during World War II. She was part of the French Resistance and she was killed. She thinks she was male during that lifetime. I commented that if she was here for the Holocaust, she must have come back very quickly. It would have been only 10 or 15 years between lives. To-Ree'-Nee' replied, "You are thinking in linear time at this level. Time, at other levels, does not exist. Time happens in a much more-expansive, non-linear, way." She also explained that she remembered many lifetimes in France. She had been a psychic at the Court of Versailles and she had lost her head to a guillotine. When she heard about the French Revolution in school, she became physically nauseous and had terrible vertigo.

Leah Taylor also remembers World War II. In second grade, she began recalling this past life and couldn't get out of bed for a week. She stayed home, under the covers, reliving the experience with all of its details. It was very traumatic.

Richard Schickel remembers his past life as a German SS Guard during World War II. He was stationed at the labor camp Theresienstadt. As the Sargent in charge of the gate where the trains arrived, he was able to work with the Underground and shuttle some people out of the camp. After his role was discovered, the Underground helped him escape to Switzerland. Following the war, he returned to Germany to find that his family had been killed in an air raid. Not long after that, he also died. The key to remembering this past life had been this life's traumatic dreams of being discovered and running from something. When he began working with these dreams, he uncovered his last life.

Can psychics help people remember their past lives?

People who do not remember their past lives can work with others to learn about these lifetimes. Some psychic readers provide bits of past-life information during readings. Other readers use hypnosis to help clients with past-life regressions. During these regressions, clients actually experience their own past lives. The clients provide their own information.

Years ago, a reader explained to me that I had been a worker in China hundreds of years ago. I had been bent over, tending crops, when someone had come up behind me and beheaded me. Prior to that, I had always wondered about my neck and shoulder aches. After that, the aches eased up.

Another reader told me that I had crossed the country in a covered wagon. This was a small insight which helped me understand why I had been interested in covered wagons and prairie dresses as a young adult.

When recalling past lives, some people experience spontaneous flashes while others have more-detailed experiences. One of people I interviewed explained that a past-life experience is not like watching a TV program, it is like being <u>in</u> the TV program. It is experiential. He could taste it, feel it and touch it. It was too real not to be real. It came to him a little at a time so that he didn't get scared. It was like seeing a movie while knowing that he was in the movie.

One energy worker told me that she had been hypnotized and had a past-life regression. Under hypnosis, she had gone to the year 1876. The information seemed to come to her very quickly; however, when she listened to the recording of the event, her voice sounded very slow. She was able to describe things which she had never seen in this life. For example, she was able to describe her Native American boots and particular weaving patterns. She described things that she didn't know existed. Later, she found them in a book.

Two of the psychics I interviewed perform past-life hypnotherapy which is another name for past-life regression. They can suggest that the client remember the pleasant parts of the experience, but not the unpleasant parts. When clients can remember the good parts, or can hear their own voices on a tape, they can better understand their past, their life lessons, and their current circumstances.

Are we living simultaneous lifetimes right now?

During the interviews, a few PRISMS mentioned the idea of simultaneous lifetimes. Raquel Spencer thought that people lived parallel lives and alternate lives, in other places and other realities, while here on Earth. It all went back to a single source.

Cynthia Rae had this experience when she was 13 or 14 years old and went to a ranch with her parents:

> "We were checking on bow hunters. There was a brook and I asked my Dad if it was safe to drink out of the brook. When I took a drink out of the water and I lifted my head, all I could see was the death and destruction of my Tribe. I didn't know what had happened. I was an Iroquois warrior out hunting for food. When I returned from hunting, I found that there had been a massacre of my village.
>
> "Some years later, I was in massage school and there was another female student. I had this reticence to work with her which I couldn't figure out. I stepped back and saw her as one of the woman in the tribe. I was a white woman who she was jealous of and she would be killing me. Even though I was a hunter/warrior in one memory, I was a white woman living with the same tribe in another memory. What that told me was that our lives and our souls are lived simultaneously. Time is not linear. We can have multiple experiences in our souls at the same time, gathering information."

I asked if she thought she had been remembering past lives, but she told me it felt like she was actually experiencing both lifetimes simultaneously with this lifetime.

Similarly, I asked an artist where the inspiration for his mask-making work had come from and he told me that he thought he was tapping into a "collective." He continued:

> "I have a lot of crystal skulls and jade pieces in my house which are part of my journey. I couldn't understand why I wanted the skulls and the jade pieces, but when I held them it was as if I had a flashback. I could see myself in Neolithic times, sitting and carving the pieces. I think I am tapping into some sort of a collective. After that, I began working on the masks. In this life, I didn't have an art background, but I think I know how to do this work because I have done similar work in other lifetimes. The only thing I had to learn in this lifetime was how to work with the leather dye on the gourds."

When I asked if his inspiration came from a collective unconscious, Spirit Guides or his own soul, he answered:

> "All of the above. I think that this is an energy. We are all impacted by what goes on around us. I am tapping into the 'cosmic library' and pulling in things that I may have done in

> Neolithic times . . . Who is to say that the past, present and future aren't all happening at the same time? There are a number of these masks which look like extra-terrestrials. I don't know where this information comes from."

The past, present and future are all happening at the same time? How many times have we heard this from the psychics? Simultaneous lifetimes in different realms, in different time periods, all at once. Is it possible?

Chapter 22 - Animals After Life on Earth

Now that we've thought about the life cycle of humans, let's find out what the PRISMS had to say about the life cycle of animals.

Where do animals (and our pets) go after they die? Do their souls live on?

This is an interesting question with a variety of answers. It is more a question to ponder than a question which has been definitively answered. Each psychic has their own idea of what happens when pets die. I have had beloved pets who have passed away and I would like to see them again so there are answers which I had hoped to hear. Setting aside my own personal hopes, this is what the psychics said:

- 20 psychics thought that our animal's spirit lives on;
- 1 psychic thought that animals have only one lifetime; they are here, then they are gone;
- 1 psychic had never thought about this topic; and
- 4 psychics didn't have this topic come up during our conversations.

Of the 20 psychics who thought that our animal's spirit lives on, eight specifically commented that we could see our animals again in the afterlife and three told me that their deceased animals had already come back to visit. Eight psychics told me that animals (living or deceased) often come up during clients' readings. Deceased animals come back to tell their owners that they are just fine.

Many psychics told me that pets go to the same afterlife which people go to. Pets have individual souls and the psychics are positive that we will see our pets again. However, there is also a theory that instead of individual souls, different types of animals may have "group souls." For example, all dogs may be part of a canine group soul and all cats may be part of a feline group soul.

This begs the question: Do animals have souls? Do <u>all</u> animals have souls? Just mammals and birds? What about insects and ants? I never thought to ask this question!

Back to the question I did ask: "Where do animals go when they die? Do their souls live on?" Here are some answers:

> ☼ Pets go to the same energy which humans go to since we are all created from that same spark that we call Spirit. It is to be fully expected that when you pass into that energy, you will be connected with your loved ones and your animals. As long as you loved them, you will still have that connection in the afterlife. *(Jackie Chin)*
>
> ☼ I don't know what to call it. If you picture the world and the Universe around it, there is a layer between the Earth and the Universe – an "ever after" holding space. Spirit energy goes there. I have seen this energy. When the spirit leaves the physical body, it is kind of a "glowy ball" and the glowing energy ends up in this space. When I look into this area, there are balls of light from people and animals. The energies can mix together, share experiences, and talk about things. *(Kat Riegel)*
>
> ☼ I think they go to the same Realm that we go to, however, it has different levels. In simple terms, I believe that there is a layer of energy that I would call "Humanness," and there is a layer above that that I would call "Divine." Above that would be a layer that I would call "The All in One (G-d)." It is not that a higher layer is better, they are all equal in "better-ness", but they are separate vibrations. There is also a vibration, or frequency of energy, for the animals of our planet, another frequency level for all the plants, and another frequency level for all the crystals.
>
> I believe that my dog who has passed on no longer has his individual, physical body, but his uniqueness is maintained in the non-physical. I believe that he has the ability to shift his energy so that he can come back into life in the animal range (probably as a dog). *(Beth Hays)*

☼ Dogs, whales and dolphins all go to the constellation Sirius. *(Delphina Nova)*

Can we contact our deceased pets?

Eight psychics reported that they can bring messages from deceased pets to their human companions. Animals often show up during readings without any effort to contact them and the psychics are able to relay the pets' messages. In addition, grieving humans often ask psychics to reach out to their deceased pets and, with the right psychic, contact is possible. In fact, the woman who works as an Animal Communicator can intentionally contact deceased pets.

Here are some examples of communication with animals who have crossed over:

☼ I did a reading in a woman's home where I was trying to talk to the woman's (living) dog. In the meantime, a big grey cat kept showing up, but whenever I looked at the cat, it was not there. I finally told the woman that a big grey cat was showing up and she told me that her cat had passed away two years prior to the reading. I told her that the cat was still there; it had not moved on. I asked if I could talk to the cat and the woman said that would be okay. The cat told me that she was a guardian and that she was not leaving the woman because the woman was going through too much. She felt the woman needed her. The woman admitted that she did still need the cat. One day they will know when it is time and they will let go of each other. A lot of animals hang out with their people for a long time. Some animals are ready to move on and others hang on to make sure that their humans are okay before they go. *(Kat Riegel)* [This scenario is similar to the psychics' explanation of ghosts.]

☼ I know they come back in spirit just like the other spirits do because animals come through when I do readings. They come back to tell their owners that they are just fine. *(Laurie Hays)*

☼ I helped a friend's pet transition when the pet had to be euthanized. What I heard from the pet, was that it was okay and that the pet understood what the person was trying to do. I saw the spirit leave the pet. *(George)*

☼ When an animal has passed, people want to know how the animal died and why the animal passed away. I read for a person who knew how the animal passed and wanted me to ask the animal about it. In that case, the dog gave me a sharp pain in my back, almost as if there had been an impact. However, it felt more like there had been a tumor on the spine. It turned out the animal had had cancer of the spine. The person said that the pain had been gradual, but at the end the tumor was so big that there had been a lot of pain. *(Kat Riegel)*

☼ A friend of mine had to have her boxer put down due to a cancerous lesion which was preventing the animal from having a good quality of life. She had loved this dog for 12 years and didn't know what she was going to do without the dog. A few days after the dog passed, the woman was laying on her bed and felt something laying next to her in the exact space where the dog used to lay. She called me the next morning, upset, anxious, and full of questions. I told her that I had never worked with animal energy before and was not sure that I was capable of this kind of work. I suggested that she call a pet psychic. I figured I was out of my element and it was best to leave this to an expert. However, my friend insisted that I try to find out more about her dog. She was a dear friend of mine and I wanted to help so I said, "Alright."

I told her what side of the bed "Raven" was laying on and what time of the night she had made her presence known. I also received the impression that my friend needed to know that Raven had not been upset that she had been put down. She had suffered for so long with arthritis and cancer that she was ready to go. I don't feel like I did very much, but for my friend it was enough. I have since learned that animals can relay information from beyond. We just have to accept that we can hear them too. *(Jackie Chin)*

Can deceased pets initiate contact with us?

Two of the psychics mentioned that their deceased animals had returned to comfort them. These pets had shown up on their own.

Delphina Nova shared:

"I have had my animals come back to me. One time I was on a sailboat and the main sail ripped. It was a very serious situation and the sailboat nearly went down. I was alone at the helm in the middle of the night. My grandfather and my dog, who had both passed over, showed up and joined me at the helm. I was going through the ocean during the night with 30' waves in a 42' boat. They stayed there, watching over me and guiding me. I could see their essence and their spirit as they told me to hang on."

And To-Ree'-Nee' Wolf recalled:

> "My cat, Flag, has shown up since he died. I had a dream that he and my other cat were on the bed together. Then I felt someone get up on my bed and there he was, twice his size, and I realized that this was actually happening. I tried to wake my husband up to see Flag. Then, the only way I can describe this is that I blended awake from another reality. I blended awake on this level of reality and I knew he was doing really well."

Do animals experience reincarnation?

Five psychics discussed animal reincarnation. Kat Riegel, an Animal Communicator, commented on her experiences:

> "People want to know if their animal will come back as another animal. That has been interesting. I have been told by animals that they want to come back, but it is not their time. I had one animal tell me that they were coming back, but their time with that person was done and they were coming back to a different family. I have had other readings where the animal had already come back in a different body."

Do animals always come back as animals or can they evolve?

One psychic who believes in animal reincarnation commented that she always sees people being reincarnated as people; she doesn't see people coming back as animals. She thinks that dogs will usually be reincarnated as canines, and cats as felines. She sees them within the same genus. Sometimes they stay with their owners on the other side. She sees a lot of people with their animals on the other side and believes that our animals wait for us.

However, several psychics, including the Animal Communicator, believe it is possible for animals to evolve and return to Earth as a different species. Kat Riegel commented:

> "I feel that pets can pick if they want to be something different. For example, they may have been a cat this time because their human needed that perfect companionship. Cats can give people personal satisfaction and calming. For me, watching a sleeping cat lowers my blood pressure. Dogs tend to be guardians. If a being is here as a cat this time so that they can calm their human, they might choose to come as a dog the next time because they understand that their human is going to need protection."

She added:

> "Animals can come back as other animals and people can come back as other people. Animals are one level and people are another level. Once an animal has accomplished everything it wants to accomplish as an animal, it can become a "people energy." Once it becomes a people energy, it does not go back to being an animal energy. Animals can evolve. I don't want to say that animals have all of the feelings and emotions of humans, but I see that they have similar emotions. They have more than basic instincts. There is caring, growth and friendship among animals. Animals do things which are very similar to the things people do."

This idea was echoed by Erik Assman:

> "Animals are evolving and they have their own Karma. Some of them have become so advanced that they are becoming pseudo-humans; they have a human form but they don't experience the same capacities as the rest of us. When they die, they die like animals and return to a group soul. They come back as something which will help them to continue their spiritual growth and to experience higher realities. Anything that contains spirit is evolving. Animals can come back as 'amateur' humans."

Two more psychics agreed that it was possible for humans to return as animals and for animals to return as humans:

> ☼ I think we change forms and a dog can be born again as a human, and a human as a dog, or a rabbit, or a cat, for example. I think we change forms. Why? To get the lessons we need to learn. We all come to this life to learn our lessons and to become the best that we can be. *(Shirli Millmond)*

> ☼ I believe that we can be reincarnated as a plant or an animal or a building. *(Gina Stanfill)*

What else might animals do once they have crossed over?

Trish Silay explained that deceased animals go to the spirit realm just like everything else. They can be our Guides, assisting us in different ways. She wasn't sure about all animals, but she knew that her own animals had been Spirit Guides for her.

As for my own experience, years ago when I as going through a particularly stressful week, I had a dream where my deceased dog came to comfort me and give me strength. Every time she was ready to fade away, I begged her to stay for another moment and she was able to fade out then come back, twice. It was so good to see her again! This dream felt very real and it actually did give me strength by helping me to feel that unseen entities were supporting my efforts. Perhaps this is my direct experience of animals helping us even after they have passed.

• • •

This Section of the book has explained why people are born on Earth and what we are here to accomplish. We are cycling around on a Wheel of Incarnation trying to learn to love ourselves and understand who we truly are, so that, eventually, we can evolve off of the Wheel and move on to different realms and realities. Just knowing that some people can communicate with invisible entities and bring messages to the rest of us will be enough for many people, but some people will want to know more about their own abilities and potential future. The next Section has hints for developing personal, intuitive, connections, and discusses how we may all share a common future. We may be able to break free from the Wheel of Incarnation and move on to other adventures. The people who are interested in spirituality may go first, then help others. What am I talking about? Personal spiritual development and the new opportunities which may open in 2012. Read on.

Section V

The Future

Chapter 23 - Developing Your Psychic Abilities

This Section discusses "The Future." The first chapter is about each person's personal future and their opportunities for psychic development. The second chapter presents the psychics' views on the period of time around 2012, the new energies which are coming to Earth, and the future of humanity.

Do most people have intuition?

Yes. Everyone has a certain level of intuition and can work to develop their abilities. People with high levels of psychic ability automatically hear, see, feel or know information. Or, words just pop into their head. They don't struggle to access information, it just comes to them. Other people can learn these skills.

How can people develop their own intuitive connections?

Working on this Project, I have learned about psychics, psychic phenomena, and how the Universe works. I meditate and I try to enhance my connection, and I am only just beginning to receive intuitive information. Everything I explore, you can explore too.

Here are some ideas for learning about psychics, spirituality, and your own gifts:

1) Go to places where you can learn about psychics, what they know and what they do.

    <u>Psychic Fairs</u>

    In addition to consultations with psychics, many fairs have speakers who discuss what they do and how the Universe works. Look on-line for a fair near you and find out if there are informational sessions during the fair.

IONS meetings

IONS is the Institute for Noetic Sciences ("Noetic" means knowing). This organization is based in northern California and has groups all of over the world which seek the intersection of science and consciousness. They have a website at www.noetic.org. In addition, local groups have their own websites and sponsor meetings.

Each month in Tucson our local IONS group presents a lecture, a movie, a book group, a Universal Energy Event (Reiki) and a Psychic Explorers group. I am part of the Psychic Explorers group and each month we try a new technique to discover our capabilities. For example, we tried bending spoons with our minds, viewing an object hidden in a bag, accessing medical intuition and sending telepathic messages to each other.

Conferences

There are conferences all over the world relating to consciousness and metaphysics. Some are highly scientific and some are just for fun. A good place to start looking for these kinds of events is on the Internet.

Lectures

Check with your local university and find out if there are lectures about the brain and the mind. Or try a beginner's lecture on quantum physics (really, it's more interesting than you might think).

Classes

Many psychics offer development classes. They teach Reiki, Tarot card reading, palm reading, past-life regression, etc. When you meet psychics, ask if they offer classes, or take their cards and check their websites. In addition, some people offer weekend retreats full of classes and guided meditations.

Spiritualist churches also offer classes. Some churches offer "unfoldment" classes.

Another good place to start is your local metaphysical shop. Most of these shops either sponsor classes or can tell you who might be teaching a class which interests you.

Movies

Movies can provide some insights about psychic ability. However, you need to be wary of Hollywood's fictional movies because they take a gem of truth and sensationalize it. On the other hand, there are many good documentaries.

2) If you prefer to work alone, you can read about psychic abilities.

Books

Start with your local library and check out books written by psychics. These books explain how individual psychics connect to the Universe. There are also books about life after death, why we are here, and how you can contact your own Spirit Guides. Then, branch out to your local bookstores or to on-line bookstores.

Magazines

There are plenty of national psychology and New Age magazines. In addition, there are free, local papers around the United States entitled, "Natural Awakenings." These publications list local psychic fairs and events. They also include interesting articles about New Age topics and health. You can find them in libraries and metaphysical shops.

The Internet

There are many websites about psychics. Try to find an educational website, not just an advertisement. Look for personal experiences. Check out blogs written by psychics. In addition, Facebook has groups for people exploring psychic ability.

Oh yes, remember my favorite website: www.MyPsychicSearch.com. Always interesting!

3) Talk to people.

Psychics

Talking to psychics about what they do is my favorite way of learning. I find that listening to real experiences means more to me than anything else. Psychics live between worlds and they have fascinating stories to share.

Friends

You might be pleasantly surprised if you asked your friends about psychic phenomena. Have they seen a ghost or felt a deceased relative? Again, listening to people with this kind of direct experience really opens minds. In addition, your friends may have recommendations for psychics with whom they have had great readings.

4) Experiment.

Try it yourself! Sometimes, we don't know what we have until we try it and succeed. If you are trying to connect with your Guides and they are trying to send messages to you, experiment with a variety of techniques and see if any of them work.

Meditation

Sit quietly, close your eyes and see what happens. Stay with it for 10 or 15 minutes each day for a few weeks. Meditation centers your mind so you can listen to Spirit. It helps moderate emotions throughout the day so that you are not just reacting to the situations which arise. Meditation provides access to infinite wisdom. You can ask anything and have a quiet period to listen for answers.

Breathing techniques

Many people with psychic abilities use specific breathing techniques to enhance their connection.

Reiki (or any kind of energy work)

Try Reiki at a psychic fair. It's very relaxing. Or ask friends if they can recommend Reiki Masters.

Chakra cleansing and balancing

There are many techniques for chakra cleansing and balancing. You can find books at libraries and bookstores, and you can go on-line to find websites with instructions for chakra balancing.

Automatic Writing

Sit down with a piece of paper and a pen. Close your eyes, meditate and ask a question. Start writing and see what happens. If nothing comes, just start writing your name or doodling. Ask another question and see if the answer flows out of your fingertips.

Psychometry

Ask a friend if you can hold one of his or her belongings. Once you have it in your hand, close your eyes and see if you can get any information about your friend by tapping into the energy of their item.

Pendulums

Using a pendulum to glean information is known as dowsing. Yes, this includes the old-time dowsing for water which we saw in western movies. Instead of using dowsing rods, use a small pendulum on the end of a chain. When you begin, you and your pendulum must agree on what is a "yes" and what is a "no." Much has been written about how to use pendulums.

Tarot cards

Purchase a deck of Tarot cards, read the informational booklet, and give it a try. Alternatively, it might be easier to start by taking a class from a local metaphysical shop or a psychic.

5) Listen to Blog Talk Radio and other Internet Radio Programs.

These programs present speakers on metaphysical topics.

6) Watch TV.

When it comes to TV, you have to distinguish between fiction and non-fiction. There have been some great non-fiction shows and interviews regarding spirituality. A few years ago, I was able to watch John Edward's show "Crossing Over" on TV. I enjoyed watching John do readings because he explained how being a Medium worked. He discussed his connection and noted how symbols appeared to him. He had to interpret those symbols and one of the reasons his readings weren't completely precise was because of this need for interpretation. After the show, the producers checked with the audience members to corroborate the messages in the readings. This show opened my eyes to what it is like to work as a Medium.

In addition, the Biography channel presents a show entitled, "I Survived . . . the Beyond." On this show, people who have died and been revived tell their stories. While each NDE story is different, it is fascinating to hear what people say they experienced on the other side.

There are also shows about Psychic Kids. Check your local TV listings.

On the fiction side, there are shows which give a hint of what it is like to be psychic, but things have to be magnified and sensationalized for TV, so take them at face value (that means, they are entertainment, not education).

Everyone is born with intuitive abilities. Think of yourself as already being psychic and see if that changes your perspective. According to the PRISMS, we are not learning anything. We are remembering. It emerges from the inside out. When we hear someone say that "Aha" thing, it activates a memory and we remember who we are and why we are here on Earth. Developing our psychic abilities and advancing our own spirituality may help us as we move into the turbulent years surrounding 2012.

Chapter 24 - Looking Forward to 2012

The year 2012, and the subsequent years, should be interesting ones. According to some people, 2012 is the end of the Mayan and Hopi calendars and this signifies the end of the world. Other researchers dispute that this is the end of the calendars and most people disagree that this will be the end of the world. However, there is much speculation that big changes are coming. Some people believe that 2012 will be the year in which some of Nostradamus' predictions are realized. Many people believe that we will survive 2012, but that there will huge changes in the ways we think and live. Other people think the Mayans just ran out of the space to keep writing a calendar.

Some of the psychics who were interviewed for this Project think that the Earth will go through a period of violent re-organization which will peak in 2012, but people will remain on Earth and learn to work together. Other psychics think that 2/3 of the people will leave Earth either through natural disasters or through the process of ascension. Some psychics believe that the remaining 1/3 will work together, in an age of enlightenment, to help the Earth to heal. Others believe that these people will think they are on Earth but will actually have been transported to a very similar world where they can live as if on Earth while the actual, vacant, Earth has time to heal. While these theories sound like science fiction, we will know in just a few years what actually happened.

What do psychics think will happen in 2012?

I didn't ask all of the psychics about the year 2012, but it often came up during the interviews.

According to the 12 psychics who commented on 2012:

5 thought that there would be catastrophic Earth changes (floods, earthquakes, tsunamis, fires, etc.) and that much of the Earth's population would leave; after the devastation, there would be a period of great peace;

4 thought that there would be huge changes in the way people think;

1 thought that this would be the end of "mechanistic" time and that we would have a different dimension of natural time to replace "clock" time;

1 thought that this was similar to Y2K where people had feared that all the computers would fail and it would be catastrophic, but really nothing changed; and

1 thought that the end of the Mayan calendar didn't mean anything in particular; the "Mayans had just run out of stone."

This chapter contains the PRISMS' ideas of what may come. The psychics are quoted so that you have a true sense of what they said.

1) There will be catastrophic Earth changes and many people will leave Earth.

In 2009, Denise Singerline had this prediction:

> "I believe that a lot of Earth changes are coming. There will be tsunamis. Continents will break away and old continents will re-surface. However, my interpretation of the 2012 Mayan prophecy is not that it is going to be the end of the world, but that it will be a new beginning. In addition to the Earth changes, there is going to be a spiritual shift of consciousness and awareness.
>
> "I think that things will accelerate until 2012. The catastrophes are getting worse and are becoming more frequent. Things will happen in the U.S. too. I think NY and FL will disappear. I think that CA will break away. I think that we are blessed to be in Tucson at this time. It is a safe place to be. We may become beachfront property!"

In 2010, Delphina Nova agreed with this position, adding:

"A lot of Earth changes are happening right now. It's like birth. The baby doesn't come out in one push. This is like a birth process. We make progress, then we go back, then we make progress again . . . and it hurts! Finally, the waters break and the baby is born. Now, ask yourself which waters are breaking right now around the planet? We just had an earthquake in Haiti and an oil spill in the Gulf of Mexico. A lot of things are happening which are like birth pangs. We ask, 'Why are these things happening? Why does G-d allow this?' It's all part of the birthing process and birth is messy. Even the waters in the Gulf have turned red like blood! Oil is the blood of Mother Earth. We have to trust in the birth process. Part of that process is letting go of the things we no longer need. We don't need the amniotic sac after the baby is born.

"I believe we are on the brink, we are at the 11th hour on our planet. Indigenous cultures around the world, as well as western scientists, are telling us that we are at the 11th hour and I think we are being brought to this place where we actually want something to happen. Our actions are creating things. We are going to be given a huge gift. I am not focused on the December 21, 2012 Mayan prophecies because not all indigenous prophecies point to 2012. We are at this point where we have a choice about how we are going to conduct our lives, how we are going to treat each other, and how we are going to take care of the environment. I believe that in the blink of an eye we will choose love. It is up to us. How we treat ourselves and the world around us is what we are going to receive. The person in one house may be living in hell, and the person next door may be living in love. I believe we can be living in a pile of dung somewhere and still be living in complete bliss. You can see the person in front of you as your enemy, as separate from you, or as your friend.

"We are going to go through planetary changes, but we are not alone. I think many of us will be pleasantly surprised by helpers who assist in the Earth's transition. There are things which exist outside of our dimension which are here to help us. There is help from other galaxies. There are unseen angels who surround this planet with love. A lot of people are beginning to feel the helpers. Ask for angels to help. Ask for the guardians of this area. Surround the desert with your Light. We have the right to call on the Light."

In 2008, Cecilia Nemmers had also spoken about major catastrophes, but had her own spin:

> "In the next couple of years, we are going to have catastrophic happenings on Earth and people are going to disappear. You will see them, then you won't see them. What will happen is that some people are going to be able to see spaceships. They are going to get telepathic messages to come aboard. They are going to say, 'Yes,' in order to avoid what is going to happen here: earthquakes, volcanoes, etc. Not everybody is going to see the spaceships because not everybody is going to want to see them. Someone next to you may not see that spaceship and you may just disappear. They will be looking around and wondering where you went.
>
> "If you are one of the people who sees the spaceships, it's best to get on board because when you go, you will remember who you are. A lot of us are Divine masters. We were born here, but it doesn't mean we are from here. We are from different stars. While we are up there, and all the land changes happen, two-thirds of the world's population is going to leave, one way or another. There is going to be a polar shift. If Nostradamus is correct, the polar shift will happen in the year 2012. The Earth will stop rotating and it will tilt. By the end of 2009, there will be no ice on the polar caps.
>
> "After the Earth changes, people will return to Earth and they are going to have to work together to save the animals. It's not just the polar bears, it's the hippopotamus which will also become extinct. Hippos have a very limited diet and they will lose their food source. About a third of the current human population will live on Earth after the changes. Earth is still going to be here and people are still going to be here. They are going to be the people who chose to stay here to help the Earth heal. But being here during the cataclysmic part may not be a wise idea. People can always opt to come back."

I asked Cecilia how we could protect our children and families and she reminded me that our children volunteered to be here too. They have their own destiny. They have a mission to help.

She noted that catastrophes didn't strike everywhere at once. Events such as volcanoes and tsunamis affected only a limited geographic area. People were already getting the urge to move so that they would get to the place where they needed to be. And, even with a tsunami or an earthquake, some people lived through it.

Delphina Nova also commented that people may choose to leave the Earth at this time. They could die without needing to wait for a catastrophe. She remarked:

> "I believe in Divine compassion. If you know that you are going to go through a hard time, yet you are experiencing Divine love, it makes things easier. There is a part of Divine love which doesn't want you to experience the hard time and if you are ready to leave, and you have learned the lessons, you will not need to stay behind and watch the changes. We are not our bodies. Out of compassion, you can leave (unless you are needed)."

One thing we must be keenly aware of is the idea that what we focus on expands. If we focus on end-time disasters, they become a self-fulfilling prophecy. If enough people share a negative belief, the collective fear creates that reality. If we focus on whatever good comes out of these difficult times, and on the things which we hope to see, we can expand the positive impacts.

2) After the devastation, there will be a period of peace.

Delphina Nova has had visions of a long peaceful period after 2012.

> "Right now, in India, scriptures tell us that we are living in a period where things fall apart. Things which need to go, go. That is part of the Earth changes. These things need to happen and we are in this period of things coming down. Scriptures also talk about a golden age. Things are going to be shaken up. This shaking needs to happen, so that we can go into a time of peace which will last a long time. We are going through this shaky period as Earth births itself because we are part of Earth, part of Mother Earth. We too need to go through the changes and release the things which no longer are working in our own lives: relationships, music, food, etc. We are in the end times right now. I don't look at 2012 as a date; we are already in the end times. This is it for me. I have felt this for 20 years. We are in it right now. Timing can be totally off. Anything can happen at any time right now . . . in the blink of an eye. I am not waiting for 2012. There is no such thing as time, there is just human time.
>
> "I am encouraging people not just to look at the date of December 21, 2012, but to think about what they are doing right now. That date is like a portal, but everything is coming down right now and the rate of change will increase until we go through that doorway. When we go through the doorway, we are going to drop all that no longer serves us on the planet. As that happens, the more we cling on to our stocks, our relationships, our

> cities … we don't know how things are going to be. We just have to let go and know that the changes which are happening are happening for the highest and utter love. I really feel that something wonderful is coming, but we need to let go of things. Sometimes when you need to let go of something, it makes you want to hold on that much more tightly.
>
> "My sense is that we are only focusing on what is happening right now. It is like giving birth. When you are giving birth and the baby is in the birth canal, it is hard to focus on the baby. You don't know what the baby is going to be like. In the moment, you are focusing on the pain and the process. Because we are in the process, we are in the messy stage right now. No one knows what the outcome will look like. I have had glimpses, but I'm not sure of the whole picture.
>
> "Several years ago I had an image of the destruction. I was filled with sorrow as I saw things coming down, cities changing, people dying. At that moment, Jesus appeared and put his arm lovingly around my shoulders and said, 'Do not look at this. This is what I want you to look at.' He turned me around and put his hand in front of me and there was a Golden City. He said that this is what stood before us, our future. The past is past. This is what is coming. Don't focus on the destruction, focus on what is coming. With that image, I have been filled with hope. That is why I don't see the end of the world . . . I already see the new world. It is a time of peace and rest. We will go through a purification process and we will be relieved. It will be huge, but what awaits us is like a mother who rests after giving birth. This is my vision, this is what I see. People who haven't seen that vision, who just see the crashing economy and the volcanoes can be dismayed, but all of this needs to happen in order for the new world to be born."

Rhonda Harford had heard that 2012 was supposed to be the year of Peace; no more war. However, she doubted this outcome. She felt that we would still have war because so many countries believed that woman were worthless. She didn't think we would be able to change the world by 2012 because too much work remained to be done. However, she agreed that many people would be eliminated. There would be natural disasters such as earthquakes, tsunamis, and volcanoes. The food chain would change and she suggested that people strengthen their immune systems.

Cynthia Rae saw a different future:

> "The world may not come to the end, but there may be a re-birthing . . . like 1929, when everybody had to work together if they wanted to make it. We have been on this planet

> for 35 million years as human beings. I don't think we are going away. I think that life as we know it is going to be very, very different. We may not be able to live in the desert anymore; that kind of thing. Or it could be the reverse. 2012 is another Presidential election year. Who knows? It might be that we elect a new kind of President. It could be that we become more prosperous, or more psychic, or more intuitive. People look at it as a doomsday, but it doesn't have to be that."

3) People will wake up and there will be a shift in perception.

Raquel Spencer commented that she didn't see big catastrophes or the end of the world in 2012, but she saw a shift in perception:

> "I think there is going to be enough awareness that there will be shift in perception and a shift in consciousness. People will begin to create a more-positive life illusion. We are all co-creators, and it is all about how we perceive our creations. Some people can always see the good and have a perfect life. Others struggle. This will be a shift in awareness, a shift in being able to co-create your illusion."

Gigi Sample believes we are already in the Aquarian Age and it is about the waking up of humanity. People used to think that this would happen in 2012, but it is already happening. People are waking up and shifting. She observed:

> "This lifetime is very different. I don't know how I know that, but I just know it. It is very different from other lifetimes. I am not concerned about the Mayan calendar, I just know we are in the Aquarian Age and the Aquarian Age is about consciousness shifting, humanitarianism and unconditional love. Pinky-orange is the color. It is a high vibration energy which is coming to the Earth plane for this time."

She added:

> "This is the lifetime we have been waiting for. We are in the 'past-life teacher reunion.' That is why you click with some people. I call it the past-life teacher reunion because every teacher from a past lifetime is here this lifetime. We might have skipped other lifetimes together, but everyone is here (or coming) this lifetime, to make this shift."

In 2010, Gigi likened what was happening to a chessboard:

> "The Guides are showing me a chessboard and saying we're putting the knights here and the kings there . . . everyone is getting where they need to be for 2010. I don't care about 2012, I care about 2010 because all of the teachers are going to figure out their life purpose. Teachers have to figure out where they are going to be and how it is going to look so that when 2012 comes and the masses wake up, we are ready. What if the masses wake up in 2012, consciousness is shifting, and there is nowhere for anyone to turn? That is why competition among psychics isn't necessary. There will be too much work for everybody. There will be so many people seeking. It's already starting to happen. There's going to be chaos along the way, but there has always been chaos. We just have more newspapers now. It's actually lighter now than it used to be. More people want to do good things than not. They just don't get on the news."

Denise Singerline was also excited by the idea that it was time for humanity to wake up and create a more-positive, civilized, society. She commented that as we approached 2012, G-d was calling all Light Workers and telling them that it was time to turn on.

Cherie Fraine mentioned that people's ideas about how to live would go through rapid changes:

> "People will either get things together or they won't. People who get it together will survive and people who don't, won't. I think there is going to be a big house-cleaning. I don't know what form it is going to take, but I have a big feeling that there is going to be a house-cleaning. It isn't about survival in the sense of having five years worth of food in the house, it has to do with where your head is. It has to do with what you think about, how you move in the world and how you treat other people. Guys who are boozing it up and hitting their wives aren't going to make it.
>
> "The Universe is an abundant place. There is no reason for some people to have so much money they can't spend it all and for other people to be grubbing in the garbage can for their next meal. That is ridiculous. I think there is going to be a much more level playing field in the future."

Laurie Hays agreed that 2012 would bring a new state of mind:

> "There is going to be a shift, but it doesn't mean that we will be obliterated. Just think how you think now compared to how you thought 10 years ago. We are the hippy/baby boomer generation. We were rebels from the start and we are going to change the way people think about being senior citizens. I have no doubt I will be here."

4) There will be a change in the way people think about time.

Trish Silay commented that 2012 would bring the end of time as we knew it. We won't have to be concerned with clock or calendar time because we would be in another dimension of time. We were becoming cosmic humans. Instead of mechanistic time, we would work in natural time.

5) 2012 is an election year, but the nature of elections may change.

Cecilia Nemmers thinks that there won't be any more elections. President Bush was the last president. There is something different about President Obama because he has the new energy, the unity.

Can PRISMS help heal the world?

Yes. PRISMS bring in information and ideas. They pray for the Earth and for all people. They ask Spirit, Spirit Guides and angels for assistance. They bring in positive energy to help solve problems and to promote peace and tranquility. Some Light Workers are helping to raise the vibration of all people so that they can ascend to new dimensions. They inspire people to be kinder to themselves and to the rest of the world.

What can people do to help with the 2012 transition?

Jackie Chin encouraged everyone to engage in spiritual work. She remarked:

> "Those of us who are in touch with spiritual energies understand that there are many Earth changes which are affecting our personal lives as well as the life of this planet. If we continue to worry and not take any action, it will be much worse. Those who are aware need to form groups of like-minded people and teach others how to connect to the life source by prayer, meditation, and energy healing. As long as they are doing positive

spiritual work, it will magnify for the good of the planet. Each color, thought, and living thing has a healthy vibration. It is up to those who understand this concept to teach others how to build up their vibrations and heal themselves. Once they have learned how to do that, they can give back to the planet."

What is "Ascension"?

Ascension is the concept of awakening to a higher level of consciousness. At the ascended level, people understand who they really are and what they have been learning on Earth. Some people liken ascension to entering Heaven alive, with a body. Death is normally the end of life. Through ascension, people no longer need to go through the pain and fear of death in order to return to the spiritual world. Some people believe that, eventually, everyone will go through the ascension process. Ascension may be one way in which people leave Earth in the period of time around 2012.

I spoke with one psychic who explained, as best she could, the ascension process. According to this psychic, people who go through the ascension process will wake up, move up a level of consciousness and remember who they really are and the journey that they are on. The most gentle description she provided was that people could be sitting at a table talking to each other then, suddenly, they would wake up, realize that they were powerful, magnificent, spiritual beings, understand how all of their past lives worked together, then keep on talking. Alive, in a body, knowing things. After that, each person could lift into his or her Higher Self and decide where to go and if he or she wanted to take the body along. There would be choices. No one is quite certain what the ascension process will be, but it is nice to think it could be as easy as just waking up and knowing things.

In previous chapters of this book, many psychics shared their thoughts on reincarnation. People live, learn, die, leave their body behind, go to the other side, integrate what they have learned, and can choose to return to Earth to continue their education. People go around on the Wheel of Incarnation. Once people have learned their lessons and had all of the experiences which they have sought, they are supposed to graduate from the Wheel and move on to other realms, planets and dimensions. However, due to outside influences, many people who have already learned their lessons have become stuck on the Wheel of Incarnation and have not been able to break free and move on to other realms. Ascension will give these people the extra energetic push which allows them to break free from the Wheel. This energetic push will come from non-physical entities who are helping the people of Earth. As soon as people go through the ascension process, they will realize that everyone is here to help each other and they will volunteer to help others.

According to the psychic with whom I spoke, we are already in the ascension process and people are waking up. This process will accelerate over the next few months and continue through 2012 and beyond. This process is available to everyone and is not based on religious belief. People who are on a spiritual path and who are ready for ascension will go through the process first. People who are wondering about ascension, but who aren't quite ready, will have the opportunity to live on Earth and learn more about who they are and why they are here. They will have the time and choices they need to determine what they want to do. When they are ready, they will go through the ascension process.

The people who have no idea that there is a spiritual component to life, and who are not interested in spirituality, will have other opportunities to continue their lives and may not even be aware that things are changing. However, things will play out over the next five years or so and there will be huge changes on Earth. Eventually, most people will leave Earth but they will all have choices as to where to go. The Earth needs time to heal.

Looking forward

In 2010, Gigi Sample summarized her thoughts on 2012 beautifully:

> "To me, '2012' will be a couple of years of people figuring out themselves. This is like people getting called to service. The year 2002 was a huge shift for most healers. It was the year that bad stuff had to come up so that they had enough time to get through their own stuff to be ready to help in 2012.
>
> "In addition, all of these new kids are coming in. They don't believe the media. They are not conditioned the way we were when we were growing up. I have tons of clients who are in their late twenties and I call them 'the new lawyers,' 'the new doctors,' etc. The old people will die off with their old ideas. To me it's not an overnight thing. Little by little we will see things change. Little by little, the economy will shift. Businesses which don't have integrity will go out of business. Banks will be re-organized. The new kids will come in and they will be the new bankers.

"The Guides say that this is the time to fine-tune things. You know how scout ants work ahead? In the 1960s we were testing the waters, now we are going to see changes. Our planet is the farthest it has ever been from the Milky Way Galaxy. Now it is turning back towards the Light. As dark as we have gotten, now we will move back towards the Light.

"We are the way-showers. We have been testing the waters; now is the time for change."

My Interpretation

We are all in this together. In our lifetime, we have already experienced huge changes in consciousness. We were raised on dogma and harsh enforcement of "right" and "wrong." Then, we began to understand civil rights and see how all people could be equally-valuable contributors to society. Attitudes shifted. The unacceptable became acceptable. As a society, we are moving forward and preparing to greet a new paradigm. We can look around the globe and see how people are finding their voices for change and democracy. New technologies are supporting our connectedness and our forward movement. The Internet and social media provide the engineering which allows us to share new ideas and to organize around these ideas.

This shift in consciousness is accelerating. One way or another people will wake up and be curious about the nature of man, and the nature of nature. Will it take violent Earth changes? If need be. Will it take violence among people? I hope not. Have we gotten the hints along the way that we need to see things differently or do the hints need to become messages spouted from volcanoes and heard in hurricanes? Up until this point, we have allowed suffering. We have tried to dominate each other, the animals and the planet. We are the ones who need to clean up our messes and preserve our planet. Things are spinning out of control. The environment is heating up, economies are cooling down, and it is very difficult to determine how to regain our composure. We need a "re-boot." Maybe that is what 2012 offers. A chance to start over. A chance to update our understandings and renovate our Earth school.

If we listen, 2012 may provide the opportunity to develop a new understanding of the energetic nature of the universe. We are energetic beings and our outputs influence other people. We need to master our own energy, putting out kind and compassionate thoughts, words and actions, so that we don't harm anyone else, any animals, or any other parts of the planet. Words, actions and volatility shut people down. We have to persuade other people to restrain their negativity so that they stop putting out poor-quality energy. We are energy in physical form. When we send out energetic waves, we have the choice to influence people for good or for bad. Imagine if everyone understood this and agreed to work together to put out a high vibration so that we stopped harming each other. Suffering would end. We would live in peace because we knew that if we, personally, didn't agree to the heightened energy exchange, neither would anyone else. It's like the nuclear arms race. Everyone has to agree to restraint or everyone gets taken out by catastrophes.

Right now, Texas has a drought, but not a famine. Meanwhile, Somalia has a drought and a famine. Why the difference? In America, we have the infrastructure and the willingness to move food wherever it needs to go. In Somalia, military groups stopped food from moving into the devastated region. The rest of the world was shocked, took action, and the groups backed off. This is a prime example of how people with negative intent are harming others. Somehow we need to elevate mindsets. Genocide cannot be tolerated. People have to understand the impact of their actions. They need to see that when they harm others, they are also harming themselves. Their actions and energy circle back. We might not be able to prevent drought, but once we are aware of the situation, we can work to minimize the impacts on living systems.

2012 is also bringing the opportunity for us to see how "the other side" and this side interact continuously. Spirit, Spirit Guides and angels are available all of the time. Some people already have these experiences, but 2012 may allow masses of people to have their own direct experiences of unseen energies. Seeing is believing. This is not traditional religion telling us to believe in invisible entities, but a new understanding based on what people actually experience. Ideas are being brought forward by the people who are perceiving the lifting of the veil between the worlds. This lifting of the veil may be the beginning of the ascension process.

If we take this opportunity seriously, we can develop a new way of thinking about the universe so that it can be explored by science. First we have to realize how little we know, then we have to develop the questions to be answered. Spirituality should not require a choice between blind faith or science. It can have both. We can begin with anecdotes and end up with science. The key is to take the anecdotes seriously.

But . . . I am going way beyond what I understand. I am thinking too much. I need to get back to what the psychics, the connectors, had to say. They say that Earth changes are going to happen and that tragedies will escalate until we decide to heed the messages and act in a different way. There is more to life than material gain. There is more to life than dominating another person, animal, or nation. There is joy to be found in working together to preserve nature so that everything on the planet has a chance to survive. Everyone has their own gifts and a unique role to play in this transition. However, if we choose to ignore the messages, we may be asked to leave the planet. Just like when the teacher told us that if we couldn't behave, we were going to have to leave the room . . .

Those of us who are interested in spirituality right now are the vanguard. We are the people who walk between the worlds. We are the Light Workers. We grew up in the era of religious dogma and power plays, yet we are holding the Light for the new era. We can pull together and make the most of this upcoming period of evolution on Earth. This is 2012.

Section VI

Conclusion

Chapter 25 - Conclusion

People ask me, "Are psychic experiences real? Do people really gather information from an invisible universe?" I think they do. I have an advantage over most people when it comes to assessing psychic ability because I have spoken with so many psychics about their lives and their talents. I don't completely understand how they do it, or why it works, but the people I talk with have a direct line to energy and information. They know things about the universe and they have a broad view of life on Earth. They see the big picture of why we are here. It's fascinating.

During psychic readings, people have told me things about my life which I know are true, but which they had no logical way of knowing. By nature, I am a bit skeptical. I wonder, "If I can't hear information from the ethers, how can they do it?" But time after time they prove to me that they are bringing in fresh ideas and verifiable information.

So, what did I learn on ***My Psychic Search?***

<u>About the Psychics</u>

I learned that each psychic does something different. They all have specialties. You have to find the reader who can answer the kinds of questions which you ask. If you go to a psychic who doesn't do what you seek, you'll think the psychic isn't very good. You have to find the correct person and the best way to do this is through a personal recommendation from a friend.

I found that the psychics shared much wisdom. They gathered information from unseen sources and gave good advice. I was able to use their suggestions to improve my life and the life of my family. They provided insights about my children and how best to raise them. They weren't 100% accurate, but they gave me useful hints and glimpses of possibilities.

Some PRISMS were able to read photographs of my relatives and tell me things which I knew, but which they had no way of knowing. I am always looking for proof and I keep finding it. Some psychics were able to convey messages from my deceased relatives . . . by name. Still amazes me.

I discovered that psychics are here to learn their own life lessons. Although they may tap into invisible information sources and bring messages into this dimension, they still need to learn about love, trust, parenting, or how to be non-judgmental. These challenges help their souls evolve. There is a broad acceptance of reincarnation and a deep knowing that there is more to life than a single lifetime here on Earth.

I also learned that certain psychics actually are better than others. As they evolve and become professional psychics, they figure out how to use and share their abilities. It can be challenging to learn to set aside their egos so they can share messages cleanly, without filtering the messages through their own belief systems. In addition, PRISMS must determine how to convey messages so that people hear the information and feel empowered. People don't want to be frightened by the news a reader shares. Figuring out how to be a good psychic takes time and expertise. The best readers have mastered these skills.

However, age doesn't matter. Some young psychics are as good as older, more experienced psychics. Are they old souls? Have they done this work for lifetimes? Or, were they born understanding their gifts and their roles? For whatever reason, good readers can be found at every age.

I also discovered that psychics are kind, friendly people. No woo-woos. No turbans. Nothing crazy. These are people who you would like well enough to choose as friends . . . wise friends.

<u>About Psychic Ability</u>

Psychic ability is real. People can access unseen energies and bring new information forward. However, this information is in pieces and impressions, and often needs to be assembled into a clear message. The ability is real, but I don't want to oversell its impact on clients' lives. Talking to a psychic will bring interesting hints and new ideas, not complete pictures. Listen with an open mind and use the information which helps, but don't expect to change your life based on what a psychic said.

About Me

I learned that the most fun part of the Project was interviewing psychics, hearing about their lives and hearing about my life too. Writing and sharing are great, but not nearly as much fun as talking to psychics. I loved the psychic channeling event and I want to do that again.

I really enjoyed talking to psychics about my life journey. I want to know my future. I want to know that I am co-creating with some unseen force; that I don't have to do it all myself. I want to know that if I work hard, there will be a reward; that the Universe will step up to greet me and support me in moving forward. The psychics told me to set my sights higher.

What else did I learn about myself? I have deceased relatives and friends who surround me and watch out for me. I am in some sort of a supportive energy which has kept my calendar open enough to allow me to work on this Project for three years. That is a lot of support!

So, am I psychic? The psychics say, "Yes, but everyone has a different role to play." This is not a good enough answer when I'm looking for a direct connection to energy and information. I may have a different role to play than that of a professional psychic, yet I still want to feel the connection. I've had a few intuitive moments, many deep meditations, and a few poignant dreams. In fact, during the course of this Project, I began to receive bits of information about other people as well as some guidance on writing. I am opening my abilities. I want to try some of the modalities mentioned in this book and see if they enhance my connection. I want to have my own experiences. However, I'm still going to talk to a psychic when I need firm insights.

What is my current role? I am a scribe who is bringing psychic stories into physical form. I am a thinker and a writer. I am a point of connection between psychics and a curious audience. I am a person who promotes kindness and respect. Kindness counts. Kindness is not about being a pushover. It is about putting out a compassionate energy then standing up for ourselves in a responsible way.

I have been guided to write this book. This book is the apex of an energetic pyramid. It is the point of connection where all of our energies swirl together: Spirit, psychics, you and me.

About "regular" People

"Regular" people have much to share. People tell me all about their experiences and abilities, but they don't consider themselves to be psychic. They tell me that they can see death coming, see spirits, read other people, or see thoughts moving from one person to another, but they don't tell me that they are psychic. There is much information below our mundane level of chat. If we go deeper and ask friends if they have experienced psychic moments, and if they are willing to tell the truth, there are many stories to share. Direct, personal, experience is the best evidence for psychic phenomena.

When people talk to me about their intuitive experiences, they generally start very slowly and cautiously, but once they find out that I understand what they are talking about, they tell me amazing things. I have heard stories from people who regularly see ghosts and spirits. I have heard about parents sending telepathic grocery requests to children who were at the supermarket. I have heard the hushed stories of how people knew they had psychic abilities, including one woman who didn't know she was psychic until her deceased boyfriend's children asked how he was . . . and she knew.

Occasionally, people tell me stories which they have never told anyone else. These stories can be very emotional in terms of content and also because people have held them closely for so long. People want to share this aspect of their lives, but are afraid that others will belittle them. They want to talk with someone who takes psychic abilities seriously. I feel humbled when people share their intimate stories with me. I feel honored to be able to provide a safe space for questions and answers. With this book, I hope people will begin to see how normal they are. People who feel isolated because they have no one with whom to share their extraordinary experiences will find many other people in the same situation. Really, they are more normal than they think.

About You

I learned that is okay for everyone to talk to a psychic and to think deeply about their own life. It is okay to get a fresh perspective. It's okay to allow the information to influence your decisions. Not to dictate your decisions, but to influence them. Every bit of insight you gather, from whatever source, enhances your life. Keep asking your questions and moving along your life path. You can benefit from psychic expertise.

About Science

Reliable scientific data supporting psychic phenomena exist, but scientists don't know what to do with these studies. There aren't enough puzzle pieces to figure out the picture. There is no frame of reference for the data. Scientists tell me that the principles of quantum physics work, but they don't know why. I think this is very similar to psychic ability. We know it works, but it is hard to replicate the results and we don't yet understand the mechanisms. In time, scientists will figure this out.

Rhonda Harford, the Astrologer, has a photographic memory. She mentioned that after working with a client, she may not remember their name, but she can remember their chart and all of their information. Perhaps psychic ability is like having a photographic memory? Recently, a phenomenon has been documented which is called "Superior Autobiographical Memory." People with this ability remember everything which happened on every day of their life. To me, it sounds like they have a direct connection to the Akashic Records. Photographic memory and Superior Autobiographical Memory don't occur very often and if they don't happen to you, they can be hard to believe. However, these skills can be scientifically demonstrated. Someday science will catch up with psychic ability.

About G-d

G-d is a benevolent, all-encompassing universal source of positive energy. We all live within this source, and this source lives within us.

About Life and Death

It is reassuring to hear that death is just another part of the life process and that there is nothing to fear. The only thing which dies is the physical body. The spirit, our true essence, lives on. We come to Earth as students and teachers to help each other learn and grow. The important thing is to make the most of this physical experience and to learn the lessons which propel our souls forward. We are here to taste and to see, to fall in love and to fall out of love; just to see what those experiences feel like. We are here to fulfill our life purpose and to learn to love ourselves. And when we have learned our lessons, we travel back to the other side, look at the big picture, take a break, then decide if we want to go around again.

Understanding the cycle of birth, learning, death, integrating, and birth again, allows us to enjoy life and passion. We can live with gusto, taking risks, knowing that the reason we are here is to try new things and to learn from our experiences. There is nothing to lose in exploring life because, if we blow it this time, we can come back again. Alternatively, we can savor contemplative time because we don't have to try everything in a single lifetime. We can make the most of this chance to see, hear, taste, travel and meet people. We can love our kids and send them off to enjoy their own lives. We don't need to make every moment so important that we cling to it for too long and get stuck. We can keep going, keep enjoying, and keep exploring because that is why we are here! And when it's over and our physical bodies are worn out, we can go around again. But we don't know what the circumstances of our next life will be . . . so if we have the chance, we should enjoy this one!

About the Future

There is no future which is set in stone. We all have to make wise choices in the moment to attract the future we want to create. We can do this by selecting the choices which feel right and rejecting the choices which do not lead to the future we seek. This is true for our personal lives and it is also true for humanity. The time period around 2012 will bring many opportunities for awareness. We can work together to birth a new world based on justice and equality.

Alternatively, we may find that we wake up to a higher level of consciousness and choose to leave Earth. A new reality on Earth or a new adventure elsewhere? I don't know what may happen but, either way, the best course of action is to look out for each other and help each other along humanity's path.

The psychics have told me that there is a bright future for ***My Psychic Search*** Project, but I have to step up to make it happen. I have to be willing to move to the next phase: information sharing. According to the psychics, if I so choose, I can make information sharing my life's work. I can help provide the knowledge people seek as we move forward with humanity's evolution. This work is not who I am, it is what I do. Who I am is a wise, eternal soul, playing out my role on Earth. Just like everyone else. We are bright lights trying to make smart choices so that we fulfill our life purpose, learn our lessons of love, have a little fun, and help each other.

Once I have released all of this information to the public, I can continue to do what I truly love: interviewing psychics, recording their stories, and sharing their information. As a bonus, during the interviews I may hear information about my life and my family. Along the way, I can further develop my own psychic skills.

Conclusion

I started ***My Psychic Search*** with an interest in how psychics accessed information and I have learned so much more than that! I have learned what it is like to be psychic. I have heard from my Spirit Guides. I have learned why we are here on Earth, what happens when we die and why we keep coming back. I have learned about the Wheel of Incarnation and how all things are connected. I have learned this information from a variety of people who live this kind of connected life. Not just from books, but from real people with direct connections. What proof do I have that there is a world beyond our five senses? Just the direct experiences and knowledge of the people who tell their stories to me and the surprising bits and pieces of information which are beginning to pop into my own mind. Right now, that is enough.

In the next phase of my life, I want to travel and I can't wait to see the sea again. California, here I come! I'm on my way, on my own life adventure. Know any psychics who I should interview? Who are your favorites? Please send your ideas and recommendations to me.

If you want to follow this journey of discovery, you can read my blogs at www.MyPsychicSearch.com. Thank you for being part of this adventure. As always, ***My Psychic Search*** can be ***Your Psychic Search***.

Section VII

References

Chapter 26 - Glossary

Akashic Records: The non-physical Akashic Records contain information on each soul's thoughts, words, and actions. They are the vibrational records of each soul and its journey.

Angels: Angels are messengers who have not lived life in a physical body. Angels offer advice and wisdom, but don't interfere with our free will unless we are in mortal danger. People have Guardian Angels who protect them, along with angels who come in for special purposes.

Animal Communicator: Animal communicators are able to connect with pets (living and dead) and other animals. They act as interpreters for the animals.

Ascended Masters: Ascended Masters are individuals who were formerly embodied on Earth and learned their life lessons during their incarnations. They are enlightened beings who have undergone a process of spiritual transformation referred to as *Ascension*. From the realms of spirit, the Ascended Masters teach mankind. Examples of Ascended Masters include Jesus, Buddha, Confucius, Mary the Mother of Jesus, Kwan Yin, Saint Germain, Djwal Khul, Elijah and Saint Patrick.

Ascension: Ascension is the concept of awakening to a higher level of consciousness. Some people liken it to entering Heaven alive, with a body. Death is normally the end to an individual's life. Eventually, all people will go through the ascension process and move forward in spiritual evolution.

Astral Plane: The astral world is the realm into which we pass on the way to be being born and at the time of physical death. This is the realm of angels, spirits, Devas, nature-spirits, and fairies.

Aura: The personal energy field around the body.

Bodhisattvas: Those who are on the path to Enlightenment, but have not yet attained it and become buddhas.

Chakras: Chakras are circular, rotating, energy vortices in the ethereal body. Seven main chakras in the human body circulate the energy of life, along with many smaller chakra points. These chakras connect our personal energy systems with universal energy systems.

Channeler: A person who communicates with non-physical entities such as Spirit Guides, angels and the deceased. "Conscious Channeling" involves a conversation in the mind. "Trance Channeling" allows spiritual entities to enter a person's body and speak through their voice.

Clairalience: Clear smelling. Psychic perception through smelling without a physical cause for the smell.

Clairaudience: Clear hearing. Psychic perception through hearing. This can either sound like an inner voice or an actual voice.

Claircognizance: Clear knowing. Psychic perception through "knowing." It is the feeling of simply knowing without clear evidence of how or why the person knows what they know.

Clairgustance: Clear tasting. Psychic perception through taste, without anything physically touching the tongue.

Clairscentience: Clear feeling. Psychic perception through feeling, such as intuition, a hunch, or a gut feeling. Also, the ability to feel another person's emotions or physical pain.

Clairvoyance: Clear seeing. Seeing an image in the mind's eye.

Cords, cording people: Cords are attachments which are created by thought. They are energetic links between people and they can be positive or negative. Frequent, obsessive, or emotionally-charged thoughts can create permanent energy cords between people. Cords can continue after death and into future lifetimes. Healthy relationships are free of cords.

Devas: The flower angels for each type of plant.

Djwal Khul: Djwal Khul was a Tibetan Master. Now, he is a Spiritual Guide for mankind, an Ascended Master. Djwal Khul is working to further spiritual evolution on Earth.

Empath: A person who feels the emotions of other people. They don't just think they know what someone else feels, they actually feel it.

Empathy: The ability to experience another person's emotions.

Energy Worker: Each person lives in an energy field and has energy moving through his or her body. Energy workers direct energy into a client's body in order to assist the client. They can also remove blockages which thwart the flow of energy. Energy workers may, or may not, receive intuitive information while working.

Ether: The upper regions of space; empty space.

Ethereal Body: The ethereal body is the lowest layer in the human energy field (aura). It is an energetic duplicate of the physical body.

Etheric Plane: The etheric plane is one of the planes of existence. It represents the fourth sub-plane of the physical plane, the lower three being the states of solid, liquid, and gaseous matter.

Extra-Sensory Perception (ESP): Extra-sensory perception is the power to know by some means other than the five senses (taste, smell, touch, vision and hearing).

Gaia: A reference to the Earth, or Mother Earth.

Gifted: A person who is gifted works with intuition. This word is often used as an adjective. People think of themselves as "gifted" astrologers or "gifted" card readers. They work with a tool, but in addition to understanding the information presented through the tool, they also receive intuitive information. This information comes in at the right time and goes out at the right time. It's not always there.

Healer: A healer uses psychic, intuitive, or energy connections to assist patients. There are many kinds of healers. In general, these people facilitate healing by guiding energy into clients' bodies so that clients can heal themselves. The patient has to accept the energy in order for healing to begin.

Higher Realms: Spirit Guides, angels, G-d.

Higher Self: The Higher Self is the non-physical portion of a person's spirit. The Higher Self knows why the person has come to Earth and the lessons he or she needs to learn. It provides a direct connection to universal energy and knowledge.

Ho'oponopons: This is a prayer with roots in Hawaiian culture. It is a simple prayer which clears energy blocks and helps people take responsibility for what they have created on Earth.

Intuition: The ability to know things without knowing why. People with intuition say that information just pops into their head or comes out of their mouth. The information comes and goes at the right time.

Intuitive: Intuitive means "to know." Intuitives have the gift of spontaneously knowing or saying things, but don't feel like it is a talent that they can summon every time they seek information. Many Intuitives don't think of themselves as psychic. They explain that intuition provides a specific piece of information or a focused view of a situation, as opposed to the broad view of issues which can be seen by people who are psychic.

Karma: Karma is the energetic law of cause and effect. Through words and actions, people can create positive Karma or incur negative Karma. The energy which a person generates can be reflected back to that person during the present lifetime or can be carried from one lifetime to the next lifetime.

Kwan Yin: Kwan Yin is the Bodhisattva of compassion. She is commonly known as the Goddess of Mercy. She is one of the Ascended Masters who is helping humanity.

Kundalini: The spiritual force in every human being that lies at the base of the spine, coiled like a snake. Once awakened, it rises through the chakras, producing spiritual knowledge and mystical powers.

Light Energy: Light energy is the essence of all things. It is the essence of Spirit before it manifests into form. It is where all things begin and all things return. It is experienced as matter, energy vibration, thought and emotion. It is the energy which flows through humans.

Light Workers: Light Workers are people who volunteered, before birth, to help heal the planet and its population. They draw light (as energy and information) into this physical universe. They help human consciousness evolve. Many Light Workers are discovering innate spiritual gifts, such as psychic communication skills and spiritual healing abilities.

Mala Beads: Prayer beads.

Manifest: To create by thought.

Mediums: Mediums talk to people who have died and crossed to the other side. They communicate with the spirits of the deceased and bring messages from the other side to this side. All Mediums are considered psychic, but not all psychics are Mediums.

Metaphysics: Metaphysics is a branch of philosophy dealing with theories of existence and knowledge. It attempts to answer fundamental questions which go beyond the scientific explanations provided by physics.

Metatron: An Archangel. In Biblical myth, Archangel Metatron is considered to be the most supreme of angelic beings. He serves as the celestial scribe and maintains the Akashic Records.

Open Readings: During these types of readings, the psychic prefers to relay messages from Spirit Guides at the beginning of the session and allow clients to ask their questions after having received the initial messages.

Oracle Cards: The use of Tarot cards for divination has inspired the creation of modern oracle card decks. These are card decks for inspiration or divination which contain images of angels, fairies, goddesses, totems, etc. They do not follow the traditional structure of Tarot decks.

Precognition: Seeing the future; the ability to have thoughts or visions about events before they happen.

Presentiment: Having feelings about the future; like a hunch about what is going to happen.

PRISMS: This acronym stands for **P**sychics, **R**eaders, **I**ntuitives, **S**piritual Counselors, **M**ediums and **S**hamans. It also encompasses Healers, Energy Workers, etc. PRISMS take the light (energy and information from the other side), bend it through their minds, and shine the colors so everyone can see them.

Psi: Psi consists of extra-sensory perception (ESP) and psychokinesis. Extra-sensory perception is the power to know by some means other than the five senses. Psychokinesis is the ability to use thought to impact physical things. Examples include hands-on healing, levitation, and using mental powers to bend spoons or to sail furniture across a room.

Psychic: Psychics can see the future or see the energy, and the flow of energy, around a person. These people can reliably tap into an unseen information stream. They can ask for information from their Spirit Guides and other entities and bring that information forward. They see where people are in their lives and the direction that their lives are going. Some psychics are clairvoyant (able to see images), clairaudient (able to hear messages), clairscentient (able to feel), and/or claircognizant (able to know). Some psychics are also intuitive.

Psychokinesis: The ability to use thought to change things or to move things.

Psychometry: Knowing information about a person by holding one of their belongings.

Reader: Anyone who does psychic or intuitive readings or consultations. Readers talk to clients and provide information and insights for them.

Reiki: A Japanese technique for stress reduction and relaxation which also promotes healing. This technique allows the practitioner to transfer universal life energy to a patient either distantly or through the palms of the hands.

Reincarnation: Reincarnation is the concept that people lead multiple lives. They can live one life, die, become spiritual entities, then decide if they would like to be born into new bodies. Each lifetime presents lessons and opportunities. After people die, they review their lives and decide if they need to come back into bodies to learn additional lessons.

Remote Viewing: The ability to see what is happening in a far away location using just the mind.

Shaman: Shamans are "way showers." They are aligned with nature and help people find their way on Earth.

Soul Braid: Soul braiding allows a second soul, or another aspect of a person's spirit, to enter the person's body so that new information can be shared. This is a cooperative agreement with permission from the person's original soul.

Spirit: A universal source of energy and information. The word can either be singular or plural, depending on its use. Some psychics think of Spirit as a universal energy source, while other psychics believe Spirit is made up of multiple energies.

Spirits: Souls who have crossed to the other side. While alive, people have souls. After death, they are spirits.

Spirit Guides: Spirit Guides have lived on Earth, crossed to the other side, and chosen to aid others on their path to spiritual enlightenment. Spirit Guides can be completely separate from a person or they may be another aspect of a person. They are neither male nor female. Some Guides remain with people for a lifetime while other Guides come in to work on special projects and assist with particular events.

Spiritual Counselor: Spiritual Counselors talk with clients and help them understand why things happen in their lives and how to cope with problems. These people provide a new way of thinking about issues. Problems often surface because there are lessons which people need to learn. Spiritual counselors see the big picture of clients' lives and, perhaps, their past lives or the reasons why they are here, and can help people understand how to deal with current issues.

Tarot Cards: A deck of 78 cards with images and symbols used as a tool of self-reflection and divination. These were originally used as playing cards and later became associated with mysticism and magic. Tarot card decks bring information and inspiration to readers.

Telepathy: The ability to know other people's thoughts.

White Brotherhood of Light: Supernatural beings of great power who spread spiritual teachings through selected humans. The use of the term "white" refers to their advanced spirituality and the fact that they have a white-colored aura. It has nothing to do with race.

Chapter 27 - Information Sources and Contact Information

Psychics, Intuitives, Readers and Energy Workers
(in alphabetical order, by first name)

The following people were interviewed for this Project. However, this is not a page of recommendations as I have not had personal readings with all of these psychics.

Beth Hays - Flower Essence Practitioner
www.IntegratedEssences.com
Beth@integratedessences.com
520-850-9463

Cecilia Nemmers - Psychic
CelNemmers@yahoo.com

Cherie Fraine - Psychic, Reiki Master
KUISTAN09@hotmail.com
520-304-8706

Cynthia Rae - Intuitive Empowerment
amsearae@juno.com

Delphina Nova - Native American Dreamer and Wisdomkeeper, Spiritual Healer, Geo-Empath, Animal Messenger, Author
www.DelphinaNova.com

Denise Singerline - Medium, Reiki Master, Chakra-Balancing Specialist
www.chakrabalancedenise.com
info@chakrabalancedenise.com
520-584-1186

Erik Assman - Empath, Reiki Master, Spiritual Counselor
highmystica@yahoo.com

Gigi Sample - Psychic Counselor
www.universalpsychic.com
800-276-7460

Gina Stanfill - Intuitive, Reiki Master
Chiworksaz@aol.com

Jackie Chin - Professional Psychic Advisor
www.psychicconnextions.blogspot.com
ReadingsbyTiLite@aol.com

Jan Class - Holy Spirit Communicator
jmclass@comcast.net

Jeff Sonnenburg - Psychic, Financial Advisor, ChildFinders, Tucson, AZ

Kat Riegel - Animal Communicator
Kre8iveKat@aol.com
520-245-5120

Laurie Hays - Spiritual Intuitive, Psychic
SpiritReads@hotmail.com

Leah Taylor - Psychic, Medium, Medical Intuitive
ladywey@gmail.com

Marianne Patyk - Medium
mfpatyk@gmail.com
520-207-2663

Marta Taylor - Energy Sensitive
martat11@gmail.com

Patricia Kirkman - Numerologist, Intuitive
www.PatriciaKirkman.com

Raquel Spencer - Spiritual Teacher, Multi-Dimensional Energy Specialist
www.RaquelSpencer.com

Rhonda Harford - Astrologer
starlady@cox.net
520-320-7718

Richard Schickel - Psychic, Medical Intuitive, Healer
www.richardschickel.vpweb.com

Shirli Millmond - Psychic, Life Coach
smillmond@gmail.com
520-208-4837

To-Ree'-Nee' Wolf - Energy Tracker
trnwolf@earthlink.net

Trish Silay - Intuitive, The *One Brain* System
www.ChoicesforSelfDiscovery.com
520-886-1239

Books

Bertoldi, Concetta, 2008. *Do Dead People Watch You Shower? And Other Questions You've been all but Dying to Ask a Medium.* Harper Collins, New York, NY.

Holland, John with Cindy Pearlman, 2003. *born Knowing. A Medium's Journey – Accepting and Embracing My Spiritual Gifts.* Hay House, Carlsbad, CA.

Mayer, Elizabeth Lloyd, Ph. D., 2007. *Extraordinary Knowing. Science, Skepticism, and the Inexplicable Powers of the Human Mind.* Bantam Books, New York, NY.

Rodriguez, Constance, Ph.D., 2008. *Gifts of the Soul: Experience the Mystical in Everyday Life.* Llewellyn Publications, Woodbury, MN.

Virtue, Doreen, Ph.D., 1997. *The Lightworker's Way, Awakening your Spiritual Power to Know and Heal,* Hay House, Carlsbad, CA.

Internet Sites

Institute of Noetic Sciences, www.Noetic.org

The International Center for Reiki Training, www.Reiki.org

My Psychic Search, www.MyPsychicSearch.com

NOTES

NOTES

NOTES

CPSIA information can be obtained at www.ICGtesting.com
Printed in the USA
BVOW081607140512

290167BV00004B/1/P